GORBACHEV

With thanks to Yelena Korenevskaya, who helped me in the research for this book with curiosity, intelligence and courage.

GORBACHEV

☆

A BIOGRAPHY

Gerd Ruge

*Translated from the German
by Peter Tegel*

Chatto & Windus
LONDON

Published in 1991 by
Chatto & Windus Ltd
20 Vauxhall Bridge Road
London SW1V 2SA

A CIP catalogue record of this book is available from the
British Library

ISBN 0 7011 3747 9

Originally published in German by S. Fischer Verlag GmbH,
1990

Phototypeset by Input Typesetting Ltd, London
Printed in Great Britain by
Mackays of Chatham plc,
Chatham, Kent

CONTENTS

MURMANSK
• Murmansk

NORWAY

SWEDEN

FINLAND

• Archangel

Baltic
Sea

Tallinn •
Estonia

• Leningrad

Russia

Riga •
Latvia

• Gorki

Lithuania

Moscow ■

Kuybyshev

Kaliningrad •
Vilnius •

• Minsk
Byelorussia

POLAND

• Kiev

• Voronezh

Ukraine

Volgograd •

Moldavia
• Kishinev

• Rostov

Odessa •

• Krasnodar
• Stavropol

ROMANIA

Black Sea

CAUCASUS MTS.

Cas

Georgia • Tbilisi

Azerbaidjan

Armenia

B

• Yerevan

TURKEY

Inset of Stavropol area

• Rostov

0 Miles   200

Russia

0 Kilometres   300

Astrakhan •

Privolnoye •
• Krasnogvardeisk

Krasnodar •
• Stavropol

Caspian
Sea

• Mineralniye Vody
• Piatigorsk
Kislovodsk •

Black

Sea

Georgia   Tbilisi

Batumi •

Azerbaidjan

TURKEY   Armenia

Baku •

IRAQ

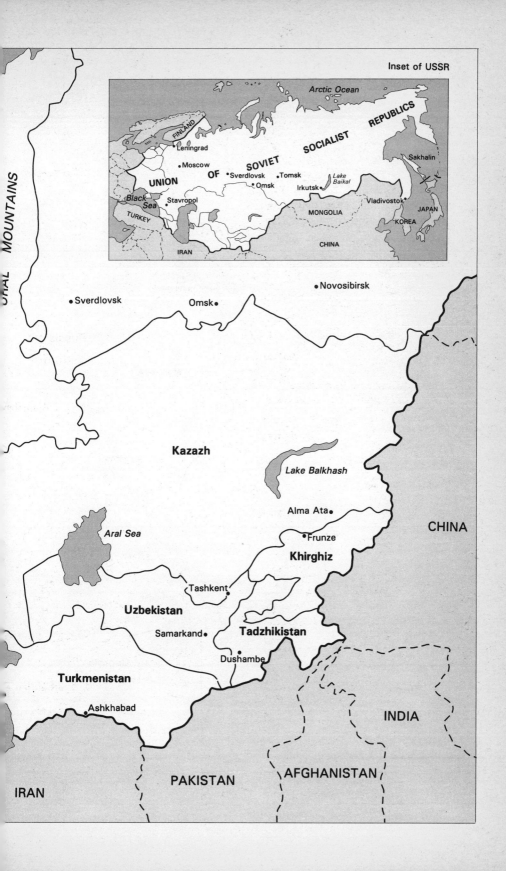

INTRODUCTION

Marxists have long disputed whether history is made by individuals or by the masses. One thing is certain: the world today would look very different without Mikhail Gorbachev. His willingness to introduce and implement fundamental reforms makes him unique among contemporary Soviet politicians. Even without Gorbachev, it is probable that the Soviet Union would have changed, as the deep crisis in the Russian system could no longer be hidden. But the changes would certainly have proceeded more slowly. No one in the Soviet Union doubts that the driving force behind the restructuring is Gorbachev, who has made the words *perestroika* and *glasnost* familiar in every language in the world. Even those Soviet critics of Gorbachev who consider the pace of his reforms too slow admit that it was he who set everything in motion.

Gorbachev once called this process a revolution. A real revolution, a total and permanent shift in power relations, has not yet occurred in the Soviet Union. What has occurred is a total change in the political climate, so that the problems of the Soviet Union can, for the first time, be openly acknowledged and discussed, the introduction of a massive programme of economic reform, and a new world political situation in which the superpowers, thanks mainly to Gorbachev's 'new thinking', have broken away from their former confrontation. Consequently, the word *perestroika* has become a symbol of hope, and the image of the Soviet Union in the West is more positive than at any time since the beginning of the Cold War. Gorbachev has become the most admired and respected head of state in the world, a fact reflected in his award, in October 1990, of the Nobel Peace Prize. In the Soviet Union, however, his popularity peaked in 1987. Since then it has wavered. In December 1989, 52 per cent of the population were satisfied with Gorbachev. In January 1990 the figure was 44 per cent, and in May only 40 per cent. This may appear reasonable for a politician who has been in power for five years, but in the Soviet Union where unanimous support for the Party leadership has long been customary, this made people think that Gorbachev was doing badly. Before the Party Congress in June 1990, when a hesitant Gorbachev seemed to have left the field to the conservatives, his popularity again sank. It recovered after his victory at the Congress, but was then again undermined when the economy deteriorated in the summer, and Boris Yeltsin overtook him for a time. Even his critics, however, acknowledge that he has good intentions, and most ordinary Russian people still see him as the only man who can save the country.

Gorbachev's undiminished popularity abroad can be explained by the fact that he has completely changed the image of the Soviet Union. For two decades the superpowers, bristling with nuclear weapons, had appeared to be on a collision course which could only end in catastrophe. With the coming of Gorbachev, however, it seemed for the first time that one of the superpowers had a leader who genuinely wanted to end the arms race.

The critical attitude of some Soviet citizens towards Gorbachev is the result of the overwhelming difficulty of reforming the monolithic Soviet system. For many Russian people life under Gorbachev is actually harder than it was before he came to power. There is also an inevitable reaction against the optimism of Gorbachev's early days in power, when Soviet citizens believed that the restructuring process would quickly bring about a better life, in a more humane society.

During this period Gorbachev himself underwent a difficult learning process. His speeches only gradually reveal the new principle that economic reform can only succeed if it is combined with far-reaching changes in the political system and in society. Many of the thought patterns Gorbachev had acquired during his rise in the Communist hierarchy had to be overcome. When he first came to power, Gorbachev was still thinking along the lines of a modernised one-party Socialist state, but in January 1990 he went so far as to say that a multi-party system need not be a tragedy. It is this ability to adapt to newly perceived reality, along with the openness of his thinking about the future of his own country and the world, that makes Gorbachev such a fascinating figure, unique among statesmen in our time. Whether or not he ultimately brings about the immense project of restructuring the Soviet Union according to his plans, whether or not the new thinking conquers the old realities, a place in history is assured for this man from a farming village who came to lead a world power.

The process he set in motion – whether one wants to call it a revolution or not – has one thing in common with all revolutions: its ultimate effect will not be the one its founders envisaged at its outset. The upheaval in the Soviet Union has only just begun, and it says much for the political wisdom of Gorbachev and his colleagues that the process has not been forced by them into a rigid, pseudoscientific mould, or channelled into the formulae of an outdated ideology, but continues to be shaped by its own development. This explains and counters the criticism that Gorbachev has not set out a timetable for his changes. Nobody, including Gorbachev, knows whether a centralised one-party Socialist state can be modernised, reformed and democratised without breaking up. Undoubtedly the empire bequeathed by the Tsars, Lenin and Stalin, and covering a sixth of the earth, cannot be transformed without major convulsions.

In 1980 I was working in Moscow as a foreign correspondent. I became aware that a number of my acquaintances in academic institutes were setting their hopes on Mikhail Gorbachev, the youngest member of the Politburo. They said he was an economic and agricultural specialist with proven organisational ability, who could well make his way to the very top. But in the Soviet Union at that time it was not possible for a coming politician openly to express his own ideas. If he deviated from the official line, if he failed to show unlimited appreciation for the leadership, he risked losing any chance of succession. I first became aware of Gorbachev's name when I spoke to an academic from the Institute for World Economy and International Relations, which had been severely attacked for its critical assessment of the Soviet economic situation. I asked my acquaintance how the institute coped with problems of this kind. 'Oh,' he said, 'we write exactly what we did before. In any case, in the Politburo only Gorbachev reads it.'

It was, I believe, Gorbachev's assumption of power in March

1985 that saved me from difficulties when I continued to work in the Soviet Union. I had published a book the year before in which I had been critical of conditions in the Soviet Union (and also, incidentally, in the United States). Soviet colleagues warned me that I would now be denied an entry visa to the Soviet Union. But a malicious newspaper criticism of my position was stopped before it came out, and when under Gorbachev the floodgates of self-criticism in the Soviet Union opened, my book appeared as a relatively mild foretaste of the criticisms that would now be made of Soviet conditions.

In the debate beginning in the Soviet Union I was reminded of my first years in Moscow, during the time of Nikita Khrushchev. I had come to Moscow in 1965 at the time of the Thaw and the exposure of Stalin's crimes. Tens of thousands were returning from the camps, the wretched life of the peasants in the villages around Moscow was beginning to improve visibly, and there was a feeling of hope in Moscow.

The new openness in the theatre and literature in 1985 reminded me of the fifties, when Vladimir Dudintsev's book *Not by Bread Alone* appeared, and Khrushchev succeeded in getting Solzhenitsyn's *One Day in the Life of Ivan Denisovich* printed. That had been an exciting and moving time, although talking with ordinary Soviet citizens was still difficult. Many were afraid of contact with foreigners, which had been officially discouraged for decades. Mostly I spoke with Soviet colleagues who had permission, or instructions, to disclose some piece of information. Some of these people remain my friends to this day. But other people also began to express their views more openly. The writer Ilya Ehrenburg, whose book *The Thaw* gave the period its name, was one. Another was the composer Dmitri Shostakovich. There were poetry recitals by young authors such as Yevgeni Yevtushenko, Andrey Voznesensky, Bella Akhmadulina and Bulat Okudzhava. Now in Gorbachev's spring, their voices were clearer and more urgent. I had seen a forerunner of Gorbachev's 'Moscow Spring' in 1957, when thousands of young foreigners had come to Moscow for the World Youth Festival, and young Soviets discovered the relaxed lifestyle of foreign young people as they danced in the streets. Even Communist Youth League leaders, who had organised the festival, were carried away by the fun and enthusiasm.

I had also experienced how quickly the new climate could change. I slipped away to see Boris Pasternak, changing from a taxi, to the underground, to a suburban train, to avoid being followed. He spoke sadly of colleagues who condemned and persecuted him. I learned that, after he had been awarded the Nobel Prize for Literature, organised hordes of factory workers and Young Communists had demonstrated in the woods in front of his house, calling him 'Judas' and a 'pig that shits in its own trough'. Poets who recited their verse on Mayakovsky Square were arrested and condemned. It was in the Khrushchev era, which brought with it so much hope, that the state began to use psychiatric hospitals as prisons.

With the coming of Gorbachev I was reminded of what, despite everything, had given us hope under Khrushchev. Gorbachev was more matter-of-fact than his predecessor, but it was clear that he knew the situation in the country, and refused to close his eyes to it.

Gorbachev had, I read, studied in Moscow at the beginning of the fifties. I remembered conversations I had had with Moscow students in 1956 in which they had talked excitedly about a better, democratic Socialism. I asked myself whether Gorbachev had been formed by the spirit of that time. I saw that friends and acquaintances who had supported change in the Khrushchev era were moving up into new jobs or again having their works published. In the Brezhnev era, some of them had made it clear to me that the victory of the apparatus over change had robbed them of years of important work, even if they had done well, and been promoted to good positions.

I was excited by what I learned about Gorbachev. At an agricultural conference the Soviet participants no longer read out prepared statements, but energetically debated the causes of the crisis in Soviet agriculture and the ways to overcome it. At times the roles in East-West discussions seemed to have been reversed: it was the American participants at the beginning of the Reagan era who were suspicious and dogmatic, while Soviet experts were freeing themselves from their former rigidity.

The climate in Moscow was changing rapidly. I was curious to learn more about the man who had effected this transformation. What were his origins? How had his political ideas come about? How new was this 'new thinking', and how deep did it go? When had he begun thinking about *glasnost* and *perestroika*? What role had been played by his own experience? I thought of Pasternak, who had spoken to me about the double life that even high Party functionaries had to lead, concealing their true thoughts and giving the impression of unquestioningly following the Party.

In 1985 I hoped to make a television programme with an American colleague about Mikhail Gorbachev. It was to include an extensive interview with Gorbachev himself, interviews with his friends, and documentary pictures from different stages of his life. We wanted to seek out the intellectual roots of *perestroika*, which seemed to have dawned so suddenly. We wrote to Soviet embassies and to Mikhail Gorbachev, but our letters remained unanswered. I made another attempt with Swedish colleagues, and another with the Dutch Alerdinck Foundation, in which Soviet television wanted to participate. President Reagan would also have been interviewed, but that project fell through when Nancy Reagan insisted that her husband receive written questions in advance.

In 1987 I went back to Moscow as a television foreign correspondent. I found my friends in Moscow talking about modernisation as if Russia was soon to be a second America. I was hungry for details about Gorbachev, about the origins and effects of his policies. But real information was still hard to get. The functionaries in Old Square, the seat of the Central Committee, remained reticent. It was only possible to learn about the style and content of Gorbachev's reform projects at second hand, from academics and writers.

A friend who had shared a room with Gorbachev at university did not mention the fact, though he knew I was aware of it. Gorbachev only gave interviews to television stations of countries he was about to visit. These revealed something of his way of talking and thinking, but nothing about him as a person. In the Soviet Union itself nothing appeared – not even hymns of praise of his work. In his home region of Stavropol, I had heard, a television crew had wanted to make a film about his youth, but had been refused permission – by Gorbachev. Nothing about his life was published in the Soviet Union until May 1989, when the Central Committee information bulletin carried an interview in which he spoke fairly personally. (This interview appears as an appendix to this book.) It appeared at approximately the same time that my own efforts seemed to produce results. Perhaps my letters had finally reached the right people, or perhaps they convinced Gorbachev that it was time to present himself to the world in a more personal, human way.

The American colleague with whom I had begun the project had retired when an acquaintance in the Soviet Foreign Ministry suggested I try again. Just before Gorbachev's visit to West Germany would be a good time. He advised me how, and to whom, I should write. I also spoke about Gorbachev to one of the deputy chairmen of Soviet television. He himself comes from a village, and is keenly interested in the lives of Soviet farmers and Gorbachev's agricultural policy. He understood why I wanted to discover the roots of Gorbachev's political thinking, and was persuaded that I did not just want to dig up sensational information about the private life of the Party leader. What happened next, and who made the decisions, I have never discovered.

One day, not long before Gorbachev's visit to Bonn, a friend phoned me from a call-box at Moscow airport. He was on his way to Peking to prepare Gorbachev's state visit, which I would be covering. 'It's okay,' he said. 'They're letting you do it.' What I had been given permission to do, he did not know exactly. Perhaps pictures of Gorbachev with his advisers on the China visit, perhaps interviews with some old friends and colleagues, he said. On my flight to Peking I told the press officer of the Foreign Ministry that I was being allowed to stick close to Gorbachev. 'Quite out of the question,' he said. 'We know nothing about it.' I turned to the Speaker of the Central Committee. He was also unable to help. In Peking, amid the confusion of the student demonstrations, which overshadowed Gorbachev's visit, nothing could be done in any case, as events on Tiananmen Square fully occupied the film crew and me.

So, when I returned to Moscow I still had nothing to show. But Soviet colleagues told me I had been given permission to make a film about Gorbachev, and had been given access to his home village and friends. At my request Soviet television gave me an editor, who could show his pass and reassure potential interviewees that I was allowed to ask questions about Gorbachev. I phoned an old friend and asked her to assist me. I knew that she would be willing to help, although not every Soviet citizen would dare to start researching the early life of the Party boss.

We began making phone calls. For some years I had been collect-
ing the names of people who were said to have known Gorbachev
well. Now I had to find them, and talk them into giving interviews.

We flew to Stavropol, in Gorbachev's home region. The head
of the television studio there, Ivan Ivanovich Shlakhtin, was
extremely helpful. We had brought with us the names of some
farmers in Privolnoye, Gorbachev's village. Ivan Ivanovich knew
some of them, as well as the head of the *kolkhoz*, or collective
farm, whose co-operation we would need, and who was waiting
for us on the outskirts of the village. He had prepared a lavish
country meal, and gave us the customary lecture on the *kolkhoz*
and its success. I began to despair. It looked as if we were being
given the routine treatment.

While I ate and carried on the conversation, the crew filmed
whatever they could get: the village streets and houses, old farmers and their ducks, motorcyclists and shepherds and the river
in which Gorbachev had bathed when he was a boy. But Ivan
Ivanovich did not want us to see Gorbachev's mother's house.
The road was closed, and you couldn't drive on it anyway, he
said, but eventually we persuaded him, and it turned out only to
be rather muddy and full of potholes. I had already been told in
Moscow that an interview with Gorbachev's mother was quite
out of the question. We finally got hold of a short film that had
been shown on Chinese television during Gorbachev's Peking
visit. In 52 seconds that must have been part of a longer conversation, Gorbachev's elderly mother, speaking in Russian tinged
with Ukrainian, told how hard it had been at the end of the war
to get a pair of boots for Mikhail. We didn't seem to be making
much progress, but, if nothing else, at least we were the first film
crew to be allowed to film Gorbachev's native village.

And then, suddenly, things improved. We visited the small
village school, where Gorbachev's first teacher was waiting. We
met some older men, in their Sunday suits, in the *kolkhoz* administration building. They were friends from Gorbachev's youth,
and they sat at the long table in the chairman's room under a
portrait of Gorbachev by a local artist. A few farmers, the village
teacher, and a former fellow student of Gorbachev's, a woman,
were sitting a little awkwardly at the table. A retired agronomist
spoke learnedly about Gorbachev's peace policy. The *kolkhoz*

chairman, who had introduced us to the farmers, said he had something more important to do, and left.

Gradually, as we got into conversation, the farmers became friendlier. One was a tractor driver, who lived in the house next-door to Gorbachev's. He had worked with Gorbachev's father. We talked about the new agricultural policy, which they expected would improve things on the land. One farmer said, half seriously and half joking: 'All they have to do is give us the dollars with which they buy grain. Then we'll buy modern machinery and seed, the lads'll get to work, and we won't need expensive wheat from abroad.' The two women sat back from the table, almost against the wall. The fellow student of Gorbachev seemed uncomfortable. She said she couldn't really recollect what he'd worn at school. All she remembered was that he had been handsome. It took some time for them to remember details about the friend of their youth.

In the neighbouring village of Krasnogvardeisk, where Gorbachev went to school for three years, we met his teachers, all of whom remembered their most distinguished pupil. The headmaster, too young to have known Gorbachev, brought the school record book. He was a little embarrassed that Gorbachev had finished school not with a gold, but only a silver medal. In the local museum a retired headmaster gave us the history of the Socialist development of the district. On the walls hung a few old photos of Privolnoye, and we were hesitantly shown an album with pictures of the young Gorbachev and his father that had probably belonged to a friend of the family. There were more photos in the small museum of the Young Communist League in Stavropol. The first floor of the old department store had been Gorbachev's first workplace in Stavropol. Now a small corner of the room was decorated with official pictures of the Party leader. We spoke with friends and colleagues from the time when he was a Young Communist League functionary and Party Secretary. They were rather reserved and careful, preferring to talk in general terms, not because they were afraid but, it seemed, because like the Gorbachevs themselves they respected the privacy of others. But slowly they became more talkative. We talked with the professors of the institute and the schools where Raisa Gorbachev had taught and her daughter Irina had studied, saw the houses in which the Gorbachevs had lived, and heard about their lifestyle and personalities.

In Moscow it was easier to get into conversation with Gorbachev's friends from his student days. Today they are professors, editors, public prosecutors. Some are already retired. One professor had taken the precaution of asking a colleague, an adviser to Gorbachev on foreign affairs, if he could talk about their student comrade Zdeněk Mlynář, who had been Czech Party Secretary under Dubček in the Prague Spring. He was advised against it: perhaps it was still too early for that. Twenty years previously the professor had been extensively questioned by the KGB about the relationship between Mlynář and Gorbachev. In May 1989 he told me that he did not want to talk about this friend of Gorbachev's. Six months later the climate in Moscow had changed to such an extent that he was willing to talk openly about Mlynář. In the meantime it had become known that in 1989 Zdeněk Mlynář had visited Moscow, and had seen Gorbachev.

We had scarcely three weeks in which to film, edit and provide a text for our film on Gorbachev, which was to be shown on the evening before Gorbachev's Bonn visit. We therefore had no chance of doing more than casting a narrow spotlight on a few decisive moments in his political development. Soviet colleagues in West Germany who saw the film learned something about Gorbachev's past for the first time. Some of them wrote reports on it, and asked when Soviet citizens would be able to see it. But Soviet television decided it was still too early. One of the Soviet officials who had backed the project took a video cassette of the film for Gorbachev, who watched it on his second evening in Bonn. Perhaps this reminder of his youth moved him, because on the following day the security men who accompanied him had a sudden urgent desire to be photographed shaking hands with me.

We continued to gather information in Moscow. It became clear to us that it is still very difficult to discover how policy originates in the leadership of the Soviet Union, or exactly how the path of a career leads to the high ground of the Central Committee and the Politburo. But a noticeable change occurred in the course of 1989: it became much easier to talk to people about Gorbachev. Even so, people who have collaborated at various stages in the forming of his policies are seldom sure exactly what motives Gorbachev had for his decisions. Some, whose hopes for reform have not been fully realised, have become critics of Gorbachev. Others see him as the country's last hope, but many of them would have liked clearer decisions from him, and fewer compromises. The nationalist leaders in the republics say that Gorbachev did not understand their problems, or understood them too late, but even they avoid attacking him personally. The most frequent comment I heard about Gorbachev was that he is a mystery. Only in Boris Yeltsin's statements is there a hint of true personal animosity. But there was increasing criticism of Gorbachev in Moscow, and after the outbreak of unrest in Azerbaidjan it took the form of anxiety about how Gorbachev actually intended to cope with the future. Still, hardly anyone spoke of him without respect. Nobody doubted his essential honesty and decency. Naturally, we looked for negative aspects. What we heard seemed too good to be true. But we never encountered the routine flattery given to former Party leaders. If my portrait of Gorbachev seems deficient in warts and wrinkles, this is not because I am an unquestioning admirer, but because no one I spoke to, including his critics, appeared to harbour any resentment of him.

This book on Mikhail Gorbachev is neither a piece of academic Sovietology nor a psychoanalytical study. It is the book of a journalist, about an ordinary human being who, in a time of worldwide political upheaval, became an extraordinary leader.

CHAPTER 1

Childhood

Mikhail Sergeyevich Gorbachev was born in a small village, to a genuine peasant family, facts which distinguish him from all previous leaders of the Soviet Union. None, not even Nikita Khrushchev, who could seem a peasant in his speech and behaviour, grew up on the vast Russian flatlands. Like the leaders of the Revolution, they all came by their experience in cities or industrial districts. Gorbachev was the first major political figure in Soviet history to have spent his youth in a village and in the fields before rising in the Party apparatus.

Privolnoye is a typical Russian village, one of many in its district. Few streets are paved or asphalted, the houses are one-storey, with small yards where the farmers keep a few cows, chickens and ducks. Just over three thousand people live in the village and on the surrounding farms. In the centre of Privolnoye are the single-storey administration building, a slightly larger House of Culture, and a club where films are shown and festive evenings and meetings are held. In the motor and tractor depot are the agricultural machines – by Soviet standards they are in good condition. The soil is fertile, and the district produces a good crop, even if the herdsmen and their cows by the river where Gorbachev and the village boys once bathed still look as if they were from a pre-industrial world. The village lies a few kilometres from the main road to the south. Where the houses end, the narrow, unpaved streets peter out into country lanes. Cars rarely drive through the village – tractors are more commonplace. At the weekends a lorry takes the women to Krasnogvardeisk twenty kilometres away to shop. At the edge of the village lies a small cemetery. Among birches and alders wooden benches stand by the graves, and on holidays the farmers come to picnic and be close to their dead. Many of the small houses in the village have television aerials on their roofs, but every Easter the farmhouses are still freshly painted blue and white, as was the custom before the Revolution. The gardens are attractive, and full of flowers. One of the first was planted and tended by Gorbachev's mother, who still lives in the small house her husband built. The villagers know her as Grannie Manya. They approve of the fact that her life has hardly altered since her son rose in the Party, and that she still lives in her old house, draws her 36-rouble pension and keeps a few chickens and small animals. Since spring 1990, however, a secret service man has been stationed in the small yard to guard against the inquisitive or petitioners.

The city of Stavropol lies 170 kilometres to the south. Visitors from other parts of Russia are often struck by the good condition of the villages in the region. Elsewhere in the country many houses have been abandoned, and those still inhabited often show signs of decay.

Although the village of Privolnoye was not originally a Cossack settlement, the customs and traditions of the Cossacks have helped to mould it. It was the Cossacks who conquered this land for the Russian empire. In the eighteenth century, under Catherine the Great, they established themselves in the south, founding military stations around which they settled. They forced the native population into the foothills and mountains of the Caucasus, and they interbred with the tribes of the Chechen, Karabadin and Karachayen. The Greeks, Ukrainians and Russians had all previously left traces of themselves on the faces of southern Russia. These people are said to be versatile, good at business and energetic. The peasants here have not been serfs for centuries. Here the adventurous and the self-reliant settled, the peasants with the greatest desire for independence. Even the name of Gorbachev's village tells a story. 'Privolnoye' means the expanse of land that was steppe when the first peasants came, and it also means freedom. Some of the peasants who came to the district had run away from their owners, others had come from the Cossack settlements. Space and freedom are concepts that in this part of Russia are bound up with the traditions and the history of the Cossacks.

The Cossacks were soldiers and peasants who, at the Tsar's orders, settled the frontiers of the empire and pushed them ever further south and east. They did not think of themselves as vassals, but as independent and free. In their settlements it was they, not the landowner or government official, who made the decisions about the running of the community. Arable and grazing land was mostly common property. In all Russia only the Cossacks chose their own leaders, and only they could vote them out of office. In the last decades of the Tsarist empire the Cossack regiments were regarded as the upholders of the autocracy, driving demonstrators apart with whips, hard and arrogant, despising those whom they considered subjugated. A love of freedom and independence was central to their lives, and nowhere in Russia was there stronger feeling for equality before the law and democracy. In the Civil War after the Revolution some Cossacks fought for an independent Ukraine, separate from Russia, and others, including the legendary Red Army cavalry of Budenny, for the Revolution.

Mikhail Gorbachev's maternal grandfather, Panteli Yefimovich Gopalko, was of Cossack stock. He is reported to have been an independent thinker, always ready to take decisions and responsibility, and some close observers of Gorbachev believe that his attitude to life springs from the Cossack-peasant tradition. In the village it is said that Panteli Gopalko was one of the first after the Revolution to organise the peasants into a co-operative, in which the peasants kept and farmed their own land, but worked together to improve farming methods and yield. Panteli Gopalko was a respected man in the village, a well-to-do peasant who supported the co-operative movement at a time when it was being organised in most villages by poor peasants. Unlike the *kolkhozes* into which Stalin later forced the peasants, these early co-operatives were voluntary, and were intended to improve the peasants' living and working conditions. When Stalin collectivised agriculture Panteli Gopalko, like other clear-sighted peasants, saw that this development could not be opposed. He became a member of the Communist Party and undertook to organise the collective farm, of which he was chairman. Older people in the village remember that it was thanks to him that Privolnoye survived the terrible time of the famine and the persecution of the peasants in the early thirties better than most other Russian farming communities.

Nevertheless, these were hard times for Privolnoye. The former agronomist of the collective, Nikolai Lyubenko, says: 'I remember collectivisation well. In 1929 I was still very young, and my family enrolled in the collective. We gave it everything. They even took the chickens. In two years the village was almost completely collectivised. There were eight of us in the family at that time, six brothers. My father was banished for ten years and his property was confiscated. Our house was torn down. We had to move six times in a year. In 1933 two of my brothers died. They're buried in the field. Whenever it's ploughed I think their bones might come up. Those were hard times. In 1932 there was the great famine. Everything had been taken from the peasants. In almost every house in the district there was someone who had died of hunger. I think Panteli Gopalko saved the village. Because he had a strong character, the famine wasn't quite as bad here as in other places. We were all afraid he'd be arrested in the purges in the thirties, and we were grateful that he stayed with us.'

Mikhail Gorbachev was born on 2 March 1931. His mother worked in the fields, his father drove combines and tractors and was responsible for the repair and upkeep of agricultural machines. The real force in the family was Gorbachev's mother, Maria Pantelevna.

'She knew how to use her elbows, and could make quite a scene,' remembers a neighbour. The father, Sergei, was quiet and hard-working, and was respected in the village. Nikolai Lyubenko says of him that although he had had little education he had gained a great deal of experience through handling machinery. 'We young people often went to him for advice, to ask how something should be done. What particularly impressed me about him was that he always stayed calm. He always had the right approach. In the country, you know, when there's engine trouble, almost anything can happen. But no one ever heard him curse.'

A local farmer, Ivan Maliko, worked as a young man with Sergei Gorbachev: 'He never got angry with anyone. If you went to him for something he was always ready to help. It made no difference if you were senior or not.' On the land in those days it was unusual but vital for someone to take the time to teach the young people, as they received no training. Gorbachev himself remembers: 'Father's neighbours valued him as a hard-working, modest and considerate man. I'm proud of my father.'

While his parents worked the young Mikhail spent a great deal of time at the house of his maternal grandparents. He wrote in

1989 that the atmosphere and way of life in a farming family, sharing the work with his parents from early childhood, greatly influenced the development of his character and his attitude to life. Undoubtedly the experiences of his parents and grandparents also made an impression on him, although at the time of the great political purges he was only six or seven. In the present district of Krasnogvardeisk and in the neighbouring district of Petrovsk during those years 70 to 80 per cent of the cadres of the Party and administration were arrested, deported or executed: leading functionaries, activists of the Young Communist League, ordinary people. The persecution of the peasants followed the persecution of supposed political opponents of Stalin – a twofold destruction of the best and most active people in the country.

Nikolai Dorochin, who in the fifties was Gorbachev's superior in Stavropol, says of that time: 'My father was the village smith. He'd only been to school for two years, but they even arrested him, and he was given five years for some invented counter-revolutionary activity. Every night they arrested ten to twenty people. There simply weren't enough functionaries for the secret police to fill their terrible quota of arrests. So they also took peasants who could hardly read or write.'

Gorbachev's friends from the time of his later work for the Party in Stavropol, such as the former Young Communist functionary Lilya Kolodichuka, say that in the years after Stalin's death they discussed the purges with Gorbachev: 'He grew up in the years 1937 and 1938. Although he was still a young child, he saw what was happening to the people around him. To the simple, honest people who had made the Revolution, who had fought in the Civil War, who had founded the collective farms. They had all suffered, though they were innocent. Naturally he didn't accept this.'

It is questionable whether the young Mikhail Gorbachev, even at the time when he came to Moscow as a student, could have had an idea of what really happened in the time of the collectivisation and the political purges. Until recently, for most Soviet citizens, the scale of the persecutions, arrests and executions was unknown or unimaginable. After Stalin's death Khrushchev was the first to break the taboo surrounding these crimes. In the 1960s Soviet intellectuals learned more from underground texts, from the so-called *samizdat*, and from work published in the West and smuggled into the country. But only in the time of *glasnost* did articles appear with facts and figures about the terrible years of the thirties, and to this day in the Soviet Union this tragedy has not been comprehensively researched or fully described. What really happened during the enforced collectivisation was for a long time one of the best-kept state secrets of the Soviet Union. Many people remained silent about what they knew, and many reports in the West also played down the consequences of collectivisation and the famine, because journalists simply did not want to believe it.

Naturally there were rumours in Moscow and the cities of the Soviet Union, but they were spread in whispers, and most people were afraid to listen to them. It was safer not to believe what the witnesses of these unprecedented events who dared to talk about them were reporting. Mikhail Gorbachev was a baby when his native village was collectivised, and a little boy when the waves of arrests during the purges swept the land. He must have experienced the atmosphere of oppression and silence at home. Perhaps he noticed that his relatives and neighbours were living a kind of double life: public enthusiasm and agreement, and private fear of what was happening around them. Perhaps his parents and grandparents behaved like most Soviet families and did not burden their children with their terrible and dangerous knowledge. By the time Gorbachev was old enough to understand the truth about these years the Second World War was over, and a new and traumatic experience overshadowed the memory of what had come before. It was now easier for people to suppress their knowledge of the past and to believe in the Party's optimistic slogans for reconstruction. The Soviet Union had survived conflict and suffering, and now the future would begin. It was still dangerous to talk about the past. Whoever did so gambled with his life and the freedom of his family.

'For Stalin the peasants were dirt,' Nikita Khrushchev said in 1956 when he began to settle accounts with the dead dictator. But the peasant had been a little-known, reviled creature for Russian Marxists long before Stalin. Even Georgi Plekhanov, one of the first and wisest Marxists, saw them as 'barbarian tillers of the soil, ferocious and pitiless, beasts of burden whose lives do not allow them the luxury of thought'. From their earliest beginnings the Socialists and Bolsheviks were parties of the cities, with their intellectuals and workers. Before the Revolution there were only half a dozen village Party cells, and fewer than five hundred peasants were members of the Communist Party.

After the Revolution the demand for land to be handed over to the peasants won the Communists' support in the villages. But the peasants interpreted this as meaning the land of the owners of large estates, rather than that of the *kulaks*, the richer peasants. They lacked, the Communists said, an awareness of the need for class struggle. In 1918 Y. M. Sverdlov, who since the Revolution had been organising the links between the Revolutionary headquarters and the Communists in the provinces for Lenin, said before the Central Executive Committee: 'We must very seriously attend to the problem of how the villages can be divided according to class, how they can be made into two hostile camps, and we have to organise the poorest layers of the population against the *kulak* elements. Only if we can divide the villages into two camps and bring about the same class struggle as in the cities will we achieve in the villages what we have achieved in the cities.' In the decade after the Revolution campaigns of 'dekulakisation' were directed against the most successful and respected people in the villages, and by 1930 the campaign for collectivisation was so far-reaching it could seize and destroy practically anyone in any village in Russia.

In the first post-Revolutionary years under 'war Communism' the Bolsheviks had simply confiscated grain. The cities and their workers needed to be provided for. Peasants who wanted to sell their grain were regarded as capitalist speculators. Tens of thousands died in the peasant uprisings during the Civil War. Lenin understood how damaging and dangerous the fight was against the peasants, brought about by the policy of confiscation. The New Economic Policy introduced firm quotas for delivery, similar to taxes – with notable success. After a relatively short time the famine ended, agricultural production rose, and the villages grew calm.

But once Stalin had consolidated his power the policy changed. It was the villages' contribution that was to make possible the construction of a gigantic industrial state. Stalin's brutal exploitation of the peasants led to a fresh crisis in the grain supply in 1928. This was a direct result of the government's agricultural policy, but for Stalin it was the justification for a general assault on the peasants.

The violent confiscation of crops had proved costly and even dangerous. Now it was a matter of bringing the harvest yield directly under the Party control. From the beginning the Party had rejected the idea of an independent peasantry and the market economy elements of the rural economy. The collectivisation of agriculture and the integration of the peasants in so-called *kolkhoz* economies under the control of functionaries seemed logical, reasonable and necessary to most Communist leaders. A renewed campaign began against the remaining *kulaks*, though their numbers had decreased and their economic role in the villages was now of little significance. Tens of thousands of functionaries streamed from the cities to the villages, many full of honest enthusiasm for the task of rescuing the Revolution's supplies and spreading Communism by taking the peasants' hoarded grain and reorganising the villages. Some of these honest functionaries justified violent measures, hunger and misery in the hope of a Socialist future, but there were others, of whom Vassili Grossman wrote: 'The most poisonous and evil were those who settled scores. They talked of political awareness, but they were driven by envy. They stole out of naked egoism.'

All came protected by weapons and secret police, and by the time they had finished their work the country had been organised into 240,000 collective farms. Millions of peasants had perished or been forced out of their villages and taken to Siberia in cattle-trucks, many dying on the journey. In the Urals and the far regions of Siberia they found no housing. They were driven onto frozen fields in which they could hardly scrape a hole in the earth. Near Krasnoyarsk 4,000 peasants were imprisoned in a barbed-wire enclosure, and within two months half of them were dead. Wolfgang Leonhard recalled how they were supposed to live in Kazakstan. A few stakes, on which were written 'Settlement Five' or 'Settlement Six', had been hammered into the ground. The peasants were left to survive as best they could. They lived in holes, and many died of hunger and cold. Vassili Grossman said of Stalin's decree: 'It laid down that the peasants of the Ukraine, the Don and the Kuban were to be condemned to death by starvation. They were to be killed with their little children.'

Secret police and activists saw to it that the peasants were unable to leave. Viktor Serge, one of the old revolutionaries, described this in his memoirs. 'Masses of dirty people crowded the railway stations, heaps of men, women and children waiting for God knows what train. They're chased away and come back without money and tickets, they climb onto any train and stay until they're driven out. They're quiet and passive. Where are they trying to get to? Somewhere where they can find bread and potatoes or work in the factories, where workers are better fed.'

In the Ukraine in those years about five million people died. In the districts of the Don and the Kuban, and in the region of Gorbachev's native village, the famine was equally bad. These were the areas of Russia where the peasants had shown the most independence and had managed their affairs with the most success. Unlike the northern regions, where the oppression of serfdom had dulled the peasants, in these areas of southern Russia independence and self-respect were part of their being. Perhaps for this very reason Stalin's campaign was directed particularly against them. In 1933 an English traveller reported that the region was like a camp in the desert: no work, no crops, no cattle, no draught animals, only peasants and workers in a half-destroyed landscape. The cohesion of the Cossacks was shattered by death and deportation. In Labinskaya only 24,000 people remained after the deportations, and of those, 14,000 died of hunger. In Starokorsunskaya, of 14,000 people only a thousand survived. Many villages lay deserted, their inhabitants having fled to the steppes where they lived off roots or by catching marmots.

The famine in southern Russia and the northern Caucasus extended to the cities. In Stavropol, where thirty years later Gorbachev became Party chief, 50,000 people, a third of the population, starved to death.

In Privolnoye Gorbachev's grandfather Panteli Gopalko was chairman of the *kolkhoz*. He had been one of the first organisers of the co-operative, and some people in the village remember that Gorbachev's grandfathers had fought in the Revolution and the Civil War for the establishment of Soviet power in the foothills of the Caucasus. But little is now known about the beginnings of Soviet rule in the Stavropol district. These events are a mere footnote in the repeatedly rewritten history of the Party. One thing that is certain is that two months after the October Revolution a 'Stavropol Soviet Republic' was proclaimed by the 'Stavropol Government', not by the Bolsheviks but by the Social Revolutionaries. Their leader, Prime Minister Alexander Kerensky, had already been driven out of Petersburg by the Communists, but they continued to find far more support among the peasants than did the Communists. A week after the proclamation a Bolshevik force tried to take power in Stavropol, but they were arrested by the Social Revolutionaries. At the beginning of July 1918 the Stavropol Soviet Republic became part of the North Caucasian Soviet Republic. A few days later Stavropol was occupied by the White Guard, and only two years later it was conquered by the Red Army.

This is the local and early history of a revolution that ran no straight course, and that has become obscure even for those, now very old, who lived through it. Gorbachev's contemporaries are just able to remember the late thirties. Then Panteli Gopalko's reputation protected the village and the *kolkhoz* from measures that hit other villages harder. We do not know where Panteli Gopalko stood in those years. Especially in southern Russia there were old traditions among the Cossacks that the land surrounding the settlements was common property, and in some places such traditions were revived after the Revolution, leading to consent, even enthusiasm, for co-operative forms of organisation. It could have been this that led Panteli Gopalko to become *kolkhoz* chairman in Privolnoye. What he thought of enforced collectivisation is not known. In Moscow, a newspaper editor says that Gorbachev once asked him in the course of a conversation: 'Did you know that in 1937 my grandfather had been in prison for a year and a half and that our family had been declared enemies of the people?' Even in the Privolnoye district such things were not discussed openly. A local functionary says there are records indicating that Panteli Gopalko was imprisoned for fifteen months for refusing to hand over one of the *kolkhoz* cows to an official from the administrative centre. There may, of course, be more to the story. This arrest must have made a great impression on the young Gorbachev, who admired his grandfather.

Apart from this, we have no idea of how much the young Mikhail Gorbachev knew of the scale of the Soviet peasant tragedy, whether for instance he saw enforced collectivisation as necessary for the establishment of a Socialist society and regarded the stories of famine and arrests as mere side-issues in a great political process. If today he sees collectivisation as one of the causes of the agrarian crisis, it is surely because he is thinking of the terrible errors of Stalin's agricultural policy.

Gorbachev's grandfather may have been a Party member, but his family, like many other villagers, continued to live the traditional life of Russian peasants. Mikhail's grandmother took him with her to church during the war, when for a time the persecution of the Church was relaxed as Stalin needed to harness the country's forces for the defence of the Soviet Union. Maria Pantelevna even succeeded in having Mikhail christened, at a time when it was dangerous to attend church. Gorbachev remembers icons hidden behind the portraits of Lenin and Stalin in his parents' house. Apparently his father disapproved, but his strong-minded mother had her way, with the support of her parents.

The house Gorbachev's parents had built for themselves was single-storeyed, like most of those in the village. 'A little house, but everything was nice and clean, even the yard. Naturally they were poor, like everyone else. There was not much to eat, and they didn't get extra rations,' says Ivan Maliko, the Gorbachevs' next-door neighbour.

Mikhail Gorbachev was ten when the Germans invaded Russia, occupying and laying waste much of the western Soviet Union. For four years his father was a soldier in the Soviet Army. He received a medal for bravery when his unit crossed the Dnieper, was wounded in Czechoslovakia and hospitalised in Cracow. He returned from the war much decorated and a Party member.

In the meantime the war had reached Privolnoye. On the village war memorial the name Gorbachev, common in the area, occurs seven times among the fallen. Gorbachev's mother had been conscripted and loaded goods trains at distant stations in the region, rarely coming home in the evening. Mikhail had to look after the cattle and chickens, but at that time he lived mostly with his grandparents. For almost six months Privolnoye was in the occupied area, but as it lay off the main road few German soldiers ever came to the village. In other parts of the Stavropol region there were arrests and executions, but in Privolnoye there are no stories of German atrocities.

Very little is known of Mikhail Gorbachev's life at this time. During these months his mother did not return to Privolnoye. Her service in the unoccupied territory and his father's military decorations must have spared the family problems after the war, as all who had come into even brief contact with the Germans appeared suspicious to Stalin and his police. At the time of the German occupation Mikhail Suslov, who led the partisans, was Party Secretary of the Stavropol district. Later, as a Politburo member, he backed Gorbachev, which suggests that there was no suspicion of collaboration with the Germans against the young Mikhail Gorbachev and his family. In the south of the Stavropol district, Stalin and Suslov had whole tribes who had lived under the Germans deported to Siberia and Central Asia.

Russians who had been trapped in Germany during the war, including prisoners of war, never returned to their homeland. The trains taking them back to Russia were redirected to camps. All traces of prisoners who had died in German camps were obliterated, and to this day their families know nothing of their fate. For many years after the war every Soviet citizen who had lived in German-occupied territory had to enter this in their personal records and in all applications and petitions. It was a black mark against them, an added burden if they were denounced, a hindrance to their careers. Even now people in the village prefer not to say that it was in occupied territory. During his meeting with Helmut Kohl in the summer of 1990, Gorbachev evaded a question about his personal experiences during the occupation. 'You know, war is war,' he said. 'For us, for our people, it was a hard, a terrible war, and I believe even the German people were totally shattered. Both our peoples, and other peoples like the Poles, experienced a tragedy. But we lived in different times then. The front ran through the place where I lived. My father went through it all – the battle of Kursk, the crossing of the Dnieper – and he was wounded. We received a report that he had been killed. There were so many families who lost their closest relatives. That can't be forgotten.'

After Privolnoye had been liberated, normal life gradually resumed. Teaching began again in the one-storey village school. But Mikhail Gorbachev was absent from class. Life had become hard, and that winter he had no clothes to wear to school, says his mother. For three months he had to stay at home. Maria Pantelevna Gorbachev told a Soviet television journalist in an interview that was never transmitted in the Soviet Union: 'My husband wrote to me from the front, "No matter what the cost,

you have to find something for Misha so he can go to school."
So I took the sheep and drove with them to Salsk and sold them.
With the money – one and a half thousand roubles – I bought
army boots. Then I went to the head of the school, Gitalo was
his name, and he said, "Maria Pantelevna, three months have
already gone by," and I said, "Misha says he'll catch up on
everything he's missed." '

So Mikhail went back to school. He was a hard-working and
attentive pupil, but not over-ambitious, his classmates recollect.
For a Russian village boy in the years following the war there
were many distractions from schoolwork. The countryside had
been destroyed, there were few agricultural machines, and food
was scarce. Reconstruction required hard work, and the Party
and the secret police enforced it: anyone who was unable to fulfil
his tasks could count on heavy punishment or imprisonment,
even if his failure was due to a lack of seed or spare parts for the
machines. In 1944, at the age of thirteen, Gorbachev began to
work on the *kolkhoz*, and from his fifteenth year he worked at
the machine and tractor depot, often as assistant to his father.

Gorbachev worked harder than most of his fellow pupils. Perhaps his father, as a new Party member, had brought back from
the war strong political convictions that influenced his son. Sergei
Gorbachev may also have believed that hard work could compen-
sate for the handicap the few years spent in occupied territory
might come to represent in his son's future life.

Gorbachev coped successfully with his work on the land and
in school. His fellow pupils say he was an intelligent boy who
learned quickly and had a good memory. He could talk well and
convincingly. This ability served him well when he joined the
Young Communist League, the *Komsomol*, at the age of fourteen.
But some people in the village remember him as nothing special,
just a boy like the rest.

Lyubov Stuliyeva, a school friend, was leader of the Young
Communist group at the village school, the 'boss', as she likes to
put it, of her deputy Gorbachev. She describes what he looked
like then: 'In the first years after the war he wore riding trousers,
halifesht I think they're called, from an old uniform, but they
suited him. With them he wore a jacket like the ones they wear
on the steppes, also camouflage-colour, and a grey fur cap with
rose trimming at the top. And if I remember correctly, he didn't

wear coarse leather boots, but shiny ones. He looked good, I thought, and so did the other girls. Everyone thought well of him. And he was very aware of how much he knew, very self-assured. He was clever and good looking. I still remember dancing with him when I was a young girl. I was a year older than he was, that's why I was the *Komsomol* leader.' Gorbachev's German teacher, Matilda Ignatenko, remembers him as 'an inquisitive boy, who asked more questions than the others. He worked hard, didn't try to get out of any assignments, and always wanted to learn more. He got the highest marks in every subject except German. But that was because there had been no German taught at the school until I came.'

Young Mikhail rendered his German teacher an important service when some of her pupils cast suspicion on her. Today the reason seems absurd, but then, shortly after the war, it was mortally dangerous. Matilda Ignatenko had read a German poem to her pupils that began with the line *'Lenin war ein Freund und Führer'*. As a result some boys maintained that she was spreading fascist propaganda and insulting Lenin by comparing him to Hitler. At that time even such a trivial accusation could lead to arrest. Matilda Ignatenko was particularly vulnerable, coming from a family with a German background. In 1937 her father had been arrested and deported. He had settled in Russia, where he married a Ukrainian. At the beginning of the war her Ukrainian name had protected her when other German Russians were being deported to Siberia and Central Asia. 'But my first name, Matilda, betrayed me, and I fled with my child from village to village to avoid denunciation. My husband died at the front. It was hard to live as a German. When the boys accused me of spreading fascist propaganda and slandering Lenin I was terribly frightened. There was no way I could convince them. But the next day Misha Gorbachev came with his dictionary and told them that the word *Führer* was not fascist, and that it was a Communist poem. He stood up for me, and eventually convinced the other pupils.'

A few weeks after Matilda Ignatenko began teaching in Privolnoye Gorbachev told an older friend that she was an interesting, educated woman, and a good teacher. 'Even if she does have a child and is five years older than you, she's an exceptional woman, and you ought to marry her.' Matilda Ignatenko knows of this conversation because the friend later did propose to her, though not, she says, because of Gorbachev's advice.

The village school ended with the seventh class. But Sergei Gorbachev wanted his son to go on studying. The nearest ten-year school was twenty kilometres away in the town of Molotovskoye, today called Krasnogvardeisk. He rented a bed for his son in a small room shared with two other village boys. Interestingly, both of these boys were also to have notable careers: one is now a Lieutenant General, the other a university professor. The bed cost 150 roubles a year, a lot of money for a peasant family, especially as in those years school fees had been reintroduced for the top three classes. On holidays Mikhail returned to Privolnoye to work on the land and help his father with the combine.

Alexander Yakovenko, a contemporary, remembers: 'In the summer holiday Misha helped his mother and father, mostly his father, who drove a combine. I think he worked hard at school, but during the holiday he didn't rest at all, he'd be working as soon as he arrived. We worked day and night, starting at dawn, as soon as the dew had dried. We didn't get to bed until late. After work we had to wipe and clean the combines. Then we lay down in the straw. Naturally we didn't have blankets or sheets. We'd doze for two hours or so, until work started again. That's how it was. We didn't bathe. Where could we have? There was no warm water. We flung ourselves down dirty as we were. And food – well, there was great poverty at that time. For breakfast there was gruel with barley, cabbage soup in the middle of the day, in the evening dumplings or pasta. There was no meat at all. It has to be said, we're rather better off today. It was quite hard for Misha. When he came back from school he immediately took his place on the combines. Even when his workmates went to bathe in the river or to rest, he continued working until September, when school began again. So he had no holiday, no break. Our fathers both drove combines. My father was a good man, but he knew how to curse, especially when he'd had a few. But when Sergei Gorbachev was with us he always pulled himself together.'

The two Gorbachevs and the two Yakovenkos worked so hard together that they earned a reputation throughout the district. In 1948 the local newspaper even reported that Gorbachev and Yakovenko were ready to begin harvesting with their two sons.

'That harvest we brought in so much wheat that we got an award from the government,' says Alexander Yakovenko. 'Our fathers each got the Order of Lenin, us boys the Order of the Red Banner of Labour. We were awarded them in Stavropol, and each of us was allowed to buy a suit in a shop. We had no idea what size we needed. The suits didn't really fit us. They were made of coarse wool, nobody would want them today, but we were pleased with them, and when we put them on we thought we were the best-dressed lads in the village.'

It was rare for orders to be awarded to two such young men, and this undoubtedly helped Mikhail later make his way in Moscow.

But for the time being he was still at the ten-year school in Krasnogvardeisk. He worked hard, and learned a lot. Even if he had not been ambitious himself, his parents' expectations would have spurred him on. His teachers at this time remember his mother's visits and her precise, purposeful questions about her son's progress. His father came more often, and asked not only about his son but also about the achievements of the other pupils.

'Misha Gorbachev always took an active part in the class,' says Maria Grevcheva, his headmistress. 'Naturally it never occurred to us that he might one day be General Secretary, although he did perhaps stand out because he played such an active part in the school.' Another retired teacher remembers: 'He really was a very quick boy, always asking questions. And he never did anything simply on his own. He always debated with the other students in his class and with me whether something was good or bad. If there was an argument – children are like that, they argue and then there's a fight – Misha never fought. Or only unwillingly, if there was no other way, if someone else started it. If there was an argument he would keep trying to persuade his opponents until they understood his point of view, and then there was peace.'

He couldn't stand pupils who were lazy, says Lydia Chaiko, one of his teachers. Others say he helped fellow pupils who were poor in Russian or mathematics. Generally, his teachers remember, he was always polite to adults, asked them for advice and listened carefully. His history teacher remembers that there was a wood stove in the classroom, for which the teachers themselves had to chop and saw the wood. Without being asked, and without expecting praise, Gorbachev often did this for them.

His teachers and companions all say that Gorbachev was very popular. He played the accordion and the balalaika, liked to sing, and danced at the evening events. He was cheerful, and liked acting. His Russian teacher Yulya Shushkova believes that she taught him to love Pushkin: 'Gorbachev had an exceptionally good memory, and soon he knew many of Pushkin's poems by heart. He also loved Lermontov, in whose play *Masquerade* he played Tsvetsdich, who murders his wife out of jealousy.' He read the Russian classics as well as the current reconstruction and war novels, and to this day he knows poems by heart that he learned then.

Gorbachev received a solid educational foundation at school, and was introduced to literature and culture. He read a great deal, often borrowing books from the library. He liked to take part in the discussions that in schools at that time were called 'political battles'. Students would expand on what they had learned in the political training courses, taking on the roles of debating partners and putting forward arguments against each other. Gorbachev was often the victor. He could speak well and persuasively, but that in itself would not have been enough. He must have closely studied the official texts and known how to keep to the Party line, to present it convincingly without deviating. Whether out of ambition or curiosity, he read beyond the texts given in class. In the small-town school this was unusual, and gave him an advantage over his fellow pupils.

'In the tenth class he surprised me very much,' remembers his class teacher Antonina Churbanova. 'He submitted an essay on Lenin's work on the co-operative movement. I can tell you, in 1950 that wasn't exactly a popular theme.' Dealing with such a subject at the time of Stalin's collectivisation of agriculture was not without its dangers. Perhaps Gorbachev's interest in Lenin's text on co-operatives was connected with the fact that his grand-father had founded the co-operative in Privolnoye before it was turned into a *kolkhoz*.

What Gorbachev's school friends and teachers say about him today may sound almost too good to be true. Perhaps hindsight has added a certain gloss, but that alone could not be the reason why one hears absolutely nothing negative. Gorbachev, it seems, made no enemies. He must have succeeded in getting along with everyone. But at the same time he had a will of his own, a feeling for truth and justice, and an independence of mind that he could express without becoming strident. What is missing in the recollections of those who knew him when he was young is that streak of impatience, even intolerance, that showed itself later, when General Secretary Gorbachev refused to reply to the objections of opposing speakers in political debates.

The people in his native village today regard him as a very humane man. It pleases them that as his political career advanced he continued to visit his mother, that as General Secretary he dispensed with his bodyguards when he came back to the village. 'Imagine it,' says one of his old friends. 'A man comes home, and the guards won't allow even his friends to talk to him. But he got rid of them.' The villagers also say that not once has he come to Privolnoye without visiting his father's grave. 'People like that,' says the agronomist Nikolai Lyubenko. 'They see that he's human and that he hasn't forgotten what life is like in a village, and how the dead are honoured. And when he comes he always visits us. So you know he's a good man. And, after all the hard times we've had in the village, what we like about Mikhail Sergeyevich isn't just that he comes from Privolnoye, but that he comes from the people. He wants ordinary people to be treated like human beings. Before we were little screws in a big machine. Now we know we're also human beings.'

In the little village cemetery there are many wooden crosses and only a few stone monuments, one of which is to Sergei Gorbachev. After his father's death in 1976 Gorbachev came straight from the Party Congress in Moscow to the village. From the cemetery he went to the memorial for the war dead and then to his mother's house. She was standing at the door, wearing an apron and headscarf, a neighbour remembers, and when she saw Gorbachev she began to cry. He smiled and said: 'Mother, did you make brawn for us?' 'Of course, my son,' the old woman replied. 'Then there's no need to cry,' said Gorbachev. The story is still told in the village many years later.

In Krasnogvardeisk people remember that the rising politician Gorbachev visited his old teachers, that he asked what could be done for his school, that he sent postcards from Moscow with holiday greetings. Nothing extraordinary, but it all fits in with the impressions formed of him forty years ago by his school friends and teachers. Some of the stories they tell serve as early indications of Gorbachev's leadership skills and the determination with which he would later carry through his policies. Naturally the character traits that are remembered are those that fit the portrait of a future General Secretary. 'We wouldn't have guessed that Gorbachev would one day have a very high post,' says Lydia Chaiko. 'But we did know this boy would make his way through life on his own.'

CHAPTER 2

University

In 1950 Gorbachev left school with a very good Leaving Certificate. He had excellent marks in almost every subject. Only in German had his work been rated merely 'good'. Evidently he had never caught up on the years lost when there had been no one to teach foreign languages at the village school. He was awarded a silver medal, not the gold that would have won him automatic entrance to university. Still, he had a very good general report from the school and from the Young Communist League. Both at school and in the *Komsomol* he had shown himself an active and committed young Communist.

These were the last years of Stalin's personality cult, with their hymns and poems of homage which no one could allow themselves not to know by heart. In the cities, especially among intellectuals, academics and writers, there was an oppressive fear of Stalin's secret police and of Beria, his Minister of the Interior, who persecuted and arrested anyone who deviated from the prescribed course. This fear also dominated the lives of simple people in *kolkhozes* and factories, where a minor offence such as being late for work could be punished with prison or the labour camp. In the newspapers, on the radio and in schools the teachings of Stalin and the success of his policies were ceaselessly drummed into people. That the German occupiers had been driven from the country under Stalin's leadership had raised him to the status of saviour of the Soviet Union, and contributed to the credibility of his propaganda. No one could risk making even a whispered criticism of Stalin and the Party, or mentioning the hardship of life in the Soviet Union.

During his three years at school in Krasnogvardeisk, Gorbachev had come under the influence of this constant political education, and as a Young Communist he had passed it on to others. The possibility of being allowed to study in the capital may have strengthened his belief in the system. Zdeněk Mlynář, a Czech who would become a friend of Gorbachev's in his fourth student year in Moscow, wrote that Gorbachev came to the university as a 'Stalinist'. Mlynář himself, who had been sent from Czechoslovakia to Moscow University, must also have given his teachers and officials the impression that he was politically 'reliable', otherwise he would not have been selected. As Young Communists and elite students both he and Gorbachev must have at least appeared to support the system that was advancing them. That, however, did not prevent them both from becoming reformers, Gorbachev in the USSR, Mlynář in Czechoslovakia, where he was Party Secretary under Dubček at the time of the Prague Spring.

Friends of the nineteen-year-old Gorbachev say that at that time he really wanted to be a doctor. Others remember that his father advised him to study mathematics at the College of Education in Stavropol. But Gorbachev decided to apply for admission to the Law Faculty at Moscow University. In those years tens of thousands of students travelled to Moscow for the university exams, and only one place was available for every one or two hundred applicants. During the exams and holidays those who were unable to find accommodation at the hostel of the institute they hoped to enter slept on friends' floors or in the overcrowded station waiting rooms. Gorbachev apparently told his father that if he were rejected in Moscow there would still be time to apply for Stavropol.

At the end of August 1950, after a journey of almost two days, Gorbachev arrived in Moscow with a wooden suitcase and some provisions. Until then he had never seen any city larger than Stavropol, and although Moscow had been devastated by the war, he must still have been deeply impressed by the magnificent mosaics and chandeliers of the capital's underground, by the wide streets, the big theatres, and the Kremlin, where Stalin lived and worked. To the young man from the provinces Moscow must have appeared as confirmation that Stalin was right, his policies successful. But for counter-revolutionary activists and the destruction and sacrifices of the war the entire Soviet Union could have looked like this.

Gorbachev had to report to the Law Faculty for an interview with the professors. His silver medal from school meant that no examination was necessary, but he still had to prove at the interview that he was worth a university place. Although his speech was coloured by the south Russian dialect, and he lacked much of the knowledge and the manner of expressing oneself that was taken for granted among students from Moscow's intelligentsia, the professors decided to accept him.

The fact that Gorbachev had been awarded the Order of the Red Banner of Labour must have played a part, as must the good character assessment by his seniors in the Young Communist League. But many Moscow professors, especially in the Law Faculty, had cautiously retained their independence of judgement throughout the Stalin years, and did not meekly accept every politically selected candidate. Fellow students of Gorbachev believe that the interviewing professors must have been impressed by the cool certainty of this candidate from the provinces, by his quick, but considered and precise, answers. For the older professors, who cared about the academic level of the university, an applicant like Gorbachev was a pleasant surprise. They were under pressure to decrease the number of students from intellectual families and to raise the numbers of children of workers and peasants, to admit fewer Jews and more ethnic Russians. Stalin's distrust of Jews had become a guiding principle of policy. An intelligent young Russian who was also the son of a peasant had excellent chances of being accepted.

It was important to Gorbachev's development that he was accepted by Moscow University's Law Faculty. Here traces still survived of the broad-mindedness and openness of the old Moscow University that, before the Revolution and even in the twenties, had set the nation's intellectual mood. Even if the professors now had to keep carefully to the Party line, they could still encourage independent thinking in intelligent students. This may have applied less during Gorbachev's first years as a student, but after Stalin's death the Thaw set in and conditions eased.

Since the show trials of the 1930s law and justice in the Soviet Union had been completely subjected to the demands of Stalin and the Party. Torture had become the usual method of obtaining the senseless and grotesque confessions that served as formal accusations in secret, closed trials. Millions of people were sentenced without the process of law to execution or to the camps. But lawyers were needed to give a legal basis to these proceedings, and to validate them with words. The training of such lawyers perverted the thinking of an entire legal generation.

Moscow University was the oldest in Russia. The elite of the Russian intelligentsia had studied there, and only the best students in the Soviet Union gained entrance. Law, the history of European legal philosophy and the Marxist classics were taught in some depth, within the Stalinist limitations. Mikhail Gorbachev entered an atmosphere totally different from that to which he was accustomed. The students were more independent in their thinking and speech than anyone he had ever encountered. Most of them came from the educated intelligentsia. They had grown up amongst journalists, academics, higher officials. Many of them spoke foreign languages and had a wider knowledge of Russian culture than Gorbachev had been able to acquire in Krasnogvard-yesk. He may have sought diligently in the school library for material that would fill in gaps in the school curriculum, but other students had grown up with their fathers' libraries, and had read the political classics in their original languages, whereas Gorbachev knew them only through quotations selected to fit the Party line. Some had fought in the war, and had seen other European countries. In Moscow Gorbachev was an outsider, a provincial. He still wore the ill-fitting suit he had bought in Stavropol when he was awarded his Order. His accent and inexperience betrayed his origins.

Despite these handicaps, Mikhail Gorbachev was very quickly accepted by the other students on his course. Even more surprisingly, of his three closest friends, all of whom belonged to the faculty's intellectual elite, and all of whom were older than him, one was Jewish and one a Czech. That Gorbachev was also in his own way an intelligent outsider does not explain why the other three accepted him as a friend, and even less does it explain why he formed friendships with a foreigner and a Jew at a time when this could have led to suspicion and persecution.

On 1 September 1950 Gorbachev moved into room 336 in the student hostel on Strominka Street, on the outskirts of Moscow, a long journey by tram from the university. Sixteen students shared the room, which contained sixteen beds and sixteen cupboards, not quite as many chairs and a huge table where they had breakfast, celebrated birthdays or debated. Lavatories and a bathroom were on the other side of the corridor. Most students received a grant of twenty-nine roubles a month (at today's values). Those who had come with a gold medal from school and who passed their exams with distinction received thirty-six roubles. A few had more because they had been awarded a Stalin scholarship. One of these was Rudolf Kolchanov, today editor of the union paper *Trud*. He met Gorbachev in room 336 on the first day of the first term. 'We were poor students. In the fifties we didn't have enough to eat, and the grant wasn't particularly large. By the end of the month we lived off sweet tea and dry bread. No one had any money left by the time the grant for the next month was paid. Some were sent food by their parents. Mikhail for example got bacon and a few other things from his village, and he always shared them with the rest of us, even though his parcels were only small.'

Another fellow student, Vladimir Kuzmin, today a retired public prosecutor, remembers the home-made sausage and the bacon that Gorbachev's parents sent from Privolnoye to Moscow. The fare provided for the students was meagre. In a little shop opposite they could buy provisions – more, they say, than today. But mostly they had little money with which to buy anything. Vladimir Kuzmin says: 'When the grant was handed out, for two days we felt we were the richest people on earth, but it had already run out long before the end of the month. But we survived. Even if we never had enough to eat, it was still fun. We could still fall in love and chase girls and go dancing and have parties, the way students do.'

Rudolf Kolchanov remembers: 'We were quite happy in our room. Some could play instruments, others sang. Gorbachev sang really well. After lectures or on free days we sang a great deal, and did all kinds of stupid things. I still remember how Misha Gorbachev and I once sang the song "Above Russia the Sky is Blue". We sang really loud because we liked it, but it was after midnight and the house master came, and we had to stop. In the hostel our room was often called the "open room". Not because it couldn't be locked, though in fact it couldn't, but we were so poor there was nothing to steal. They called it open because in our room there was so much discussion. Students from other years would come, and we discussed all kinds of problems. There was endless discussion, sometimes clever, sometimes not so clever, sometimes about internal problems, sometimes about foreign policy. We talked constantly about everything. I can no longer remember what Mikhail Gorbachev said in these discussions. I don't even know what I said any more, but I do know that he was very involved. And he was a good listener, even when someone had a different opinion to him. He always respected the opinions of others. We were young, and it would have been easy for behaviour to deteriorate. But he always found the words that allowed the discussion to continue without our coming to blows, without the situation becoming tense. Even so, he never deviated from his principles. If he considered his position right he stuck to it. He was also good at convincing others, but if he saw that his opponent was not going to be persuaded, he accepted it. He was not inclined to extremes, that I remember very well.'

Vladimir Kuzmin remembers his first meeting with Gorbachev. 'I was sitting in the hall of the hostel when I saw a good-looking young man carrying a case approaching. He was dressed like someone from a village. He asked whether there was a place for him. That was at the end of August or the beginning of September 1950. Not all the sixteen beds were taken yet, but to play a trick on the newcomer we directed him to the most uncomfortable bed. He didn't complain, and seemed happy to have found a place. He was disarming. At first we found him a little odd. There was still some cheap vodka in the shop opposite the hostel, but Gorbachev didn't drink, and that made us suspicious. But that was only at the beginning. Soon he'd made many friends. There were sixteen of us in the room and he was the only one who didn't argue with anyone, and that was not easy, believe me. And he was helpful, good-natured. Once I had to go to the station very early in the morning. It was winter and bitterly cold, I got up at five and was just leaving when Gorbachev woke up, saw my thin jacket and said: "Why don't you take my coat, it's warmer." In our room we used to speak openly, but very quietly, and only when there was no one else there. The times were dangerous, and a careless word could mean expulsion from the university, at the very least.'

Lyudmilla Komarova, today a professor, says that in the lecture hall she immediately noticed Mikhail because he wore a medal –

the Order of Labour. That was unusual, although a few of the older students had war decorations.

'What I liked about him was that he achieved what he did on his own. He had no influential relatives or friends, he wasn't even from Moscow. He had got there on his own merits. He wasn't much older than me, but he already had a medal. As we got to know him better what impressed us all was that he was a good companion, always ready for a joke. In the faculty we voted him on to the committee of the union and then at the end of the year to the committee of the Young Communist League. But he never really showed off, and even when he became the faculty *Komsomol* Chairman he never gave himself airs.'

'Gorbachev's modesty bowled me over,' says Vladimir Liberman, another of his close friends from his student days. 'We went into a Latin exam, and I saw him take off his Order outside the door. So I also took off my war medal, and in the exam we both only got a four, the second-best mark. If we'd worn our medals the professor – he was in awe of medals – might have treated us a little better. Not getting the highest mark had quite an effect on our grants, because candidates with a four got substantially less than those who excelled.'

Gorbachev's political career began in the faculty office of the *Komsomol*, where he was responsible for the teaching and educational section. Many students had no desire to take on work in the Communist Youth League. After all, there were six days of lectures a week, as well as private study and the social activities of the unions and the Young Communist League. That left little time for a private life. The more intellectual students saved their free time for going to the theatre or reading, and avoided routine political activity.

Of those who did take on work in the Young Communist League or in the unions, some saw it as a chore, and performed it without enthusiasm. There was little of the passion that had distinguished the Young Communists in the 1920s. Now they were often young men who were preparing careers for themselves as Party workers, perhaps at the university or at a scientific institute. Some were the sons of higher officials who owed their university places to their fathers' influence. Often, it didn't take them long to realise that they were unable to keep up with the intellectual achievements of their fellow students, and that a career as a researcher or a teacher would be closed to them. They consequently took on the 'social work' of organising discussions, political courses and meetings.

If they kept the faith politically, which could mean informing on other students, they could count on being granted an additional year of study before their final examination. Although they propagated the politics of idealism and sacrifice, few of them subjected themselves to these rigorous demands. The difference between the ideology they preached and the work they did was obvious. They loudly upheld the Party line, but avoided discussing it, as such discussions would have involved unorthodox arguments, and it was forbidden and dangerous to so much as consider these, even if only to refute them.

Other students tried to keep their private lives free of political work, and avoided meetings. Many had not yet formed their own opinions or acquired knowledge that could have fed their vague, prudently unspoken, rejection of the regime. From time to time newspaper articles condemned the indifference of such students.

'Generally,' says Lyudmilla Komarova, 'we Moscow students didn't have much respect for the *Komsomol* officials. They were mostly ambitious, and they put on airs. But Mikhail Gorbachev was different. He didn't constantly refer to his village origins or his medal, which most people on their way up would have done, because it impressed their superiors. On the contrary, we saw that he attached himself to students who were doing scientific work and who were interested in culture and education. And he did this without ingratiating himself or being embarrassing.' Vladimir Liberman says: 'When we elected the *Komsomol* committee he was an obvious candidate. He could be trusted, and we knew he took things seriously. Even in his third year at university when he became a Party member he didn't become aloof and didn't behave like an official, as many others did. He stayed a good man whom we liked.'

At that time Gorbachev met Anatoli Lukyanov, a young *Komsomol* official whose circumspection and restraint, combined with a capacity for hard work and organisation, appealed to him. Today Lukyanov is Gorbachev's Deputy in the Supreme Soviet of the USSR, the highest organ of state. At his election, when many delegates turned against him as a colourless *apparatchik*, Gorbachev defended him, saying that he needed a Deputy on whom he could rely absolutely. By then he had known him for more than thirty-five years. At Moscow University Lukyanov had been Gorbachev's superior. In fact, as Secretary of the *Komsomol* Committee of the Law Faculty, Lukyanov had once publicly criticised him. An official document from October 1953 states: 'The election meeting of the *Komsomol* took place at the Law Faculty. A number of serious defects were pointed out in the work of the Faculty *Komsomol* Committee and the courses. One defect is the low standard of work. Of 750 *Komsomol* students only 633 passed the spring course with "very good" or "good" marks. The Faculty Committee took no effective steps to obtain better results. Although the section of the office responsible for education is called the "Teaching and Educational Section" (Comrades Gorbachev and Serebryakov), in practice it does no educational work. The new *Komsomol* Committee must understand that its most important work is educational.'

This should not be taken as a serious reprimand of Gorbachev. Though *Komsomol* officials liked to present themselves as enthusiastic activists, they imitated the style of the Party bureaucracy, and frequently behaved like future members of its leadership.

As a student from a peasant family, who had worked on the land and even been decorated for it, who had proved himself at school in both political and academic work, Gorbachev's prospects in student politics were better than those of the careerists among the Young Communist officials. Having come straight from a village to the most famous university in the Soviet Union, he could also be genuinely enthusiastic for the work of the Young Communist League and the Party.

The backgrounds of Gorbachev's closest friends among his fellow students were very different. Yuri Topilin and Vladimir Liberman had both fought in the war and been decorated. Topilin came from an intellectual Moscow family, Liberman from a family of Jewish lawyers. In the last student year Zdeněk Mlynář from Czechoslovakia became the fourth in this group of close friends. He spoke four languages, and had enjoyed a classical European education. 'That was rather unusual company for a boy from the provinces,' says Vladimir Liberman today. 'The other three of us had brought rather heavier educational luggage from home. And though Zdeněk was a Communist sent from a Socialist country, at this time any friendship with a foreigner was suspicious. Gorbachev certainly wouldn't have known that Mlynář was of Jewish origin. I didn't know it myself, and no doubt neither did the authorities. That would have made things even more difficult.'

When Mlynář sent a holiday postcard from Prague to Privolnoye, he found out later from Gorbachev that the local Police Chief had personally come with the card to the field where he was working with his father during the vacation. A card from abroad was a suspicious matter. Mlynář says that Gorbachev had laughed at the idea that one could only receive something from abroad via the police. In the years of the campaign against the 'cosmopolitans', as Jews were designated in Stalin's last years, contact with them could destroy a career. All three of Gorbachev's friends were Party members before he himself joined in 1952.

Gorbachev had chosen three unusual and difficult companions. Remarkably, they accepted him as a friend although they themselves came from quite a different world, and could talk with familiarity about things of which Gorbachev had not even heard. They had read authors whose books would certainly not have appeared in Gorbachev's school library, and knew quotations from the classics which were not found in Stalinist textbooks. They cited Marx's claim that in the Communist society of the future every woman would be able to choose men as freely as men chose women in a capitalist society, and ridiculed the endless appeals for class struggle made by one particular lecturer.

'After the war there was a great difference between education in country schools and those in the city,' says Rudolf Kolchanov. 'In the first student year one could feel the difference in education. But Gorbachev worked so hard that the difference constantly diminished, and by the third year it no longer existed.'

'He stood out from the other students because of his performance in the seminars, because of his thorough study of the material and sources. He had a natural intellect, there's no other way to put it,' says Liberman.

Young Gorbachev also had courage. In one lecture the friends became annoyed by a professor who simply quoted passages from Stalin's essay on the problems of the economy, long a part of the orthodox canon and known by heart. One of them wrote a note to the professor: They could do without lectures like this. After all, they could read for themselves. Such a note could easily be understood to mean that the writer was bored by quotations from Stalin. Somebody had to sign the note if it was to be sent to the professor, and Gorbachev did. A minor scandal was narrowly avoided. Gorbachev's friends are not sure what saved him from punishment. Perhaps it was his reputation as a diligent student and active *Komsomol* official.

At the beginning of 1953, Gorbachev took a further risk. Vladimir Liberman remembers: 'In January 1953, about a month after the newspapers had reported the arrest of a group of doctors whom they called the "doctor murderers", there was a Party meeting on our course. The doctors, who were accused of having poisoned high Party officials, were overwhelmingly of Jewish origin. I no longer remember exactly what I said at this meeting, but perhaps it was something along the lines of: "Must I as the only Jew among you take full responsibility for everything Jews do?" That didn't stop one of our fellow students from attacking me. His father had been a victim of the purges, so it's understandable that he wanted to have his say. Everybody was silent. Then Gorbachev spoke. It was very unusual for him to show irritation or anger. Everyone knew that Gorbachev had extraordinary self-control, which he's kept to this day. Momentary outbursts happen now and again, but only when he's really driven to it. Well, one of these outbursts happened now, with the young man I was talking about. Gorbachev said to him: "You, you're a spineless animal." With that all discussion about me ended.'

In the political climate of the time Gorbachev had taken a great risk. His outburst can be attributed to his character and temperament, but the remarkable thing is that it had no serious consequences, at the time when Stalin's terror was reaching its final climax.

Towards the end of the 1940s Stalin, the victor of the Party power-struggle and the Second World War, began displaying signs of an insane distrust of almost everyone, even those closest to him. His suspicion of the Jews was particularly virulent. In the occupied countries of Eastern Europe he had already instigated purges in which Communist officials confessed after torture to being agents of Zionism, American imperialism or – after the break with Tito – of the Yugoslavian secret service. Now he was preparing a fresh purge for the Soviet Union.

In some republics, especially in the Ukraine, local leaders were openly antisemitic. Criminal reports in Soviet newspapers were full of Jewish names. The number of Jews admitted to universities was reduced.

Nikita Khrushchev describes in his memoirs how Stalin personally gave him the order to organise a pogrom in an aircraft factory because the workers there were dissatisfied with their conditions. Stalin suggested that Khrushchev should have truncheons distributed to the workers so that they could beat up the Jews in the factory. Khrushchev remembers Stalin imitating Jewish pronunciation and openly expressing his antisemitism at Politburo sessions. In 1948 he had the surviving members of the Jewish Antifascist Committee, among them high Party officials, arrested, tortured and shot. The campaign against the so-called 'rootless cosmopolitans' led to the murder of Jewish actors and writers. Then, in 1952, came the arrest of those doctors Stalin considered conspirators against the life and health of the state and Party leadership. A woman doctor who worked for state security agencies had written a letter accusing these doctors. The Ministry for State Security had long been making use of Stalin's antisemitism.

'A letter like this was enough for Stalin to decide that there was a doctors' plot in the Soviet Union,' reported Khrushchev at the Twentieth Party Congress in 1956. 'He gave the order for a group of eminent medical specialists to be arrested. At the Party Congress was the former Minister for State Security, Comrade Ignatev. Stalin told him: "If you don't get a confession from the doctors we'll make you a head shorter." Stalin summoned the examining judge and gave him orders and instructions as to the methods of investigation to be used. These methods were very simple: beat, beat and then beat some more. When we examined this "case" after Stalin's death we established that it had been contrived from beginning to end.'

The doctors from the Kremlin Hospital were arrested and tortured on the obviously false charge of having planned the murders of the heads of the Party, state and army. The accusations were so improbable that even the Minister for State Security, Abakumov, found the so-called confessions of the doctors unbelievable, but Stalin's response was to continue to beat them until they made full confessions. On 13 January 1953 Soviet newspapers reported the alleged conspiracy of the Jewish doctors, who were described as 'the murderers in white' or 'the doctor murderers'. Demonstrations against the doctors were staged throughout the Soviet Union, with scientists, writers and officials forced to take part.

At a Party meeting of the Presidium of the Academy of Sciences death sentences were unanimously demanded. In hospitals all over the country patients refused to be treated by Jewish doctors. Everywhere there were denunciations to the secret police of alleged Jewish poisoners. Hospitals and clinics dismissed Jewish doctors. In scientific institutions, universities, artists' unions, publishing houses and factories lists of Jewish employees were drawn up. Preparations were made to deport Jews from Moscow. Forty years later, the survivors still find it difficult to understand the decade of organised insanity which followed. In this climate, to speak up for a Jewish fellow student as Gorbachev had done was almost unheard of.

It would have been less surprising had the young *Komsomol* official made a speech against Zionism and the cosmopolitans, as did so many professors, authors and representatives of the Party apparatus. In July 1989 a rumour surfaced that in January 1953 Gorbachev had made an antisemitic speech against the 'doctor murderers' at Moscow University. A Soviet emigrant remembered having read such a speech in the Young Communist newspaper *Moskovskii Komsomolets*. Soviet experts in England, America and France followed up the report, and their suspicions grew when the Lenin Library in Moscow denied them access to their files, with the excuse that the newspapers for that week were in a very poor condition.

Two weeks later, the Paris Institute for Social History found the relevant copy of *Moskovskii Komsomolets* at the Library of Congress in Washington. And indeed it contained a speech by a Gorbachev, but he was an official from the Moscow region with the initials V.I., and the speech dealt not with the doctors' plot but with routine matters of organisation. If it had been possible to attribute an antisemitic speech to Mikhail Gorbachev, his standing in the West would have been seriously damaged, even though a speech made under the conditions of 1953 did not necessarily express the speaker's true opinions. In reality, it would appear that Gorbachev had actually stood up for his Jewish friend.

At that time a new wave of fear overwhelmed the Soviet people. They felt that another purge was coming, a repetition of the mass arrests and liquidations of the late thirties. Stalin had begun to strip the highest Party officials of their authority. Individual members of the Politburo were forbidden to attend meetings because he suspected them of being British agents, and had them put under surveillance. He was preparing, as Khrushchev later said, for the liquidation of the leading members of the Politburo, and only his death prevented it.

That would have been the signal for mass persecutions throughout the entire country. In the camps, the full horror of which was only to become known later in reports from the so-called 'gulag archipelago', there were about eight million prisoners. The secret police had seven million people working for it at the time of Stalin's death in 1953.

'We were in our third student year when Stalin died,' says Rudolf Kolchanov. 'One has to remember the times in which we received our education. We were fanatics. We had blind faith in Stalin. That went through the family, through the schools, through the textbooks, and one mustn't forget it. There was a drastic rupture between the period in which we'd lived for so long, and the period that followed. I can still remember the night Stalin's death was announced on the radio. Several of us, including Gorbachev, were in our room. We hardly spoke about the news. We thought about it. Occasionally we exchanged a few words, a few brief sentences about what would happen now. Some students were even crying. I didn't cry. And Gorbachev didn't either, that's certain. The others cried as much from pain at the loss as from uncertainty and anxiety about what would happen without Stalin. That's how we were. We felt his death as a tragedy. When Vladimir Liberman hinted that he was glad Stalin was dead, Gorbachev gave him a look that stopped him talking.'

Stalin's body was laid in state in the Hall of Columns of the Union House, the former club of the aristocracy at the heart of Moscow. During the four days of state mourning, poets, journalists and Party officials wrote rhapsodic obituaries. The Politburo members who formed a guard of honour at the coffin were already preparing for the unavoidable power-struggle, but tens of thousands of people filed past the coffin in tears. Moscow was sealed off by special units of the secret police. There was panic in the inner city, and more than five hundred people were crushed or trampled to death by the crowds and by armed police. The death of the dictator who had ruled their lives day and night plunged Soviet citizens into fear and confusion. Even people who learned of his death as prisoners in the gulag told me they had cried.

The new leaders distanced themselves from Stalin's methods. A month after Stalin's death, the 'doctor murderers' were set free. The Party organ *Pravda* declared that in future tyranny and illegality would be severely punished. There was an amnesty decree. In July 1953 Beria, the head of Stalin's secret police, was arrested. In December the newspapers reported that he and six of his closest collaborators had been shot after a secret trial. In the following year other leading members of the apparatus who had led the investigations into the 'doctors' plot' and had been responsible for the forgery of evidence against leading Party officials were executed. Hundreds of thousands of prisoners returned from the Siberian camps to a world where their jobs had long been taken by others, where they again met relatives, friends and colleagues who, for reasons of envy or fear, had denounced them.

Of the reactions in the student hostel after Stalin's death Rudolf Kolchanov says: 'It was a very difficult time. In the following months and years our views changed fundamentally, especially after 1956, after the Twentieth Party Congress under Khrushchev. We discovered something of the truth. But our minds were still fresh. It was easier for us to shake off the tragedy of the past and to assimilate the new conditions than it was for older people. I think we quickly found the strength to look honestly at the past, to assess it critically and draw the right conclusions.'

Vladimir Liberman adds: 'When in the late summer of 1953 the famous substance of the July Plenum of the Central Committee became known, the Plenum that gave the reasons for Beria's arrest, it caused bewilderment and fear in many people. It didn't seem to me then that Gorbachev felt that the foundations of his view of the world had been shattered. In fact he seemed pleased that abuses that might have prevented a further development of Socialism had been exposed.'

During his first months at university Gorbachev had spoken of the true situation on the land. Vladimir Kuzmin remembers: 'He spoke of the great poverty during the occupation and after the war. There was drought and famine, and there weren't enough people to do the work. He began working at thirteen. Nowadays eighteen-year-olds don't know what it means to earn a piece of bread. Gorbachev came from the land. I learned a lot from him. Even before Stalin died I spoke with him in confidence about the problems of Socialism under Stalin. He and I weren't satisfied with that atrocious system, under which we were afraid of everything. We discussed carefully whether Socialism of Stalin's kind was good or bad. But when there was a risk of being overheard we said nothing about the subject. We were afraid. You were under threat of the death sentence. The cult had reached such a degree of inhumanity that anybody, but anybody, could be a victim of that madman, that psychopath, that murderer and criminal. After Stalin's death we spoke more openly about the fact that this wasn't Socialism, that this kind of Socialism was bad. And about what was then called collective leadership: an idiotic dictatorship by a vicious gang. We talked about that too, between ourselves.'

Gennadi Borsenko, today a professor at the Law Faculty of Moscow University, says of the time after Stalin's death: 'There was lively discussion among us of the problems of collective leadership and political change. At first we were in a state of shock at the death of Stalin. Many people were confused. They didn't know how the country would change. When the Party began to follow the line of collective leadership during the Thaw, these problems were discussed in detail. It became clear that one person alone couldn't rule a country and decide everything for everyone. We began to understand that we should have some form of participation in state matters. After the period of shock and tension in the first months after Stalin's death there came a certain animation, an upsurge, as if now it was easier to breathe. I remember the atmosphere among the students at that time. And today, when I hear certain speeches of Gorbachev's, I recognise the way of thinking that developed among us in the student collective. He's kept that, and it's what allows one to have trust in what he says and does today.'

What Gorbachev's fellow students recollect about the discussions in their circle corresponds to reports from other students at Moscow University in the years after Stalin's death and during the struggle for succession. After Khrushchev's disclosures about Stalin in 1956 during the Thaw, students dared to talk more openly about the politics of their country.

Official publications later criticised the students' behaviour. In

January 1957 the Party paper *Communist*, under the headline 'Raise high the banner of Marxist-Leninist ideology!', condemned discussions in which the leading role of the Party was rejected and a purer democracy demanded. In September 1959, when the Thaw had come to an end, a lawyer criticised student circles in the government newspaper *Izvestiya*: 'In that confused period three years ago when Stalin's personality was subjected to serious criticism state security authorities discovered that some students, alienated from reality and spoiled by an easy and comfortable life, had succumbed to enemy influence. These young people would meet and make public antisoviet speeches. They praised each other and arrogantly condemned everything else, and they went so far as to put their political views in the form of essays. Later they admitted that some of them had even suggested writing and distributing harmful leaflets.'

During this period questions were also being asked at meetings of Young Communist organisations. The Stalinist writer Kochetov, in his short novel *The Brothers Yershov*, describes students asking such questions: ' "If we want to uproot the forms of the personality cult, must we then not also destroy the old apparatus?" "Which apparatus?" "All of it, but first the bureaucratic apparatus." '

At Moscow University, according to reports in the Young Communist paper *Komsomolskaya Pravda*, unofficial student newspapers with titles like *Heresy* or *New Voices* ridiculed the fact that art was being made to conform to Socialist realism and criticised *Komsomol* leaders. News-sheets on the walls debated whether Soviet literature still had anything at all to do with the truth. In smaller groups political debate was not disguised as discussion about art. In the autumn of 1956 I met some philosophy students at Moscow University who wanted to draw up a programme for political change. Its first point was free elections (for which, however, only members of the Communist Party could be candidates). The students, as products of their political education, thought that as there was no class conflict in Russia, there was no need for different political parties. In a one-party system it would suffice for representatives with differing views of what needed to be done to present themselves to the voters.

When the authorities learned of the discussions of these students, they were expelled from the university. I lost track of them until, at the beginning of the 1980s, I again met two of them, now leading members of one of those scientific institutes at which, uncommissioned and occasionally criticised by the Party leadership, work was being done on a model of reform for the Soviet economy. At the Law Faculty of Moscow University in 1956 scientists and students printed leaflets opposing the dictatorship of the Party and demanding a return to the line of Lenin and Soviet democracy. They were arrested and sentenced to as much as eight years' imprisonment.

By 1956, of course, Gorbachev had already left the university. But the students of his time were intelligent enough to read between the lines even before Stalin's death, and to understand the half-voiced asides some professors wove into their lectures.

Between 1953 and 1958 many students were thinking about change in the Soviet system. They criticised the all-powerful bureaucracy of the state and Party apparatus. They read Lenin's *State and Revolution* and *The Next Tasks of Soviet Power* and concluded that Soviet society had increasingly distanced itself from Lenin's ideas. But they rejected capitalism and the West, and still regarded Socialism as the better system. The rule of the Party, they considered, had become a dictatorship of the bureaucracy that stood in the way of further development. They therefore demanded the restitution of democracy within the Party according to Leninist principles, and the transformation of the Party apparatus from a bureaucratic, almost hereditary caste into a genuine political party. They wanted a state in which power would lie with democratically elected councillors subject to the power and the will of the people.

There is no evidence connecting Gorbachev with groups that systematically discussed these problems. But the *Komsomol* officials were well aware of the growing tide of opinion that the system needed to be reformed and democratised. There were even demands that they themselves should stand honestly for election. In Gorbachev's last year at Moscow University such ideas were in the air, and they would resurface thirty years later in his thinking and speeches.

But there was more to student life than work and politics. There was the theatre, concerts and parties. A Moscow lawyer remembers that Mikhail visited her at her parents' flat, where he admired her father's library and saw the lifestyle of a cultivated

Moscow family. He listened quietly and seriously when she played Rachmaninov on her parents' piano, and tried to hum the tunes. 'For us Moscow snobs he was a country boy, but his interest in culture appealed to me.'

'He was drawn to a world of culture and education that he'd never experienced before, neither in the village nor in our room at the hostel. At the time we were surprised that he was so indifferent to girls,' says Vladimir Liberman. 'Yuri Topilin and I led a fairly free life. We had come back from the war, swore a lot and chased after every pretty girl. Mikhail never swore, never ran after girls, and at first we found him rather prudish. Then we realised that that was his nature, and that he didn't imitate others. He also had this extraordinary dignity, and the three of us became close friends in our second year, before Zdeněk Mlynář joined us from Czechoslovakia.

'In 1953 a poster was put up in the hostel, offering dancing lessons. The students laughed because the lessons were so expensive, and we were all short of cash, but Yuri Topilin and I thought we would put our names down and see if any pretty girls turned up. In the second lesson, the waltz, we had no partners, so the instructor brought Raisa Titarenko and her friend over to us. Yuri and I took our pick. He got Raisa, or Raya, as we called her, and I got the friend. A little later Gorbachev came into the hall. He'd already made fun of us at the first lesson. "Good lord, what are the pair of you doing?" he'd said, things like that.

'After the dancing class Yuri and I introduced him to Raya and her friend. That's how they got to know each other. Three or four days later Yuri came and told me that Mikhail had fallen seriously in love with Raisa. Until then Mikhail had shown no particular interest in girls. But a flame had suddenly been lit.'

Like Gorbachev, Raisa Maximovna Titarenko was not from Moscow. But she did not have a village background. Her father was a railway worker, and Raisa had grown up in various towns to which his job had taken him. She was born in the small town of Rubzovsk in the Altai region of Siberia, near the border with China and Mongolia. She was the youngest of three children, and they often had to change schools when their father was moved to another station. It is said, although it has never been proven, that Maxim Titarenko was one of those arrested during the Stalin period. What is certain is that during this time the family lived in great poverty. But all three children were successful students. Raisa's sister was admitted to medical school, and her brother became a journalist and writer. Raisa herself always came top of her class. In her final report she received the highest mark in every subject, and was awarded a gold medal.

At that time the family was living in Voronezh, a city 500 kilometres south of Moscow. Raisa wanted to enter the Philosophy Faculty at Moscow University, where the entry standards were among the highest in the Soviet Union. Fellow students remember her as a hard worker, well organised, perhaps a little pedantic, and strikingly beautiful with her Russian-Tartar eyes.

The period after Stalin's death was an exciting one in the Philosophy Faculty of Moscow University. One group of professors still held fast to the style of the Stalin period. Others, such as Mamdashvili, today one of the most original thinkers in the Soviet Union, and Alexander Zinoviev, who later had to emigrate, began to question the dry canon of Marxist-Leninist philosophy. Students challenged the dogmatic professors with searching questions and counter-arguments. Raisa Titarenko was at the university at a time when students could once again think for themselves and speak openly. Until the Thaw ended philosophy professors could discuss ideas with their students, even when those ideas did not conform to the prescribed pattern. Raisa was a successful student, and at the end of her five student years the faculty offered her a grant for a doctorate.

When she met Mikhail Gorbachev she was, her friends say, an attractive and self-confident but reserved young woman. Some say that at that time she seemed more intelligent than Gorbachev. She was certainly much more knowledgeable about literature and art, and the couple often went together to the theatre and to concerts. Raisa's cultural interests undoubtedly influenced Gorbachev, and added a further dimension to his education. Friends remember their courtship taking the form of endless serious discussions – not unusual among young Russians.

'When I first knew Raya she was small, delicate and fragile as a blade of grass,' Vladimir Kuzmin remembers. 'In 1953 they married, and Misha organised the wedding. For those days it was a sumptuous celebration. It was held in the students' dining hall at the hostel on Strominka Street. There were no relatives there, and fifteen or twenty of us students were invited to the meal after

Raisa and Mikhail came back from the registry office. Our Party leader, Volodia Safronov, made the toasts. There was plenty to drink, something that always interested me in those days. But Mikhail hardly drank anything at his wedding. He was dry by nature.'

The newly married couple were not able to move into a shared room together until 1954, when a new hostel in the Lenin Hills was completed. They lived there in their last student year in Moscow.

In that year Mikhail and Raisa Gorbachev were faced with the decision of what they should do after their studies. For Raisa there was the possibility of a doctorate and a highly promising academic career. Mikhail was twenty-four, a member of the Communist Party, a *Komsomol* official, and was ending his law studies with a distinction. He could have expected a good legal career in Moscow, and indeed he was offered a post in the Public Prosecutor's office. They wanted to remain in the capital, with its theatres and concerts, their circle of friends from the university and their good career prospects. But the Public Prosecutor's office could not provide accommodation, which made it impossible for them to stay.

They moved to Stavropol, in Mikhail's home region. At the time his acquaintances were unable to understand this move, and some even suspected that Gorbachev had been forced to leave Moscow for political reasons. But there is no evidence to support this. The only known reprimand he had received had been the routine matter at the *Komsomol* office two years earlier. Gorbachev's friends could not understand why he had accepted a fairly minor position in the Young Communist League in Stavropol. He himself said that he felt it was his duty, after studying in the capital, to return to his native region to work. And his father had asked him to come back to the land that had nurtured him. He had already called on the *Komsomol* committee in Stavropol during his university vacations and enquired about the prospect of a job. Many young lawyers were alloted jobs in the *Komsomol* and Party apparatus after graduation.

Some of those friends who at the time considered Gorbachev's choice a mistake now think his decision was sensible and characteristic. In Moscow Gorbachev could have had a good career, but he would have been merely one young lawyer among many.

Besides his generally acknowledged sense of duty, he might have been influenced by the likelihood that in his native region, where he knew the people and their problems, he would quickly find a significant role and be more likely to rise to a position where he could really achieve something.

CHAPTER 3

Stavropol

In January 1955, after a brief period as a lawyer, Gorbachev began work in the *Komsomol* Committee of the Stavropol region. He became Instructor for Propaganda, on the lowest managerial level of the *Komsomol* and Party hierarchy. Lilya Kolodichuka, who at the time worked in the Regional Committee of the *Komsomol*, says: 'We were a little afraid of the new man. He came with a distinction and a good reputation from Moscow University, and we thought he'd look down on us. But after only a month we were all for him because he was a good worker, a sociable, cheerful and modest young man. Although he was much better educated than we were, he didn't talk down to us, and after a while he even taught us modern dances he'd learned in Moscow.'

As an instructor, Gorbachev was not entitled to one of the flats that were kept for officials. He and Raisa found themselves a little room in a precipitous street bordering the city centre, the rent for which cost him a third of his low salary.

At that time Stavropol had a population of about 140,000. It was the capital of a region twice the size of Switzerland, with one of the richest grain harvests in the Soviet Union. After the war the city had undergone rapid industrialisation. To the south, in the foothills of the Caucasus, were spas where the sanatoriums of the Fourth Department of the Health Ministry had been built. Leading Party officials, including members of the Politburo, came for cures, in luxury undreamed of by the farmers of Privolnoye or the students of Moscow. In Stavropol's centre are buildings from the time of Catherine the Great and attractive nineteenth-century administrative offices, as well as parks laid out by the Tsars' governors to make their stay in the province more agreeable. But there was a great difference between the cultural lives of Stavropol and Moscow, and for the Gorbachevs, especially Raisa, this must have been painful.

The Gorbachevs' small room had no running water – there was a pump in the street. They could only use the stove when it was lit in the winter, so mostly they cooked on a paraffin burner. Moscow student life had been comfortable compared to this. They did not get their own flat, one room and a small kitchen, until the birth of their daughter Irina in 1957. Life was not easy, but Raisa, who was working as a lecturer on Marxism-Leninism at the Medical Institute, had grown up in similar conditions. A friend remembers: 'The Gorbachevs were always cheerful, especially after Irina's birth. Raisa was a good cook and her husband always helped. That was then rather unusual for a man.'

Mikhail Gorbachev worked in the Regional Committee of the *Komsomol*, which was closely connected to the Party organisation. The task of the Young Communist League was to propagate the current Party line, to impose discipline on young people and to motivate them to volunteer for extra work. It organised meetings, held evening entertainments with music, folkdancing and amateur dramatics, and wrote articles for the League's newspapers. Gorbachev was a popular *Komsomol* leader, whose meetings and evening entertainments were lively and well attended by young people.

This was the year of the Twentieth Party Congress, at which Khrushchev began to settle accounts with Stalin and the political climate changed in the country. Reforms were being demanded, not least in the state and Party apparatus. Initiative and energy began to count for something among *Komsomol* leaders. It was again possible to work with energy and optimism for the future. As an Instructor in the Propaganda Department, it was Gorbachev's task to stir up enthusiasm among young people for the changes and the new line. He did this with great success, according to Nikolai Dorochin, then Gorbachev's superior as the cadre boss of the *Komsomol* Regional Committee in Stavropol. Dorochin quickly realised that Gorbachev was politically gifted, and he did not remain a mere Instructor for long. After only a year he became First Secretary of the *Komsomol* Committee of the city of Stavropol. This was an important promotion, as he now had independent managerial work and was a member of the city's Party leadership. He could now expect to move up in two-year stages to the offices of Second and then First Secretary of the *Komsomol* Committee for the entire Stavropol region.

In many ways Gorbachev's outlook as a Young Communist leader suited the times. He believed in Socialism, but he was also convinced it could be, and needed to be, improved. In Moscow Khrushchev was spreading optimism. He gave the impression that the fast train of Socialism had been held up by Stalin's mistakes, and that all that was necessary was to relay a few tracks and tighten a few bolts for it soon to reach its goal, Communism. Khrushchev had eliminated his conservative opponents in the apparatus, and at the Twentieth Party Congress he overwhelmed and won over the delegates with his sensational revelations about Stalin and his system. His speech was not published, but at closed meetings it was read out to Party members by officials. It could not have been difficult for Gorbachev to take the new line.

Lilya Kolodichuka, who for fifteen years worked with Raisa Gorbachev in the Philosophy Faculty of the Agricultural College, says of the beginning of her friendship with the Gorbachevs: 'What brought us closer were the long discussions we had with Mikhail about Stalin. Even after the Twentieth Party Congress and Khrushchev's famous speech, comparatively few people in the provinces condemned Stalin. I was one, because I had seen the consequences of Stalin's politics at first hand. My mother was arrested in 1937. I was surprised at the time that Mikhail knew the names of so many people who had been the victims of repression in our district in the thirties. Mikhail was never sympathetic to Stalinism, and that didn't change in later years when there was a tendency to revise the criticism of Stalin in the Central Committee. When somebody wanted to change the name of Volgograd back to Stalingrad Gorbachev took a firm stand against it.'

The father of Nikolai Dorochin, Gorbachev's first cadre leader, had been condemned to five years' imprisonment during the purges. Many of the people with whom Gorbachev worked at this time must have had similar backgrounds.

Gorbachev's circle of friends in Stavropol was small and intimate, and he remains in contact with many of them to this day. They talk with warmth and affection of the time when they worked with him. They say he was energetic and clever, honest and cheerful, always precise about what he wanted. And he held to what he believed in with great stubbornness. He enjoyed simple pleasures, such as walking in the woods with other young people, singing as they went. 'Mikhail always sang first. He knew the words to all the songs,' says Vladimir Kolodichuk, Lilya's husband. This sounds like the archetypal Young Communist's life, as it was led in the provinces, but was no longer fashionable in Moscow.

Vladimir Kolodichuk was leader of the Cultural Department of the Stavropol region for twenty years, and often came into official contact with Gorbachev. Despite the opposition of the authorities in Moscow, he says, Gorbachev succeeded in getting a Palace of Culture built for Stavropol, with halls for concerts, readings, performances and exhibitions. The Gorbachevs were frequent users of the city library, and they kept company with Stavropol's writers, journalists and artists. Gorbachev enjoyed visiting artists in their studios, and went whenever possible to plays at the local theatre. He started a musical festival in Stavropol, to which the Georgian composer Vano Muradeli, who at the end of the Stalin period had been condemned along with Shostakovich as a formalist, often came.

'He really did have a feeling for art, a very sensitive, very human response to it,' says Vladimir Kolodichuk. His wife Lilya adds that Gorbachev was very creative. 'But so was Raisa Maximovna. Each is a person in their own right. And they've worked together all their life,' she says. Critics today sometimes claim that Raisa has too great an influence over her husband. But Lilya Kolodichuk brushes this aside, and stresses the independence of both partners of this marriage.

According to a Russian proverb, 'The wife is the husband's second destiny'. It would be hard to imagine two people better suited to each other in origins and character than the Gorbachevs. Raisa was hard-working, eager to learn and intelligent. As a university teacher she expected high standards from her students. She was always friendly and ready to talk, but at the same time somehow reserved, hardly allowing any outsider a glimpse of her family life, and keeping her circle of friends small. Perhaps her greatest influence on Gorbachev's life was her intense interest in literature and culture.

Her taste had always been much wider than the officially recognised culture. Among others she loved the poems of Nikolai

Gumilev, the husband of the poet Anna Akhmatova, who was shot as an alleged counter-revolutionary soon after the Revolution and whose name was not mentioned in Soviet histories of literature until the 1980s. She had come to university with a gold medal, compared to Gorbachev's silver, and she was the more successful in her studies. After the final examination it was she, not her husband, who was offered a substantial grant to work for a doctorate. But she was prepared to go with him to Stavropol and, given the possibilities open to her, accept fairly modest teaching work. At the Medical Institute she taught future doctors the principles of Marxist philosophy, and in her field she rose faster than did her husband in the Young Communist League.

She was promoted to the Philosophy Faculty of the Stavropol Agricultural College, which had a high reputation. Her husband's connections can hardly have influenced this appointment, as he was then at the very beginning of his career, while the professors at the college already occupied high Party posts. The Dean of the faculty, Mikhail Chuguchev, had previously been Party Secretary in Krasnogvardeisk, in Gorbachev's home district.

Today Chuguchev says: 'The leaders of the faculty at that time were two Party functionaries who had reached pensionable age. They learned that there was a gifted young lecturer, a graduate from Moscow University, working at the Medical Institute. As the two professors were receiving a pension, each gave up half his salary, and Raisa received a full salary because she'd come with a distinction from Moscow University. I think she was very moved at the time to be given such attention. She had to compete with other candidates, but she was clearly the best. From the start she was very successful and active. After only a year she was given the title of Lecturer, and a few years later she became Principal Lecturer. She taught philosophy, but continued her sociological work. She drove in rubber boots to the *kolkhozes* and state farms of various districts and from her research produced a book, *The Daily Life of Collective Farmers*. This became her dissertation, and she presented it successfully in Moscow at the Lenin College of Education.'

Sociological studies were rare in the Soviet Union in the 1950s. Since the 1930s sociology had been suspect, as its empirical research could lead to results that contradicted the Party line. The fear of discovering evidence that might provoke the anger of

Stalin prevented the central and local leadership from discovering the truth about the lives of Soviet citizens. Not until the end of the 1960s was an Institute for Concrete Social Research again established at the Academy of Science in Moscow. One of its directors was to be Raisa Gorbachev's doctoral supervisor, G. V. Osipov.

At the time that Raisa was trying, with her questionnaires and enquiries, to find out about the lives of the *kolkhos* farmers in the Stavropol region, there was no independent department of sociology in Moscow. Sociology was a circumscribed area of interest that was accommodated within the Philosophy Faculty. Those who did work in the field were people with independent minds, and contact with them was stimulating for a young student. What Raisa had learned in Moscow she made use of in the Stavropol region to investigate the conditions on five local *kolkhozes*. She discovered that there was almost no central heating, running water or sewerage in the farmers' houses. Two thirds of the farmers' families had icons in their houses, four times as many as in the homes of people who worked in administration, schools or agricultural technology. The life of women was particularly hard, and they were often allocated heavy manual work by the men.

Raisa's discoveries must have been of the greatest interest to Mikhail. They confirmed much that he already knew from personal experience, and gave him first-hand information about agriculture and life on the *kolkhozes* which was probably unique to any official in the whole Soviet Union. Raisa's findings were a collection of facts, not an ideological attack on Soviet agricultural policy. Her conclusions were restrained: the material conditions of the *kolkhoz* farmers of Stavropol were improving, but slowly. Mikhail could draw his own political and organisational conclusions. The factual nature of Raisa's work surprised some of her friends, who had thought of her as being of a more literary-philosophical bent.

When I visited the Agricultural College of Stavropol, the Dean of the Philosophy Faculty took down a few volumes of Raisa's work for lectures and seminars from the shelves. A large diagram on which Raisa had depicted the philosophical world systems still hangs in the room. Among other work of hers kept by the faculty is a brochure with the title 'Our Party Congress on the Further

Development of Socialist Culture', and she also contributed an article to a book entitled *The Kolkhoz as the School of Communism*. 'She worked a great deal with the philosophy students, but scientifically she was especially interested in the sociology of the farmers,' says Mikhail Chuguchev. 'That was why she was asked to take part in planning the social-economic development of the collectives. The *kolkhozes* and state farms asked her to develop these plans. At the time that was something quite new, and she became an authority on planning of that kind.' Mikhail Gorbachev, as a *Komsomol* and Party official, also had to propose and organise such programmes.

Raisa's former colleagues have few memories of personal contacts with her. Perhaps they prefer not to say anything about the private life of the Party leader, but a more likely reason is that Raisa cultivated few friendships. 'Raisa was pleased when delegates from ministries and the Party organs came to attend her lectures. Not all professors were. After all, the delegates came to criticise, but with her there was hardly anything to criticise, even as a formality. This was before Mikhail Sergeyevich became Party Secretary. She was a very serious lecturer and very thorough in her work,' says Professor Chuguchev. 'Naturally she took part in little festivities with her colleagues. Once we gave her a box of chocolates for her birthday, and she immediately offered them around. We sometimes asked her to have her photograph taken with us, but she refused every time. She said she wasn't photogenic. Most of the others liked to have their photographs taken, but she only would when it was absolutely essential for an official photograph.'

A colleague, a friend of Raisa's since 1959, says: 'When she came to us she was young, pretty, very well dressed, modern. She was often taken for a student. The doorkeepers sometimes wouldn't let her into the professors' room. She'd complain "They've taken me for a student again! Something has to be done!" She was a little indignant, but she also found it quite flattering. Raisa was always friendly. She joined in the voluntary work on Saturdays, cleaning and dusting. I was younger than her, still a student at first, and Raisa said to me: "Come, we'll learn together. Come to my lectures." I attended her course for research assistants who were preparing their doctorates. She always wanted her students to do well. Sometimes she would work late with us, and Gorbachev would come to collect her.'

On a recent visit to Stavropol Raisa called in on the professors' room. They noticed little change in her. 'She spoke very slowly, as if we were a class she was lecturing, and so we told her,' one colleague says, and the others laugh. Even as the wife of the first man in the Soviet Union Raisa remains the professor, a little stiff, formal and precise in her meetings with presidents' wives and queens, political visitors and inquisitive journalists, though she has a disarming smile. She has a kind of charm that gives her public appearances a cautious, somewhat aloof glamour.

In Stavropol the Gorbachevs lived a rather private life, and in Moscow today this is still the case. When Gorbachev comes home in the evening, Raisa sends all the domestic staff away and eats alone with him. She does the same on his travels, when Gorbachev goes only to unavoidable official dinners.

Those who visited the Gorbachevs' flat in Stavropol were more often friends than colleagues. The Kolodichuks were among their closest friends. Lilya had given birth to a daughter in the same year as Raisa. In the *Komsomol* Town Committee she was Mikhail's immediate superior. Her husband Vladimir was in charge of the city's cultural administration. During the Thaw they were often with the Gorbachevs. Both couples read the literary newspaper *Novy mir* which, under the editorship of Alexander Tvardovsky, was beginning to take a close look at Soviet reality. Alexander Solzhenitsyn's *One Day in the Life of Ivan Denisovich* first appeared here, as did his novel *Matryona's House*. Solzhenitsyn came from Gorbachev's part of the country, having been born not far from Kislovodsk in the foothills of the Caucasus, and he had relatives living near Privolnoye.

The two couples also read the famous anthology *Pages from Tarusa*, published by a group of liberal writers. After years of Socialist realism, in which Stalin had appointed writers as the 'engineers of the human soul', in this book the simple, human, sometimes melancholy voice of the great Russian writers was heard once again. Raisa, friends say, especially loved poetry: Anna Akhmatova, Boris Pasternak, Nikolai Gumilev. Mikhail knew entire pages of Russian classics such as Pushkin's *The Bronze Horseman* and *Poltava* by heart. He knew Lermontov's poems very well, and searched for traces of the poet in Piatogorsk, to the south of Stavropol, where Lermontov had been killed in a duel.

Gorbachev had got into the habit of reading at school. His friends were amazed at his ability to memorise poetry, and he also had a remarkable facility for remembering the names and faces of people he had met only once – an important talent in politics.

In 1960 Mikhail Gorbachev became First Secretary of the Young Communist League of the Stavropol region. In this year he also stayed at the Kremlin for the first time, as one of the delegates to the All Union Meeting of Communist Activists. Stavropol was close enough to the capital to be aware of the changes and disputes taking place under Khrushchev. Since 1957 Khrushchev had been attempting to reform the Soviet adminis-tration and economy by dismantling the country's excessive cen-tralisation and stimulating greater personal initiative. This brought him into conflict with the Politburo, but he was able to outmanoeuvre the so-called 'group hostile to the Party' led by Molotov, Malenkov and Kaganovich.

The time of the collective leadership came to an end. Khrush-chev, who for a time had shared power with Nikolai Bulganin, now took over from him as Prime Minister, and merged that position with his own of Party Leader. Only Stalin had previously held both posts at the same time. Khrushchev was now in a position of great power, even if, from apparent modesty, he did not call himself General Secretary, but only First Secretary of the Party. Now he could begin trying to reform Soviet agriculture. He knew that the inefficiency of the *kolkhoz* system and the rural poverty connected with it were among the heaviest burdens on the Soviet economy.

In the years after Stalin's death there had been a gradual improvement in the lives of the peasants, who had previously had no identity cards and, like serfs, were not allowed to leave their *kolkhoz*. The required yields for *kolkhoz* farmers and land workers had been lowered, the mechanisation of agriculture was progressing, and freedom of choice had increased: what was to be grown by the *kolkhoz* was no longer decided by the central planning authorities in Moscow, but by the rural district.

But development was often confused. From time to time Khrush-chev pressed for a system under which the *kolkhoz* farmers would become paid workers on state farms. In Khrushchev's time the number of *kolkhozes* decreased by half, and the number of state farms doubled. Khrushchev demanded that Soviet production of meat, butter and milk catch up with that of the USA within three to four years, a threefold increase. This totally unrealistic goal led once again to the falsification of production figures in rural districts. On top of that, after his visit to the United States in 1959, Khrushchev had told the farmers to plant maize. 'Maize is sausage on a stick,' he had proclaimed. But in some regions maize was a complete failure, and in others it was far more expensive to produce than the usual forms of cattle feed.

This policy of constant new campaigns and scientifically doubtful experiments led to growing irritation within the administration, which was also required to deal with a new ideological adjustment. Khrushchev now spoke of a 'state of all the people', as if the Soviet Union had entered the final phase of development before the achievement of Communism. This defused the Party's conflict with the people and served as the basis for a reform of the law and the judiciary, and also for Khrushchev's attempts to reduce social differences and improve the living conditions of the workers and peasants.

As well as such reforming moves, largely determined by Khrushchev's own character, there were outbursts against artists and intellectuals, who in the early years of his rule had been granted greater freedom. Although this restriction of tolerance and hardening of the line corresponded to the wishes of many higher Party officials, they were still uneasy about Khrushchev's unpredictable decisions and his abrupt dismissals of people he considered unsuitable. His disappointment at the lack of agricultural progress led him to repeatedly change the Minister of Agriculture, and even to consider the extreme step of splitting the Party into two apparatuses to create, as it were, an agricultural and an industrial Communist Party.

Mikhail Gorbachev knew the problems of Khrushchev's agricultural policy from his own experience. He was after all one of the few officials working in a region he had got to know from the seat of a threshing machine. He can only have known about the mood of writers and intellectuals at second hand, but he was certainly aware of the doubts about the infallibility of the Party which the Twentieth Party Congress had unleashed, and which had led to criticism of the leadership and attempts to vote officials – especially in the *Komsomol* – out of office. News of the crises in the Eastern Bloc must have reached him from Poland, and even more so from Hungary, where the Soviet Army suppressed an uprising of the people and the Party. These events showed the breaches that could be made in the Eastern European power system by more open criticism of the system in the Soviet Union, and they undoubtedly had an effect on Gorbachev's political thinking.

Of course Gorbachev understood how to interpret the official Party speeches and the positions it adopted, and how to form an approximate picture of the real situation. This applied particularly to the steps being taken towards the reform of ideology, the economy and society. Every member of the Communist Party had to study the publications that dealt with this. It was taken for granted that officials would toe the line and join in the condemnation of toppled opponents of Khrushchev, but this in no way prevented them from forming their own opinions.

Among friends Gorbachev would sometimes quote Plekhanov's aphorism that the flour with which a Socialist cake could be baked had not yet been ground. This is not to say that he doubted Socialist ideals, but their realisation seemed to him inadequate, and in his eyes the complacency of the Party leadership was unjustified. In the early sixties Gorbachev found much in Khrushchev's speeches and plans that promised a breakthrough to a better Russia. But Gorbachev was a realist, and his attitude to Khrushchev can hardly have been uncritical. Then, as later, he considered Khrushchev's destruction of the Stalin myth his greatest achievement. But there was a great deal about Khrushchev and his politics that struck Gorbachev as Utopian and unrealistic.

In October 1961 Mikhail Gorbachev went to the Kremlin for the second time, as a delegate to the Twenty-second Party Congress. This Congress not only continued the break with Stalin's crimes, but also revealed that toppled Politburo members like Molotov, Malenkov and Voroshilov had been involved in them. The death sentences they had signed of alleged enemies of the people and their families appeared in the newspapers. Overnight Stalin's body was removed from the mausoleum in Red Square and interred by the Kremlin wall. The city of Stalingrad, site of the greatest battle of the Second World War, was renamed Volgograd.

Many delegates at the Party Congress were surprised by these developments. The older ones, who had fought under Stalin in the war and had made their careers during the Terror, were alarmed and sometimes genuinely bewildered. But the condemnation of Stalin's crimes, shocking though they were, was confined to the tyrant himself and his aides. The official designation of Stalin's regime as the 'period of the personality cult' was itself a euphemism. Neither the full extent nor the causes of this perversion of Socialism was described. A number of officers and officials were punished and expelled from the higher echelons of the secret police, which Beria had turned into Stalin's most feared political weapon. Khrushchev subjugated the secret police to the Party once again.

Limits were set to the criticism of the emergence and consequences of Stalinism, but criticism of Stalin himself continued. The functionaries in the Party apparatus did not know where Khrushchev's campaign would end. Would the revelations be limited to toppled Party leaders, or could they be directed against others still in power, or waiting for power? Many members of the apparatus felt threatened, but Khrushchev now undermined himself by overstating and coarsening some of his ambitious plans. He was accused of 'bird-brained adventurism', and his belief that in the Soviet Union there now existed the 'new human being' who could take the final step to Communism was derided. By 1980, he claimed, the Soviet citizen would no longer feel ambition, envy or jealousy. Much that Khrushchev said and thought was completely out of touch with Soviet reality, and his opponents mocked his dreams of the future Communist society which seemed to him so close.

When Soviet citizens start to make jokes about their leaders, it is a sure sign that their rule is threatened. Khrushchev either did not hear what was being said about him or took no notice of it. Now the apparatus began delaying his policy of reform. Leading officials formed alliances among themselves in order to protect themselves from reassignment or dismissal. The roots of the conspiracy that would lead to Khrushchev's downfall began to spread invisibly through the apparatus of the Party, state and military.

There was no need for the younger delegates to the Twenty-second Party Congress to fear for their positions and careers. Friends of Gorbachev remember that he greatly respected Khrushchev, and never joined in when other functionaries ridiculed him during the Brezhnev years, but that he was very critical of parts of the submitted programme at the Congress. Nikolai Dorochin, who had now moved to the Regional Party Committee, shared a hotel room with Gorbachev and sat next to him at the Congress. 'When Khrushchev talked about how quickly things would progress and that we ourselves would live under Communism, we exchanged looks. We didn't shake our heads, but we knew what we were thinking. It seemed Utopian to us, because we knew the real situation in agriculture. We discussed these things openly in our hotel room.'

The thirty-two-year-old Gorbachev was too young and too far removed from the centre of power for Khrushchev's opponents to have roped him into their palace intrigues. But he had not remained unnoticed in his outpost in Stavropol. The economist Gavril Popov remembers that he had already heard of the young official in 1961, at a time when he himself was working on the foundations of economic reform in Moscow. The assistants of two agricultural specialists and later Politburo members, Fyodor Kulakov and Kyril Masurov, had come to Moscow from Stavropol. They told Popov about a young man in their home town who had returned from Moscow University to Stavropol and was being rapidly promoted in the Young Communist League. Popov remembers them saying that this young man, Gorbachev, was intelligent but modest, a disciplined worker without pronounced personal ambition. These qualities, says Popov today, were always valued in someone rising in the Party.

This was Gorbachev's first, albeit indirect, connection with Kulakov and Masurov, who would later be among his supporters. Although it was only their assistants who had mentioned him to Popov, assistants have always carried weight with the leading men in the Central Committee or the Council of Ministers. It is they who supply the isolated high functionaries with information from the outside world, and for this reason their influence is often significant, if hard to quantify.

Fyodor Kulakov was soon to come into more direct contact with Gorbachev. He had been made Minister for Agriculture, but Khrushchev fell out with him, and had him transferred to

Stavropol, as First Party Secretary of the region. In March 1962 Mikhail Gorbachev moved over to the Stavropol Party Committee. Khrushchev was once again reorganising the economy and agriculture, and new modes of administration again bound the economy tightly to the Party apparatus. The *kolkhozes* were to be transformed into enormous state farms, and Gorbachev took on the role of Party Organiser in one of the large agricultural units being created. His knowledge of the villages and farmers around Stavropol was as important as his legal training and his experience of organisation and propaganda during his *Komsomol* years, and his access to Raisa's research was an additional advantage.

If Gorbachev had reservations about Khrushchev's project, which was intended to turn the farmers by degrees into paid workers in agrarian cities, Kulakov would surely have understood them. Khrushchev's last agricultural reform was to end two years later, with his own downfall. A year later his successor, Leonid Brezhnev, criticised the attempt to create giant agricultural units. In future *kolkhozes* and state farms were again to develop separately, and the weak farmers' co-operatives were to be given assistance.

Khrushchev's removal from power is now known as the 'dacha intrigue', because his opponents met in the country houses of high functionaries. There are indications that Fyodor Kulakov, whom Khrushchev had pushed out to Stavropol, and a hunting party arranged by him for Moscow officials on Lake Mantish in the Stavropol region, played a part. What ultimately brought Khrushchev down was the irritation and alarm that his politics aroused in the Party and state apparatus. Leading men from different regions and with quite distinct interests found themselves allied in their opposition to him.

Politburo members such as Mikhail Suslov felt that destalinisation and deideologisation had gone too far. The economists in the Party turned against Khrushchev because of the erratic course of his reforms and their lack of success. Though the military had succeeded in its demands for an increase in armaments expenditure, it had not forgotten Khrushchev's earlier attempts to decrease defence spending. The Soviet grip on the Eastern European satellite states had been weakened because their leaders had been made insecure. The Party Secretaries of the regions and the leading members of the Central Committee and the Politburo felt threatened by Khrushchev's abrupt decisions. If Khrushchev still had any support it was from the intellectuals, but even they had never been sure of his politics, and were now disappointed in him. Khrushchev had overestimated his ability to single-handedly change the country from above. He spent his last days in power at the government dacha of Pitsunda on the Black Sea. The Presidium of the Central Committee unexpectedly called him back to Moscow, and Central Committee Secretary Suslov confronted him in the Politburo with a long list of his mistakes. No one came to his defence, and nothing remained for him but to agree to his resignation on the grounds of ill health. On 14 October 1964 the Central Committee met, and unanimously decided to remove him not only from his office as Party and government leader, but also from the Central Committee.

The writer Anatoli Strelyani concludes from talks with Khrushchev's former assistant that he had already lost the will to fight for reform. His political imagination, narrowed by years of dogmatic thinking, prevented him from realising that the system needed to be more deeply ploughed up than he believed.

Mikhail Suslov had organised the conspiracy, but he was content to remain in the background. Leonid Brezhnev took over as General Secretary of the Party, in collaboration with Prime Minister Alexei Kosygin and President Nikolai Podgorny.

Khrushchev was sent off to his dacha near Moscow. His old colleagues avoided him, and he remained almost totally isolated. Only after his death was he remembered as the man who had freed his country from stagnation and petrification and for a few years let it breathe. In the Brezhnev era those who had hoped for change and reform came to think of him with growing respect. Most were now forced to abandon their expectations. But for one particular Party functionary who would later strive for change himself, Khrushchev's failure must have carried important lessons.

Gorbachev was now leader of a department in the Regional Party Committee. Fyodor Kulakov had returned to Moscow, where as Secretary of the Central Committee he was responsible for agriculture. Kulakov knew his way around the power-blocs within the Party. He had played a part in the conspiracy to remove Khrushchev, and now Khrushchev's successors brought him into the Central Committee as leader of agricultural policy. He soon rose to the Politburo. Evidently he had mastered the rules of the game and the tricks of the apparatus. This was important for Gorbachev. Now there was a man close to the centre of power who knew his abilities.

In Stavropol too his influence and reputation were increasing. His colleagues were more likely to meet him at work than on the all-male drinking bouts popular among many officials in the Brezhnev era. He was now living with his wife and daughter in a three-room flat with a balcony in a house for leading officials.

Despite Gorbachev's increasing responsibilities, he enrolled as an external student of economics at the Stavropol Agricultural College. Problems of agriculture continued to occupy him, but now he was Party Secretary of an industrial city. Economic knowledge, in addition to his legal training, would be useful. Again he worked hard as a student, says Professor Chuguchev, who then held the chair. 'Mikhail was more or less the only student who really did all the work. And he did it for its own sake, he didn't just want another qualification to further his career. He went to all the seminars, because it would have embarrassed him as First Secretary to do less than the others. As an external student he received quite a broad education in economics.' Stavropol Agricultural College is best known for the quality of its agronomic research, but it also has a good reputation as a teaching institute, and it has a library of half a million books.

Gorbachev made good use of this, as he proved when he had to defend his diploma work before the state examining board. Professor Alexander Nikonov, today Director of the Soviet Academy of Agriculture, was then chairman of the board in Stavropol. Gorbachev's work seemed remarkable to him and his colleagues, as did the way in which he expounded and defended his conclusions. He had brought a number of graphs and a pointer, and spoke clearly and confidently. The professors compared Gorbachev's performance with the way in which Party functionaries usually received their diplomas: for mediocre work they had often not even done themselves. They knew that Gorbachev had worked hard, and they assumed that his wife, whose academic abilities they knew, had helped him. Only later, says Professor Nikonov, did he discover that Raisa had refused on principle to assist her husband's studies. The examining board was so impressed by Gorbachev's diploma work that the professors wanted to publish it as a dissertation. Gorbachev rejected their proposal, as he had rejected the college's plan to make Raisa a professor after she had successfully defended her dissertation in Moscow. He knew that she merited a professorship, but while he was Regional Party Secretary such an appointment for his wife was out of the question. It seems that this decision was made with Raisa's full agreement, as she herself always took care at all costs to avoid the suspicion that Gorbachev was exploiting his position.

In a city like Stavropol the First Secretary of the Party Committee is, quite simply, responsible for everything: for theatres and schools, for the newspapers (with whose editorial staff Gorbachev often spoke about the following day's headlines and articles), for the hospitals and clinics, the transport system, housing construction, industrial development and the decisions of the law courts at city level. Gorbachev was Party Leader of a sizeable centre for industry, supply and administration in a region of considerable agricultural importance for the whole Soviet Union. Power, in a very concrete form, comes with the job: the Party Secretary can reward by promotion, punish by bad reports, and he can also help a friend get a flat or a holiday in a sanatorium. Most Party Secretaries are tied to their desks by their need to keep an overall perspective and not lose sight of organisational problems.

For this reason, people in Stavropol say today, Gorbachev lived a retiring life. Constant personal contact with petitioners would have been both damaging and tedious. In Soviet cities a Party Leader is always dealing with requests for better jobs or pleas for children to be admitted to hospital. Raisa, her colleagues remember, made it clear that she would not approach her husband with requests for help from friends, except for matters of urgently needed medication.

If Gorbachev's name was becoming increasingly well known in Moscow, this was at least in part due to the fact that Fyodor Kulakov was now Secretary of the Central Committee. When in 1966 the position of Secretary of the Communist Youth League became vacant, Gorbachev's name appeared on the list of candidates. Leonid Brezhnev sent for the 'character portrait' of the young man, looked at the photograph and said, 'He doesn't have enough hair for a Young Communist leader.' That ended the candidacy.

CHAPTER 4

Party Secretary

So Gorbachev remained in Stavropol, occupied with the many practical tasks of its daily political life. This was a time of great change for industrial cities such as Stavropol. Two days after Khrushchev's resignation Prime Minister Alexei Kosygin announced a reform programme for the whole of Soviet industry. At first the reform seemed to be succeeding, but then economic growth slowed down. Kosygin had stressed that he was not attempting to introduce a market economy, and the administrative apparatus had seen to it that its central authority hardly diminished. Though industry's yardstick was no longer simply mass production, without any regard for quality, the increased evaluation introduced in its place strengthened rather than weakened the bureaucratic style of management. The reform process had bogged down once again. Meanwhile, economists were already discussing a Socialist market economy such as Ota Šik had suggested in Czechoslovakia as the starting point for a new economic structure.

The Prague Spring, and the Czech struggle for democratic Socialism, was not as remote from Mikhail Gorbachev in Stavropol as might be supposed. In 1967 he had a visitor from Prague. Zdeněk Mlynář, his Czechoslovakian friend from university, visited him in Stavropol.

Mlynář has always been reserved about his relationship with Gorbachev, and has never revealed what they discussed in 1967 and how Gorbachev reacted to the news from Czechoslovakia. Perhaps they continued their student discussions from the time of the Thaw.

On the way back from Stavropol Mlynář stopped off at Moscow, where a talk with his other university friend Vladimir

Liberman quickly turned into a heated debate. Professor Liberman, who had himself got into difficulties with the Party apparatus for his independent thinking, remained, despite everything, convinced that it was still too early for Socialism or Communism 'with a human face'. According to Liberman, Mlynář said: 'I thought your education, your origins, your liberal inclinations and your undogmatic thinking would all help you to understand my point of view, but I was wrong. Misha Gorbachev, with his very different experiences, understood me better.'

In the summer of 1968 the Socialist neighbour states of Czechoslovakia were in agreement with the Soviet Union that the Czech experiment would have to be terminated before it started an avalanche. Poland's Party Leader Vladislav Gomulka was supported by all the Socialist Party leaders when he said at a conference in July that Czechoslovakia was undergoing a counter-revolution that was particularly dangerous, as the opponent did not fight with guns. The lifting of censorship showed that the Czech Party leadership had given up attempting to influence developments.

It was this raising of censorship that caused particular unease in Moscow. After decades of Party monopoly on information and the formation of opinion the idea of renouncing control over knowledge and thought was alarming. *Rudé Právo*, the newspaper of the Czechoslovakian Communists, had said that the Party could not claim to speak for the entire nation. It described the Party's mistakes, and said that they could be democratically corrected. The Communists in Czechoslovakia were allowing themselves to be carried by a wave of spontaneous activity among the masses they had formerly led.

Well-known scientists and writers published the 'Manifesto of 2000 Words', a settling of accounts with Communist rule, which expressed the view that the state apparatus was no longer controlled by the people, and that the Communist Party had become an organ of power in which ambitious egoists and careerists fought for influence.

Tens of thousands of Czechs signed the manifesto, and this wide support made it particularly dangerous in Soviet eyes. The assurance that reform would not be achieved without or in opposition to the Communists did nothing to calm the Soviets, as the manifesto also promised to support Dubček and the other

Communist leaders, with arms if necessary, should foreign troops invade.

Soviet intervention was inevitable. *Pravda* later stated: 'The Communists of the brother countries could not allow Communist states to remain inactive because of an abstract concept of sovereignty while the country fell into antisocialist degeneracy. Anyone who calls the action of the allied Socialist countries in Czechoslovakia unlawful forgets that in a class society there is not and cannot be any classless right. Law and justice are subordinate to the class struggle and social development.' This was the basic pattern of what was called the 'Brezhnev Doctrine', which justified the use of military might to force Socialist states to toe the Soviet line. The *Pravda* article continued: 'Each Communist Party is not only responsible to its own people, but to all Socialist countries and the entire Communist movement. A Socialist state that forms a Socialist community with other states cannot disregard the interests of this community.' In reality, of course, not the community, but Moscow, decided.

During the night of 21 August 1968 Soviet, Hungarian, Polish and East German troops marched into Czechoslovakia. Alexander Dubček and other leading members of the Presidium were arrested, taken in a tank to the airport and flown in chains to the Soviet Union, where they were forced to take part in mock negotiations intended to disguise the military occupation of Czechoslovakia. Among those dragged to Moscow was Zdeněk Mlynář.

The military intervention in Czechoslovakia was received with neither surprise nor support by the Soviet people. After twenty years of propaganda, the vast majority of the population was willing to believe that the Red Army had once again saved Czechoslovakia, which it had already liberated from the West. There were few protests. Seven demonstrators, among them Andrei Sakharov's son-in-law Pavel Litvinov, briefly unfurled banners bearing such slogans as 'Hands Off Czechoslovakia' in Red Square before the police stepped in and arrested them. They were heavily sentenced, but almost a hundred Soviet intellectuals signed a letter to the Supreme Soviet supporting them.

Andrei Sakharov later called this period a turning point in his life. For some years he had been helping people who were being persecuted for their political opinions, their faith or their nationality. In 1968 he brought out his underground article 'Reflections on Progress, Peaceful Co-existence and Intellectual Freedom', which quickly became known throughout the world. In the same year he openly admitted to being a dissident. The physicist who had once been the father of the Soviet hydrogen bomb was now no longer allowed to take part in projects that were classified as secret. He lost his privileges, but remained the leading scientific figure in the Institute of Physics. Although he kept working, Sakharov was already on the path that would lead to his banishment to Gorki in 1980. There he was to live, isolated and under constant police surveillance until, in one of the most extraordinary moments of recent Soviet history, a phone call from Mikhail Gorbachev called him back to Moscow in December 1986.

The KGB naturally learned of Gorbachev's meeting with Mlynář in 1967, and fellow students who had known Gorbachev and Mlynář were questioned by KGB officials. But apparently no damaging conclusions were drawn. Gorbachev later said to a friend that Yuri Andropov and the Deputy General Public Prosecutor Viktor Naidyonov had saved him. Andropov had been Chairman of the Committee for State Security (the KGB) since 1967, and had been ambassador to Hungary at the time of the people's uprising.

Gorbachev's friends in Moscow interpret his remark as meaning that Andropov and Naidyonov, who were struggling against corruption in the Party, wanted to protect Gorbachev from denunciation. On several occasions, Gorbachev later told his friends, Andropov kept him out of trouble when his opponents wanted to damage his career.

Gorbachev continued to rise in the Party Committee of the Stavropol region, and in April 1970, at the age of thirty-nine, he became First Party Secretary. He was now one of approximately seventy men who not only had executive authority and power in their own regions, but could also make their influence felt in Moscow. Under Brezhnev their position had grown stronger and their power increased. They had more influence on political decisions than members of the Central Committee, and they ranked in importance only behind full-time Central Committee Secretaries and members of the Politburo.

In 1971 Gorbachev was elected to the Central Committee. Its members held regular plenary sessions at Moscow Party headquarters, which made possible the cultivation of connections with other leading officials throughout the country. Gorbachev had an advantage over most of the other members: the spas in the south of the Stavropol region drew leaders of the Soviet state for cures and relaxation. Some, like the Party Ideologue Mikhail Suslov, had houses at their disposal in the area. If Gorbachev had been a First Secretary in the far north of the country, or in Siberia, there would, as he himself says, have been fewer opportunities for him to establish contact with the most powerful men in the Party.

Gorbachev and his family now occupied their own one-storey house in Stavropol. In its small walled garden he could plant apple trees. Three times a week an old woman called Aunt Xenia came to help in the house, because Raisa was still working at the Agricultural College. But when friends came to the house Raisa preferred to rely on the help of her husband and daughter rather than on a waiter or a domestic help, to which she was now entitled.

Alexander Nikonov, then director of the Agricultural College, once found the eleven-year-old Irina at the stove preparing the evening meal for her father. 'What can one do?' said Gorbachev. 'Raisa is on an official trip.' Irina's former teacher still has a note Gorbachev wrote informing her that Irina's mother was ill and that Irina had to stay at home and look after her.

Irina, born in 1957, was no 'Party princess', but was brought up very simply. She spent the summer holidays with her grand-mother in Privolnoye, often working in the garden. Like her parents, she worked hard at school. Her teacher Valentina Mirosh-nikova says that the striking thing about her was her sense of discipline. She was interested above all in literature and the arts, but succeeded in getting excellent marks in every subject, includ-ing science. Like Raisa, she left school with a gold medal. 'She was a very reserved girl,' says her teacher, 'and never exploited her father's name. In fact she tried to avoid any connection with him or his position.'

While Raisa came regularly to the parents' evenings, Mikhail only visited the school twice – on Irina's first day, when he brought her to the class, and on the day she received her gold medal. Then he was invited to sit on the stage with the teachers, but he declined, smiling and saying that he was only there as a parent.

The teachers thought that Irina would choose to study literature or philosophy, and were surprised when she went instead to the Medical Institute in Stavropol. Some say the desire to study medicine was awoken in her by a fellow student, Andrei Virgansky. In their third student year they married. Reveka Polyak, head of the Surgical Department of the Institute, says today: 'Until that third year I didn't even know Irina was the daughter of our First Secretary. I knew that Andrei and Irina were excellent students. And they were a nice-looking couple, all of us thought that.'

The wedding celebration of the daughter of the First Party Secretary of Stavropol was rather similar to that of Raisa and Mikhail in the lean fifties. Nothing was spared on food and drink, but it was unlike the lavish celebrations that in those years were taken for granted in the families of high functionaries. After the ceremony at the registry office two cars drove to the Gorka restaurant in Stavropol. In one car were the young couple and their witnesses, in the other the parents. The celebratory meal was held in a small room, and only fellow students and friends of the couple were invited. The bride's parents soon left. 'I wanted them to have a wedding like Misha and I had,' Raisa said to friends who were surprised that she and her husband had left the restaurant so early. 'They don't need us now.' There was naturally a good deal of talk about this wedding in the city, and some people thought the First Secretary had been mean not to give his daughter a grander wedding.

The women of Stavropol had already noticed that the wife of the Party Secretary did not, as had become the custom, wear diamond rings, and that her daughter did not even have a sheepskin coat, at that time a status symbol for young people. When a colleague mentioned this to Raisa, she said: 'Sheepskin coats are not openly sold, and for that reason I don't want my daughter to run around in one.' During the Stavropol years Raisa was never seen in a fur coat. But she dressed well. Perhaps she was a little too self-consciously chic, which aroused the envy of some women in Stavropol. Photographs of the time show that she knew how to wear even a raincoat and a headscarf a little differently from her colleagues or the mothers of Irina's classmates. She gave a personal style even to simple clothes.

Gorbachev had already begun taking Raisa on most of his

official trips. While he attended official meetings she went to the markets and the shops, looked around and asked questions. 'So Gorbachev always had information at first hand, and moreover of professional quality,' says Professor Nikonov. 'Sometimes at the end of a visit he knew more about the real problems of the place than the local officials with whom he had sat at the conference table.' Nikonov thinks Gorbachev may have taken Raisa on these trips because he was an essentially emotional man who had had to learn to exercise rigorous self-control in public. He needed the presence of one person who was emotionally and intellectually close to him. Today, at the weekend he takes to the wheel of his official car and drives out into the country with Raisa. They leave the car somewhere and go on long walks together. This is not only relaxation, but also an opportunity to escape the throng of officials and advisers with whom a Party Secretary constantly has to deal.

As a provincial Party functionary Gorbachev led a comfortable, but not luxurious life. His house was simply furnished, with none of the antiques so beloved of the upper levels of the Party. Instead, the Gorbachevs had built up a good library. One thing that struck Gorbachev's colleagues was that, unlike his predecessor, he did not have himself driven to his office in a black limousine in the morning, but walked through the park and across Lenin Square. People would meet and talk to him as he walked, and in this way he learned a great deal about their problems. That he learned to drive and often drove his car himself would not have been unusual in the West, but in the Soviet Union in the seventies it was an open break with protocol, almost an insult to fellow functionaries, and is still unusual today.

Gorbachev did not simply follow instructions from Party headquarters. He made changes on his own initiative, which entailed a certain amount of risk. Functionaries who kept to what was prescribed by the apparatus were reasonably safe if things went wrong, but anyone who undertook something different on his own responsibility could run into difficulties even if he was successful. Colleagues who worked with Gorbachev in the Party Committee think that even then his actions showed the beginnings of *perestroika*.

Nikolai Dorochin, Gorbachev's first cadre leader in Stavropol, remembers proudly: 'I can say without a doubt that Mikhail's personality as a great politician developed here in Stavropol. Later, when he was General Secretary, he said that *perestroika* as an idea did not come into being at the Plenum where it was first mentioned. The situation then was favourable for a new beginning, but the thoughts and deeds that brought *perestroika* into all areas of life existed much earlier. Here in the Stavropol region, for instance, we worked out a programme with Gorbachev for the mechanisation and electrification of agriculture. Electrification reached every last settlement, every last farm.

'Mikhail Sergeyevich didn't sit at his desk, but was out there himself. He always said you had to go out to the people and study the problems on the spot. There were irrigation projects, which were very important in our dry region. And the building of the Stavropol Canal. These were all the fruit of Gorbachev's work. They had to be cleared by the government and the Central Committee, which wasn't easy, but Misha didn't give in when he wanted something. That was his character: if he was convinced about something he took it to its logical conclusion. And he's still like that. The most important thing in our region was to improve living conditions. After all, the life of the workers and the farmers is the basis of industrial and agricultural production. We had to solve many problems by going against the instructions from Moscow and the official line. On our own we built schools, kindergartens, hospitals and clubs, and not just a few for show, but hundreds. That encouraged people to stay here. It helped us not only to prevent the flight from the country to the cities, but even to create the conditions that brought people here. That's what explains our success.'

Dorochin and other former colleagues are convinced that as Regional Party Secretary Gorbachev had already begun to introduce elements into the economy of his region that would later be typical of his policy of *perestroika* throughout the entire Soviet Union: financial independence for enterprises, greater emphasis on profitability, material inducements and market-economy structures. Many people who held important posts in the city and region say that under Gorbachev things were very different in Stavropol than in neighbouring regions.

Viktor Postnikov came from Privolnoye to Stavropol, and is today a member of the Congress of People's Deputies and the general director of the largest and most modern poultry farm in the Soviet Union. He remembers: 'In about 1974 I read about a poultry farm in the magazine *America*, which comes out in Russian. I was so impressed that I wanted to try its methods out right away in Stavropol. Without Gorbachev that wouldn't have been possible. From the first day our enterprise was associated with his name. He was involved in all the plans, decisions and problems. He helped us to switch to economic management. That was something quite new at the time, and it was only possible with his help. He helped to overcome the entire bureaucratic apparatus, which we still constantly criticise in the Soviet Union, and he showed what freedom of action can mean for an enterprise. We were given increasingly more independence, especially after 1983. Nobody interferes any more with our production, processing and sales. When he was Secretary for Agriculture in the Central Committee I often went to see him, and he helped us to overcome bureaucratic obstacles. We had always wanted to finance ourselves, we didn't want money from the state, and we had to make the people in the Finance Ministry understand that. Without Gorbachev we wouldn't have been allowed to restructure our whole business. The person running an enterprise must be able to feel he's the master and owner, and we've had that since 1983. Gorbachev left Stavropol in 1978, but to this day we feel we're reaping the benefits of what he sowed.'

In 1976 Gorbachev won approval for Postnikov to start his enterprise experimentally, and it now produces just about everything that can be made from poultry, from duck-liver pâté to quail's eggs. It has its own supermarket in Stavropol, which is modern and clean, unlike most in the Soviet Union. It has shops in Moscow which are among the most popular in the city. And it brings hard currency into the country by exporting its products.

Another delegate from the Stavropol region also speaks of Gorbachev's early attempts at *perestroika*: 'Our *perestroika* began the day, 20 April 1970, that Gorbachev became First Regional Secretary. But he had to fight hard to get most of the changes through. For example, there was the question of whether to expand the specialised breeding of sheep. In Moscow they were against it, but Gorbachev supported it and his tenacity helped us. He bravely went to the Politburo itself, to Brezhnev. The matter was finally settled in our favour, and since then wool production has almost doubled. On another occasion, towards the end of his time with us, the Politburo wanted to develop new land, reclaiming regions of the steppes rather than intensively cultivating the land we already had under the plough. Gorbachev wrote letters against this, and was afraid he might be removed from his position because of it. But things turned out well, and a few months later he became Agricultural Secretary to the Central Committee.'

When Gorbachev was responsible for agriculture in the Stavropol region a system of achievement-rated premiums was introduced, and the old system of detailed controls and norms was abolished. Working parties made up of farmers and their families entered into contracts with the *kolkhozes* and were rewarded according to the economic yield. The system also reduced the cost of production.

In the mid-seventies it was claimed that such working parties could increase the harvest yield by 30 to 50 per cent, and it seemed to be Gorbachev's aim to introduce the system into the entire Stavropol region. But at the same time he adopted a system devised by his supporter Fyodor Kulakov, by which the harvest would be brought in more quickly through the massive use of agricultural machines. Columns of threshing machines drove from *kolkhoz* to *kolkhoz*, followed by huge lorries for transporting the grain to the silos. With the tractor drivers and technicians came everything they needed: medical care, field kitchens and even entertainment ensembles for the evenings. The new system was called the 'Ipatovo method' after the district in the Stavropol region where it was first used.

At first the innovation was remarkably successful. The yield per hectare, always high in the Stavropol region, went up even more. But the concentrated use of travelling brigades of technicians was based on exactly the opposite principle to that of the system of small, independent working parties introduced a little earlier. These working parties had an interest in not only exploiting the land, but in improving it for the future. Now the mechanised columns thundered through the *kolkhozes* and the opportunity to use the farmers' experience and initiative was lost. Like all purely technocratic innovations, the Ipatovo method brought only short-term improvements, and failed to deal with the basic agricultural problems.

The initial success of the Ipatovo method brought Gorbachev official recognition. In May 1978 the Party Ideologue Mikhail

Suslov came to Stavropol to present him with the Order of the October Revolution, his second decoration. Gorbachev's photograph appeared in all the newspapers of the Soviet Union, a sign that he was now coming to be regarded as a potential future leader in Moscow.

A few years later the Ipatovo method was abandoned, and the introduction of farmers' working parties, working independently and sharing in the yield, was again promoted. Gorbachev, as Agricultural Secretary of the Central Committee, had engineered the change.

In Stavropol, Gorbachev regularly brought the agricultural specialists of the region together in seminars to discuss new methods and local experience. He turned to the Agricultural College for laboratory analyses and for help with problems. He would come to the College's research station immediately if scientists thought they had found a solution to some problem with sheep breeding or the cultivation of grain.

During the mid-seventies there were a number of bad harvests in the Stavropol region because of drought. Gorbachev met with the scientists of the Agricultural Institute and the Director of the Agricultural College, Alexander Nikonov, and together they went through the yearly reports on agricultural development that the district's governors had been required to send to the Tsar before the Revolution. These revealed that in times of drought at the turn of the century those regions where the land had been allowed to lie fallow for one or two years had had good harvests. In the 1970s the Party in Moscow backed the mechanisation of agriculture, and the theory of fallow land was considered virtual heresy. Gorbachev called a Party conference in Stavropol and presented the evidence of the old reports. Before the officials realised what they were letting themselves in for, they had agreed to ask the authorities in Moscow for permission for a fallow land project in the Stavropol region.

Moscow rejected the project. 'We were told straight out: "Fallow land is to farming what an epidemic is to breeding livestock",' says G. Starshikov, then First Deputy Chairman in the regional administration responsible for agriculture. 'But that didn't frighten Mikhail Sergeyevich. We discovered that the central agricultural authorities had no information about fallow land. Mikhail Sergeyevich went to Moscow and succeeded in getting all the secretaries of the Central Committee to come to a meeting where he submitted our evidence, convinced them and overcame their doubts. To do this he even had to talk to Brezhnev himself. As a result of reintroducing fallow land, and despite periods of drought and sandstorms, we were able to bring in decent harvests.'

For Professor Nikonov, Gorbachev's fallow-land initiative proves his courageous determination to seek out better agricultural methods than those prescribed by Party headquarters. He always tried to make the local conditions the basis of agrarian-political decisions, and to defend the experience of farmers and scientists when it contradicted the abstract and dogmatic policy of the functionaries. Gorbachev was never rigid in his thinking, says Nikonov, but was always ready to consider new ideas. At the same time he was a practical and cautious man, who would carefully consider every political step and would weigh up the tactical factors in his disputes with the apparatus.

It is almost impossible to develop and systematically impose uniform methods in a region like Stavropol. From the 4000-metre-high Dombai in the Caucasus to the marshy lowlands of the River Mantish there are many varied landscapes and climatic zones. With three million people, speaking numerous different languages and having different traditions, the region presents many problems for a Party leader. While the areas of wheat cultivation produce a good average yield provided it rains, in the mountain and desert regions little is possible beyond raising sheep. More than 150 *kolkhozes* and almost 250 state farms produced approximately 3½ million tons of grain in the mid-seventies, as well as sunflower seeds for oil production and vegetables to supply the cities. They kept 1.4 million cattle, a million pigs and 600,000 sheep. The produce of this region was vital to the whole Soviet Union.

As well as agriculture, the First Party Secretary was also responsible for the development of industry, for the exploitation of natural gas and oil deposits and for the food-processing industry, which was of major importance to the region. During Gorbachev's time in Stavropol the emphasis in industry switched to machine-building, chemical products and building large power stations. He was in charge of setting up production organisations in heavy industry and large combines for the processing of meat, fruit and vegetables. He was also responsible for seven colleges with 30,000 students, for the school system of the region and for cultural facilities such as theatres, cinemas and youth centres. There were over thirty towns in the region, and Gorbachev was the supreme authority for all decisions.

In just twenty years Stavropol had doubled its population, and Gorbachev had to personally ensure that the structure of industry and supplies kept pace with this rapid growth. 'In 1976 a bakery and confectionery combine we urgently needed was built in Stavropol,' says Alexander Alexeyenko, at that time First Secretary of a District Committee. 'Things kept grinding to a halt, and Mikhail Sergeyevich phoned me and said: "Shura, you know what we need to do? You have to assign the builders to particular groups until the combine's ready. That way there's somebody to whom we can turn and whom we can hold responsible. Then building will go ahead faster." And when it came to renovating the meat-canning combine he phoned me again: "Shura, I'm told you go round with a slide rule. Could you come and go over the figures?" So I went to see him. There was Mikhail Sergeyevich pacing the room and dictating his thoughts about the renovation to a secretary. I was amazed. I'd never come across anyone like that before. But I could see it was a good method if you had to solve a problem. He asked me to check some calculations and to read his notes. That kept us busy for two or three hours. Then he worked out the suggestions for the city Party Committee, how the production range of the meat-canning combine could diversify so people could also buy chicken and pasta. For me this was an object lesson in working out an idea collectively.'

Alexeyenko remembers Gorbachev's good memory for faces and names. 'He always addressed people by their first name and patronymic, almost never by their last name. And if he knew someone he'd turn to him like one Young Communist to another: "Shura, I urgently need this information. Could you get it for me?" I never heard him talk down to anyone, he always spoke in a calm, friendly way. And if someone treats you like that you want to do your job well.'

In his work as Party Leader in Stavropol, aspects of Gorbachev's character that had already been apparent in his earlier life came to the fore. He worked hard, but did not give the impression of being personally ambitious. He was open to new ideas and vigorously tried to bring about changes he considered right, but he did this without harshness towards his colleagues, and he always confirmed his plans with his superiors before he tried to put them into practice. This pragmatic method was the most likely to succeed, as there was no way the apparatus itself could be changed. Gorbachev's experience in Stavropol forged his leadership style, and also strengthened his conviction that the state and the Party would have to find more rational methods of implementing their policies. But until these existed one had to keep to the rules.

The most important stage of Gorbachev's rise occurred during the Brezhnev years. After Khrushchev's fall, the Party drew breath. Organisational reforms were withdrawn. The highest offices of Party and state, which Khrushchev had united, were again separated. Their old functions were returned to the ministries, and the top functionaries once again felt secure in their posts. Brezhnev's plans for the economy and society were more realistic than those of Khrushchev's last, Utopian, Twenty-year Programme.

It was soon clear, however, that the country would have to cope with further problems that resulted from bureaucratic and centralised control. None of the economic and administrative reforms of the Brezhnev era went deep enough to bring about real improvements. Prime Minister Kosygin promised greater independence to state enterprises, but then tied them closely to central planning, to detailed direction by ministries and state planning committees. The discussions among economists about the role of market forces and operational independence ceased after the invasion of Czechoslovakia had put an end there to the development of a Socialist market economy. Clearly Brezhnev had no high opinion of scientifically elaborated economic reform. He seemed to rely above all on patriotic and moralistic appeals to the Soviet people. Kosygin's economic reforms came to nothing, and ten years later, towards the end of his life, he told colleagues he should have withdrawn earlier, as soon as it became clear to him that under Brezhnev his influence would be extremely limited.

Under a system in which the next economic change of direction could not be anticipated, a rising Party functionary needed to react quickly and with circumspection if he wanted to achieve success. Gorbachev energetically and imaginatively supported the leaders of the larger enterprises in his region. He wanted to make life easier for the people, by means over which he himself had control. He allowed profitable enterprises to raise their workers' meagre pay, which was in conflict with Moscow's policy. His interest in art and literature led him to promote projects that won Stavropol a high reputation among Moscow artists and writers. As well as the music festival he introduced an annual Lermontov festival, which attracted writers, performers and journalists from Moscow, principally to honour Lermontov, but also perhaps because of the warm climate, the hospitality and the rich choice of fruit at the farmers' markets. A further bonus for them was Party Secretary Gorbachev himself, who liked to meet and talk with the writers, and the atmosphere created by his wife and his colleagues.

Gorbachev would ask the actors and writers who came to Stavropol for information about what was happening in the world of art and literature in the capital. Even as First Secretary of a region he received only the official accounts of such events as the expulsion of Solzhenitsyn, whose books had so impressed him. The festivals he introduced to Stavropol gave him an opportunity to keep in touch with the mood in Moscow.

Some of Gorbachev's guests at the time remember him as a sociable, uncomplicated man who liked to sing and recite poems, usually by Lermontov and Pushkin, when he was with friends. He was not a fanatical opponent of alcohol, but he got rid of the heavy drinkers in the Party and administrative apparatus. 'Several leading people were excluded from the Party because he couldn't stand boozers who had no conscience and no self-control,' says Vladimir Kolodichuk. Gorbachev would sip a glass of brandy when he was with the hard-drinking Moscow intellectuals, but that was all. In Stavropol people remember how he saved nearby Mount Strishament, on which grow some unique aromatic herbs, from agricultural cultivation. Today Stavropol citizens credit Gorbachev with having saved their 'Strishament brandy'.

General Secretary Gorbachev, nicknamed the 'Mineral-water Secretary' in Moscow because of his anti-alcohol drive, did not attempt to break his friends and acquaintances of the habit of drinking. Even later, when the full-scale campaign against alcohol consumption was under way, a friend who called on Gorbachev in his office in the Central Committee one morning had the surprising experience of being offered a brandy by the General Secretary. It was too early for him, said the friend, and Gorbachev – visibly relieved – ordered tea instead. In Kiev during the anti-alcohol campaign workers asked him how they could be good hosts without offering their guests a glass of *gorilka*. Gorbachev answered that it was all right to drink, but not too much. Although Gorbachev has been represented as an ascetic enemy of alcohol, and the instigator of the unsuccessful crusade against wine and vodka, in reality its main supporter was that steely non-drinker Yegor Ligachev. Of the many people who met Gorbachev in Stavropol not one remembers any sign of asceticism, fanaticism, or even unsociability.

The spas in the south of the region were often visited by high-level officials – Politburo members, Central Committee secretaries, ministers and their deputies. The sanatoriums and country houses, with their springs and baths, lie hidden in large private parks. The much-praised mineral water of the Caucasus was seldom the officials' main drink, however. They came to the spas to enjoy the company of male colleagues of equal rank, out of sight of their wives, their subordinates and the general population, with good food, vodka, champagne and gypsy singers, where they could sing sentimental folksongs as they slapped each other on the back and drunkenly assured each other of their eternal friendship.

It was Gorbachev's responsibility to see to it that these officials enjoyed their holidays. There was no need for him to organise their pleasures himself, as most of them stayed in the sanatoriums and country houses of their own institution or ministry, where everything was taken care of. The Politburo, the Central Committee, the KGB, the army and other big ministries had their own establishments, and most functionaries liked to be with colleagues from their own section of the apparatus. It was the First Secretary's duty to greet the highest dignitaries from Moscow at the airport and to drive with them to their dachas and sanatoriums. Gorbachev had to take care that Politburo members felt honoured and well looked-after. Every Party functionary knew how important it was for his future career to make a good impression on the mighty.

Gorbachev had one problem: that he hardly drank made him appear suspicious to some visitors. Would this man, they might have asked themselves, remember everything that was said late at night over the last bottle of vodka? The number of higher functionaries who came to the spas was so great that Gorbachev eventually got special permission from the Central Committee not to have to meet them all. This enabled him to spend more time with the most important visitors from Moscow. He would frequently go to the dachas and sanatoriums to see them, and he knew how to make a good impression.

An influential Union Minister who liked to play billiards found a partner in one of Gorbachev's closest colleagues. Gorbachev gave this colleague urgent instructions to lose to the Minister in order to keep him in a good mood, in the hope that the Stavropol region might then receive more money from the Ministry.

Not all of the Moscow Party leaders appreciated the lifestyle of Brezhnev's circle. Some disliked the all-night drinking sessions as much as Gorbachev. Two Politburo members in particular deliberately and clearly set themselves apart from the Brezhnev clan. These were the Party Ideologue Mikhail Suslov and the KGB chief Yuri Andropov. Both frequently spent their holidays in the Caucasian spas, and it went without saying that the First Secretary of the region looked after them with special care.

Suslov and Andropov were regarded as puritans by Brezhnev's closest associates. They were better educated than the functionaries who surrounded Brezhnev, and thought of themselves as intellectuals. Andropov wrote poetry in the classical style – a fact which only became public knowledge after his death. Suslov, like Gorbachev, knew long passages of Pushkin by heart. In conversation with them Gorbachev, with his phenomenal memory, was able to quote facts and theories from economics, politics, history and law, and he impressed them with his clear and considered judgements. 'That's a really intelligent young man,' Suslov is reported to have said about Gorbachev after one of their first meetings. The word 'intelligent' in Russian implies not just cleverness, but also that a person belongs to the educated classes, the 'intelligentsia'. Andropov's wife was apparently charmed by Raisa's seriousness and education, and particularly by her modesty.

In a period when the wives of functionaries liked to adorn themselves with gold and diamonds Raisa undoubtedly made a striking impression – especially on the wife of a man such as

Andropov, who himself scorned ostentatious display and luxury. It may have touched Andropov that, like himself, Raisa was the child of a provincial railway worker – he had grown up at a small railway station on the line between Stavropol and the Caucasus, which he passed on his journeys from Moscow to the spa.

To this day Moscow intellectuals and journalists differ as to who most smoothed Gorbachev's way to the top – Suslov, Andropov, or Fyodor Kulakov. Little is known about how decisions of this type are made in the Soviet leadership. In the Brezhnev years personal connections and loyalty were important, but it is difficult to assess the role of ideological loyalty or success on a practical organisational level. Since the beginning of the sixties Fyodor Kulakov had openly supported Gorbachev, but it is hard to see in the level-headed Gorbachev a close follower of Kulakov, who was given to outbursts of Russian temperament and sentimentality, and who loved the leadership style of a powerful functionary.

From the mid-seventies Gorbachev also received the support of Yuri Andropov. But this was very different from the kind of mutual promotion by which members of Brezhnev's team clambered up the Party ladder. Gorbachev worked for more than twenty years in the *Komsomol* and the Stavropol Party apparatus before he was called to Moscow, and his reputation was founded on his work, not on personal connections. The move to Moscow, to the power centre of the Party, was nevertheless only possible with support from the very top. Gorbachev's restrained lifestyle must have impressed Andropov, who bitterly opposed the corruption and extravagance of other Party officials.

Mikhail Suslov, who had himself been Party Secretary of Stavropol in the early 1940s, may have valued Gorbachev because he lived simply, recited poetry and could talk intelligently about the practical problems of the Soviet Union without overstepping the ideological guidelines. But none of the personal or political connections by which people in Moscow today try to explain Gorbachev's rise conclusively link him with any of the cliques which at the end of the seventies decided political careers.

The economist Gavril Popov, formerly a supporter but now a harsh critic of Gorbachev's economic policy, thinks Gorbachev was able to rise in the Party by his cleverness, but also by his character traits, some acquired, some natural. 'He didn't drink or join in the dacha parties. He worked hard where he was and didn't take part in the complicated power intrigues in Moscow. He didn't tie himself to one of the clans or the Kremlin camp. And, remarkably, no one held this against him. He had little to offer by way of connections, and he was modest. But he was an agricultural expert at a time when those at the Central Committee headquarters considered agriculture a difficult area. He was a workhorse, and in Stavropol he never tried to do anything really radical. He allowed the instructions from central headquarters with which he disagreed to lose their momentum and he had had some successes. If someone had to put his head on the block as the new Agricultural Secretary of the Central Committee, they may have thought, why not Gorbachev?'

Among Gorbachev's most trusted agricultural advisers was Alexander Nikonov, then a professor at the Stavropol Agricultural College, today Rector of the Soviet Academy of Agriculture in Moscow. In the 1970s Nikonov knew that changes were necessary in Soviet agriculture. He was adamant that the farmer needed to be the master of his land, and to be able to go to market with his products himself, whether he owned the land, leased it, or belonged to a co-operative. He needed a better vocational education and better machines. The villages needed an adequate infrastructure, good road connections and decent housing. And the economic system which was crippling the farmers' initiative and discounting their knowledge needed to be replaced by more freedom of choice and a move towards a market economy. These beliefs formed the basis of the opinions he passed on to the Party Secretary. Gorbachev, who had to obey the instructions and production demands from Moscow, could only incorporate vague hints of such plans in his work and his speeches. The time had not yet come when he could propose his own agricultural programme. But he cautiously and successfully built these ideas into his concept of agricultural policy.

Nikonov, who went from Stavropol to Moscow two months before Gorbachev, does not believe that either Suslov or Andropov played a personal role in Gorbachev's appointment as Agricultural Secretary of the Central Committee: 'This was one of the rare moments in Soviet history when a man's personal qualities brought about his rise. Gorbachev was young and energetic, he had made a name for himself in the Central Committee with his speeches on agriculture, but he belonged to no clan and no one was afraid of him or jealous of him.'

For the 1978 June Plenum of the Central Committee Fyodor Kulakov, responsible for agriculture in the Central Committee, entrusted Gorbachev with the main speech on agricultural policy. Gorbachev had two and a half months to prepare his speech. He consulted with the leaders of agricultural enterprises in his region and the scientists of the Stavropol Agricultural College. At that time most high Party functionaries had their speeches written by advisers – or better still, by people from the central apparatus.

'Gorbachev worked for weeks on his speech. He went around with a dictaphone and even recorded his thoughts in his car,' says Alexander Nikonov. 'I knew he could work hard, but I was astonished that he could bear this workload.' Did the First Secretary of the Stavropol region know that the speech on agricultural policy would be the decisive event in his career? Nikonov believes that Gorbachev gave this no thought. He was aware that it was an honour for him to make a policy speech before the Central Committee of the Party, but he did not prepare it with a view to being appointed to Moscow's highest Party committee.

Gorbachev's speech was well-informed and full of insights and information that had not previously been presented to the members of the Politburo and the functionaries of the Central Committee in such a forceful manner. But he knew the rules of the game for the period, and introduced no proposals that would have required a radical change of direction in agricultural policy. His speech was a compromise between what he considered necessary and what was possible, in the judgement of his friends and advisers. 'He wanted to be quite certain that every fact and every figure was accurate,' says Alexander Nikonov. 'And he checked them all himself.'

Gorbachev's speech impressed the Central Committee. He had clearly done a lot of work in his field, and he argued from personal knowledge and with figures taken from practical experience instead of with ideological formulas and manipulated statistics. Most of the listeners, to whom Gorbachev's name meant almost nothing, were surprised. By Moscow leadership standards Gorbachev was a young man, but he presented his agricultural programme with commitment and persuasiveness. The older members of the Central Committee and Politburo were very taken by his performance. After the session some of them commented that one could see that there was promise in the rising generation.

By the end of the seventies it was clear that the state of agriculture in the Soviet Union was rapidly getting worse. In fact the experts of the scientific research institutes forecast that a catastrophe was imminent. Buying grain from the USA, Canada, Argentina and Western Europe had concealed the true state of affairs and postponed the crisis. Even so, three times as much grain as was imported from the West was lost through bad storage and distribution. Even the Party leadership knew that a change in policy was necessary to get Soviet agriculture back on its feet.

Fyodor Kulakov died in July 1978. He was sixty, an age at which the Party leadership still considered him a young man, a future candidate for the highest posts. The official announcement of his death stated simply that his heart had stopped. Today it seems certain he committed suicide, for unknown reasons. His death unleashed a flood of rumours in the capital. For twelve years he had been Secretary of the Central Committee, for six a member of the Politburo, but neither General Secretary Brezhnev, nor Prime Minister Kosygin, nor Politburo members such as Suslov and Chernenko came to his funeral.

Gorbachev gave one of the funeral speeches. That a Party Secretary from Stavropol should give a funeral speech for a Politburo member appeared to prove that Kulakov had fallen out of favour with Brezhnev. If this was the case, it would also suggest that Gorbachev was not a member of any of the ruling clans.

In 1990 one of the last surviving insiders of the Brezhnev years, Pyotr Shelest, recollected Gorbachev's rise. Shelest had been Party Secretary of the Ukraine, a Politburo member, and First Deputy Prime Minister. He first met Gorbachev in 1973, and says he struck him then as a sensible young man, eager for knowledge, who asked many questions and seemed interested in everything. 'After the mysterious death of Fyodor Kulakov, Gorbachev was brought into the apparatus of the Central Committee. Kulakov had supported Gorbachev since the time of their collaboration in Stavropol, where Kulakov was First Secretary of the Party Committee and Gorbachev was Secretary of the *Komsomol*. After the death of Suslov, who had kept strict control of the hierarchy of the Party, Gorbachev went over completely to Andropov who was gathering supporters for the battle to succeed Brezhnev. It

91

was more or less in this way that Gorbachev established himself in the Kremlin leadership, and after Andropov's death, under Chernenko, he was already the second man in the Central Committee.'

No one at Kulakov's funeral knew that Gorbachev would be chosen as his successor. The way in which such decisions were made in Moscow had become completely obscure even to high functionaries. Personal connections obviously played a part, but officially all important posts in the Party, state, economy and culture were filled according to the process called *nomenklatura*. A Party manual defines it like this: 'The *nomenklatura* is a listing of the most important posts. Before their nomination for these posts candidates must be recommended and accepted in the responsible Party Committee of the district, town, region etc. Members of the *nomenklatura* can only be released from their posts with the agreement of the responsible Party Committee.'

Only those whose names are on the *nomenklatura* list are considered for appointments as editors, heads of research institutes, ministers in the government of a republic, chairmen of Party committees and countless other posts. Not every Party member belongs to the *nomenklatura*, only those who have reached the inner circle of the Party. Nothing can happen to a member of the *nomenklatura*, even if he commits a crime, unless the Party functionaries responsible give the law permission to prosecute. The highest levels of the *nomenklatura*, the Politburo and the Secretariat of the Central Committee, are not mentioned in the Party manual.

In the Brezhnev era there were no longer any clear rules. A former member of the Politburo remembers how in 1977 Brezhnev appointed himself Chairman of the Presidium of the Supreme Soviet, in other words Head of State. The position was held by Nikolai Podgorny, who together with Brezhnev and Kosygin had come to power after Khrushchev's fall, but who was gradually being divested of his political influence. At a plenary session of the Central Committee, Podgorny, sitting next to Brezhnev, was astonished to hear a speaker propose uniting the office of General Secretary with that of nominal Head of State. Podgorny turned to Brezhnev and said, 'Lonya, what's this?' Brezhnev looked at him gravely and said: 'I'm surprised, too. But if that's what the people want . . . '

The witness to this episode was himself later removed from his position by Brezhnev. Why members of the Politburo and the government accepted such acts is unknown, but no individual dared question the decisions of the General Secretary and the Party.

Two months after Kulakov's burial, Leonid Brezhnev's special train stopped for a break at the Caucasian spa Mineralniye Vody. Konstantin Chernenko, the sixty-seven-year-old Central Committee Secretary and Brezhnev's closest colleague, was travelling from the Black Sea back to Moscow with Brezhnev. Waiting at the station were the sixty-four-year-old Yuri Andropov, who was being treated at a nearby sanatorium for a serious kidney ailment, and the forty-seven-year-old Mikhail Gorbachev. He was at the station because it was his duty as First Secretary of the Stavropol region, but also because Andropov wanted to help his career.

Kulakov's post as Secretary for Agriculture was vacant, and Andropov wanted to use this opportunity to bring Gorbachev to Moscow. Of the four men at the station that day, one was General Secretary of the Party and the other three would be his successors. Gorbachev's rise in the apparatus of the Central Committee dates from this meeting at the station of Mineralniye Vody.

It was obvious to Gorbachev that he was now only a step away from the centre of power, the Politburo. Brezhnev, Chernenko and Andropov would not have seen Gorbachev, in their eyes still a young man, as a rival. Only Andropov was aware of Gorbachev's personality and political expectations. Perhaps he, himself aspiring to the post of General Secretary, saw a possible successor in Gorbachev.

Gorbachev was more than just a provincial Party Secretary. As a Deputy of the Supreme Soviet, which met twice a year to unanimously approve government bills, he may have had no real political power, but since 1974 he had been Chairman of the Commission for Youth in the Soviet Union, and in this role he had received an insight into legislative work and collaboration with government officials. In the years to come he would gain further experience in the Supreme Soviet. In 1979 he was Chairman of the Commission for Legislative Proposals, an important link between Party, government and the nominal legislative body. In 1982, when Andropov was General Secretary, Gorbachev became Chairman of the Foreign Policy Commission, which introduced him to another important field, and also brought him into contact with the veteran Foreign Minister Andrei Gromyko. These were important steps on the road to the highest office of state, and added to the experience and connections he had already gained in his political career. This was not a calculated progression to the top, but anyone thinking of promoting Gorbachev would have been aware of how useful his experience of the apparatus of both state and Party would be.

CHAPTER 5

Moscow

The vote to choose Kulakov's successor as Secretary for Agriculture took place in the Central Committee in November 1978. There were three candidates: Sergei Medunov, First Secretary of the Krasnodar region and one of Brezhnev's cronies; Fyodor Morgun, First Secretary of the region of Poltava in the Ukraine; and Gorbachev. It seemed that Medunov had the strongest support in Moscow. Twice Brezhnev had made him a Hero of Socialist Labour, and many members of the Central Committee owed him favours. But there were also arguments in favour of Gorbachev. His speech before the Central Committee had won him a reputation as a young and energetic agricultural expert. Two influential Politburo members, Suslov and Andropov, saw him as the hope of the new generation. He was an ethnic Russian, was intelligent and hard-working, and had a modest lifestyle. He was obviously concerned with the social and economic condition of the people, a point in his favour with Chernenko, Brezhnev's right-hand man, who saw social policy as the starting point for the stabilisation of the Soviet system. Above all, Gorbachev was not a member of any of the rival Party clans, and he was unlikely to make any fundamental criticisms of Party decisions. The old men of the Politburo would accept him without fearing him as a rival. The combination of all these factors probably decided the vote for Gorbachev.

The Brezhnev years are today called 'the time of stagnation' in Moscow. Russians remember them as a period during which development ceased and belief in progress collapsed. But what distinguished Brezhnev's regime from its very beginning had been the promise that he would bring about a period of tranquillity and order. Khrushchev's rapidly changing reforms, and his impatient reprimands and perfunctory dismissals of longstanding officials, had made the Party nervous. Brezhnev, on the other hand, as the strong-man of a collective leadership, presented himself as the father of the people, from whom the apparatus need fear no unpleasant surprises. In his first years as Party Leader, Brezhnev and his Prime Minister, Kosygin, promoted reform of the economic system. From 1970 he gave the Soviet people, who for years had been living with the dread of nuclear war, hope of a new security in Europe and an improvement in economic and living conditions.

By the late 1970s, towards the end of Brezhnev's period in office, the Soviet population was becoming frustrated. Some things had grown worse under Brezhnev, and nothing had improved. People complained that under Stalin and even under Khrushchev there had been sufficient food in the shops, whereas by 1980 Muscovites had to queue for hours to buy potatoes, imported from distant Cuba. Vegetables in the *kolkhoz* markets could not be afforded by people on average incomes.

Today, when the lack of supplies is again compared unfavourably to former times, the citizens of Moscow seem to forget that even in 1980 they could only buy meat and butter in limited quantities. The ordinary citizen bore the brunt of cuts in government spending. Social services were reduced, child mortality rose, one had to wait weeks for a hospital bed. Public kindergartens refused to take children whose parents could not give them donations. Nurses would only change the sheets on hospital beds if they were bribed with presents or cash.

The leaders themselves were less affected than ordinary citizens by the problem of supplies. They, and their friends and relatives, had access to a supply system that was not available to the rest of the population. Indeed, they could obtain cars, flats and luxury goods more easily than before. Imports and Western credit concealed the shortcomings of Soviet agricultural and industrial policy. American wheat, for example, became Russian bread or vodka. Despite this, dissatisfaction grew even in government circles. Complaints about the growing importance of personal connections and bribes, and anger at the injustice of the social system, could no longer be ignored. Party functionaries who knew the real situation gradually became aware that the Soviet economic system had reached the limit of its capacity for development, and in its present condition stood rigidly in the way of any improvement or reform.

The younger people in the scientific research institutes, the ministries and the Party who saw this were particularly embittered, because it was not possible to openly write or talk about these matters. Brezhnev and his administration had declared the age of 'genuinely existing Socialism'. At first this had been a defensive move against reform Communists in Eastern Europe and Eurocommunists in the West who criticised the Soviet system. But soon it became a formula which meant that reforms to the Soviet system were impossible. Many Russians lost any hope of an improvement in their living conditions.

The Brezhnev regime may have suppressed criticism, but only those who fundamentally criticised the leadership or the system needed to fear sudden arrest by the secret police. One could make oneself comfortable within the system. But cautious heads of scientific institutes still removed forecasts of failure from their colleagues' work, only allowing optimistic reports to be published.

Officially, the Party blamed the lack of supplies on the Americans and NATO, who had forced the Soviet Union into an arms race that devoured its resources. But many Soviet researchers were aware that the failure of the economic system had internal causes which could only be overcome by reform. To Brezhnev and his entourage the situation looked quite different. By its very nature the Brezhnev regime balked at a true examination of the poor living conditions and lack of development of the country. Its style of leadership was determined neither by ideological analyses nor by sober politico-economic considerations. The cohesion of the leadership was based on intrigue and personal connections.

When the leaders did make criticisms, they were directed against individuals rather than the system itself. At fairly regular intervals Brezhnev lashed out in the Central Committee against the weaknesses of Soviet industry and its managers. He also attacked high representatives of the state apparatus, but those he denounced were by no means necessarily the worst or the least successful. Colleagues in a large ministry could suddenly discover from the newspaper that General Secretary Brezhnev had rebuked their chief for incompetence. No doubt this was painful for the Minister concerned, but in many cases it led to nothing. Indeed, sometimes public humiliations of this kind were rapidly followed by promotion. Such contradictions raised doubts about the rationality of the leadership, and weakened the authority of the ageing Brezhnev.

Although Brezhnev repeatedly announced that the military-industrial complex would use its highly developed capacity to meet civilian needs, Soviet citizens were accustomed to fending for themselves at high prices in the shadow economy. The managers of industry had long known that to reach their state-planned quotas they not only had to juggle their statistics, but also had to make use of gifts and bribes to ensure that their supplies arrived.

Under Brezhnev the bureaucrats of the Party and state apparatus felt relatively secure, but they were uneasy that talk about the liberalisation of the Soviet system, which had reached its peak after Khrushchev's revelations about Stalin, had not ceased. In 1965 the new leadership wanted to show that it would ruthlessly clamp down on intellectuals who refused to toe the Party line. The writers Andrei Sinyavsky and Yuli Daniel, who had allowed their books to be published abroad under pseudonyms, were sentenced to seven and five years' imprisonment respectively. This was a signal: for the first time since Stalin's death, writers could again be sent to prison. But Sinyavsky and Daniel, unlike the accused in the Stalin trials, steadfastly refused to admit guilt or show remorse. A number of Soviet intellectuals risked putting their names to petitions in support of the condemned writers. On the 'Day of the Soviet Constitution', the 5th of December, about a hundred people demonstrated on Pushkin Square for the observance of constitutional rights. Many among them, including Andrei Sakharov, were taking part in an unauthorised demonstration for the first time in their lives.

Now the persecution of those who 'thought differently', the dissidents who at first only regarded themselves as a loyal opposition, began in other cities of the Soviet Union. Most of those arrested were members of the intelligentsia who had openly demonstrated for human rights. Others continued to work, apparently unhindered, in leading positions in cultural and scientific life, but there was a constantly shifting dividing line. In 1966 more than twenty respected scientists and artists had warned the Twenty-third Party Congress against rehabilitating Stalin. Among them were writers such as Ilya Ehrenburg and Kornei Chukovsky, the ballerina Maya Plisetskaya, the cellist Mstislav Rostropovich and the atomic scientists Pyotr Kapitsa, Igor Tamm and Andrei Sakharov. They were all protected by their famous names, and the Party had no wish to turn them into martyrs.

In May 1967 Alexander Solzhenitsyn sent each delegate to the Congress of the Writers' Union a letter protesting against censorship. It read: 'Censorship, by censors not publicly named, not provided for in the constitution and therefore illegal, weighs on our literature. It perpetrates arbitrary acts by illiterates on our writers.' Not one of the 300 delegates risked openly reading out the letter, but nevertheless a third of those present asked for the question of censorship to be discussed at the Writers' Congress.

The persecution of dissident intellectuals grew fiercer. With increasing frequency the KGB used psychiatric hospitals to frighten, punish or even destroy them. Fewer and fewer people risked putting their names to protests against censorship or demands for the human rights of imprisoned colleagues. For a decade and a half from 1970 only a small group admitted to being dissidents, thus voluntarily exposing themselves to persecution. They continued to proclaim and spread those ideas which had been openly discussed during the Thaw after Stalin's death.

The members of this courageous group lost their jobs and access to clinics and hospitals. Many of the older ones lost their pensions. Most of them would have starved if colleagues had not helped them with money or anonymous work – the dissidents were not in fact as isolated as they seemed. This made the Party leadership uneasy, and they tried once again to suppress all original thought. The Institute of Philosophy, which in the sixties had been open to new and undogmatic thinking, received a new Director, a philosophically educated engineer who was supposed to wean the Institute's members from the bad habit of independent thought. Scientific and literary journals were again submitted to harsh controls, with entire editorial offices dismissed overnight.

Andrei Sakharov, who had become an open dissident, could still, as a member of the Academy of Sciences, take up the cause of those who were being persecuted. But his position became more difficult. When officials tried to expel Sakharov from the Academy the nuclear physicist Pyotr Kapitsa asked whether there was a precedent for this. He himself, he said, could think of only one: the expulsion of Einstein from the Academy of Sciences in

Berlin. The disciplinary action against Sakharov was dropped, and he remained a member of the Academy even after he had been transported to Gorky and cut off from the outside world. No other member of the Academy risked openly backing Sakharov. He was forced to live in a distant outpost that was closed to foreigners, and where even Russian friends who wanted to visit him would be arrested and turned back at the station. If he went on hunger strike, he was forcibly fed.

Andropov, Suslov and Brezhnev may have persecuted the dissidents, but they failed to prevent the spread of their ideas. They were prepared to make great personal sacrifices, and their secret strength lay in the fact that more and more people in the Soviet Union shared their thoughts, even if they did not dare express them.

It was Yuri Andropov more than anyone else who brought about Gorbachev's move from Stavropol to Moscow in 1978. At this time Andropov was lining himself up as Brezhnev's successor. Brezhnev's favourite, however, was Konstantin Chernenko, who as Central Committee Secretary and Leader of the General Department of the Central Committee was in effect general secretary to the General Secretary.

Gorbachev shared Andropov's aversion to corruption and nepotism. Like Andropov, he took pride in being contented with the more modest official privileges. This distinguished him from the circle surrounding Brezhnev, who liked hunting lodges and foreign cars, and who crammed their flats with antiques. But Gorbachev did not want to make an enemy of Chernenko. He was Brezhnev's closest ally, and Gorbachev knew he could not implement his agricultural programme without the support of both men.

Later, as Central Committee Secretary, Gorbachev came into remarkably little conflict with other Politburo members. Some of them, like the Moscow Party leader Viktor Grishin and the Leningrad Party chief Grigori Romanov, were openly ambitious to become General Secretary. But they felt too secure in their positions to regard Gorbachev as a threat. Gorbachev was not drawn into the power-struggle which followed Brezhnev's death.

A Politburo member who is today one of Gorbachev's severest critics confirms that the Gorbachev who came to Moscow in 1978 did not appear to be motivated by personal ambition. He qualifies this by saying that what people thought about Gorbachev and what Gorbachev himself thought were never the same thing. The apparently modest agricultural specialist could in fact have been a committed politician striving for power.

Most of the people who had dealings with Gorbachev in the Central Committee cannot recall having noticed any indication then of far-reaching political ambition. The economist Gavril Popov, who today belongs to Boris Yeltsin's camp, says that Gorbachev did not take part in the palace intrigues of other top functionaries jockeying for position. 'He was not a bootlicker, and that means something here. Even before the Revolution Russia was a country where the bureaucracy was all-powerful, and many careers were built on flattery. Gorbachev always worked hard and long. Other functionaries regarded this as a sign of short-sightedness and naivety. They knew that the ones who made careers for themselves stayed close to the mighty on the upper floors and won their favour.'

Gorbachev, who disliked going to dacha parties or on hunting trips, knew that he was not making himself popular by this kind of stand-offishness. Occasionally he told friends that he was not worried about his future. If his political career ended, he was a trained lawyer, he could teach at a university, and if the worst really came to the worst he could be a chauffeur or drive a threshing machine. His listeners would laugh politely. Nobody who wanted to make his way to the top in Moscow talked like this, especially during the late Brezhnev years. But it was generally acknowledged in the Central Committee that Gorbachev was a good boss and colleague, always ready to take on assignments and work. A working day of ten or twelve hours had long been normal for him. Most other members of the Politburo, however, felt overloaded, and were glad if work was taken away from them.

His colleagues found his manner pleasant. He did not swear or bang the table, as was the custom with others, including Brezhnev himself. It was difficult to get close to him, say some who knew him at this time, but he compensated for this by being polite and businesslike. Because of this, and because of his interest in many aspects of politics and culture, Gorbachev was able to attract people from varied fields and get information from them. 'He didn't flatter, but he was also not condescending,' says one of his former colleagues. 'He offended no one, even those whose views he rejected. He always tried to find a compromise, to establish a consensus. He was a master at creating the impression that a decision had been arrived at by general agreement, even if in reality it was his decision alone.'

One year to the day after Gorbachev became a Secretary of the Central Committee he became a Politburo Candidate. Eleven months later he was a full member, one of the fourteen most powerful men in the Soviet Union. For such a rapid advance one not only needs supporters, one must also not make enemies.

When the Gorbachevs came from Stavropol to Moscow, they looked forward to rediscovering the city they had known as students almost twenty-five years before. During short visits they had been to theatres, concerts and museums, but now they again wanted to form a picture for themselves of the entire city. They went on several of the bus tours provided for Soviet tourists. For a Secretary of the Central Committee this was extremely unusual. He had a fleet of cars at his disposal, and taking a tourist bus-ride with his wife seemed a little ridiculous to some of his colleagues and staff.

Gorbachev lived simply. He did not offend the apparatus by pointedly refusing official privileges, but took only what was his due as Central Committee Secretary, asking for nothing extra. With his wife, daughter and son-in-law he moved into the three-room flat provided for him at 12 Alexei Tolstoy Street, furnished by the Central Committee administration. Friends from Stavropol were surprised that Gorbachev had a less well-furnished flat than his brother Alexander, who as an army officer also had an official flat in the vicinity of Moscow. In the Gorbachevs' flat there were only the standard furnishings for senior officials: cupboards from Riga, a kitchen made in the Moscow *experimentalnaya fabrika*, synthetic carpets. Unlike other high functionaries, they had no foreign refrigerator or imported television. The flat was small: a bedroom, a living room, and a room for Irina and Andrei, who now had a daughter. Even Boris Yeltsin, who today accuses Gorbachev of providing himself with luxurious dachas, admits that in his first years in Moscow Gorbachev lived simply and modestly.

In his first year as a Central Committee Secretary Gorbachev earned 700 roubles, and the next year, as a Politburo Candidate,

800. The average worker's income at that time was a little over 200 roubles. In Stavropol it had been easier to live on less money, Gorbachev remarked to a friend from his student days, because then his parents had still been able to send him meat and vegetables from the village. The only advantage to being in Moscow, said Gorbachev, was that he could order books from every library in the country. But he did not have enough money to buy better furniture or to install his daughter and son-in-law in a flat of their own.

His friend Dmitri Golovanov, to whom he talked about these problems, found this hard to comprehend, and asked him: 'Why don't you get the Central Committee administration to give you a flat for your children? Other people's grandchildren even have official flats, and many of them are constantly changing one flat for a better one.' Gorbachev replied that he was new in Moscow and that he did not want to be the subject of gossip. The parents of his son-in-law were prepared to contribute 5000 roubles towards a privately-owned co-operative flat, but Gorbachev was too short of cash to come up with the same amount. Finally he borrowed it from Golovanov, who was glad to help, but thought that Gorbachev was too modest for a Central Party Secretary. It seemed to him that the Gorbachevs felt themselves strangers in Moscow, and Gorbachev once told him he would rather be back in Stavropol.

With every step up the hierarchy in Moscow the living conditions improve. As General Secretary Gorbachev moved to Shchusev Street, only a few hundred metres from his first flat, but with four rooms, a Japanese television and a bath imported from Scandinavia. Friends who visited him there say that there were still no ornate antiques or the heavy crystal vases so beloved of Moscow's upper stratum. What they noticed instead were the traditional Russian knitted covers that Raisa spread over the tables, the photographs of friends and the bunches of flowers. Today, Gorbachev lives in a large, almost elegant house in Kosygin Street, looking down on Moscow's inner city. On the ground floor are reception rooms, the communications centre, and accommodation for the guards and the domestic staff. The Gorbachevs have six rooms on the first floor, and above that are private guest rooms. Raisa, it seems, has developed a taste for Meissen figures and pre-Revolution silver. There is a sauna and a beautiful garden, but in his free time Gorbachev is said to prefer staying at the dacha in Rasdory, forty kilometres north-west of Moscow. 'Then we sometimes go for a stroll in the woods, but I wouldn't call our walks athletic,' says Raisa. Gorbachev apparently likes to recall how he went riding as a boy in Privolnoye, where there were many horses. Today his love of animals is confined to a poodle, Daisy, and a bird called Gray. Raisa sometimes talks nostalgically of the open country, flowers and mushrooms, wild animals and trout of the Caucasus, where in his last years as Stavropol Party chief Gorbachev had a government dacha built on the edge of a nature reserve.

The wives of Politburo members and Central Committee Secretaries made up a fairly enclosed social circle, which they rarely left. But their lives were less regulated than those of their husbands, and Raisa socialised more with members of Moscow's intelligentsia than most Party wives. She could tell her husband about the most interesting plays in the capital, and it was with the two liveliest and most controversial theatres, the Taganka and the Sovremennik, that she came into closest contact. As an unknown woman from the provinces she could move with greater freedom in the cultural circles of the capital than the wives of older members of the leadership. Theatre directors who learned who she was cultivated contact with her. The wife of a Central Committee Secretary and Politburo Candidate could be a useful contact if the Ministry of Culture and the official critics put pressure on them.

Raisa was also able to revive her contacts with the philosophers and sociologists of Moscow University. This helped her to gain an impression of the thinking of young scientists, to get to know their work and to bring to Gorbachev's attention those people who were looking for alternatives to the prevailing domestic and foreign policy. Word got around that a young man had moved into the Central Committee Secretariat and the Politburo who was interested in a critical appraisal of economic and social problems. Increasingly, workers at the University and at research institutes sent analyses and proposals for reform to Gorbachev at his Central Committee office or direct to his home. Many scientists, it appeared, had been waiting for someone in the Party leadership to show real interest in the country's grave problems. An entire library of scientific work accumulated on Gorbachev's book-shelves and in his safe.

Raisa also discovered the fashion designers of Moscow, including some who still work for her today. For state visits or special occasions the wives of leading Ministers would have entire wardrobes created for them. In 1978 Raisa embarrassed the directress at the House of Models by asking what she should pay for two dresses she had had made. Nobody knew what the dresses cost. That was the concern of another department, and the bill would be sent as usual to Gorbachev's assistant at the Central Committee. But no one knew exactly how, if ever, such bills were settled. Raisa declared that no one else needed to know what she spent on her clothes, and asked for her bill. After an hour of confusion, she was finally allowed to pay. Naturally she, inexperienced in these matters, had brought money with her. According to the House of Models she still always pays for the dresses she has made, and always enquires about the price before ordering them.

This, however, has not protected her from the Moscow rumour-mongers, who have occasionally seemed to be running a campaign aimed at Gorbachev himself. A photocopied pamphlet spread the false information that Raisa was a niece of Andrei Gromyko, and that Gorbachev had risen through her connections. The anonymous text cited non-existent articles in the German magazines *Spiegel* and *Stern*. Raisa's work for the Culture Fund of the USSR, which independently promotes contemporary art and spiritual traditions, was represented as social climbing. In the markets badges could be bought which read: 'I Love Gorbachev', and others reading: 'I Don't Love Raisa'. It was said that she had too much influence over Gorbachev, and that she pushed herself to the fore. Many people in Moscow thought that she was drawn to glamour and power, luxury, foreign couture, jewellery and country houses.

Raisa Gorbachev's clothes purchases were naturally recorded in the KGB files, as was almost everything that members of the leadership and their families did. In Stavropol there had been no gossip about the Gorbachevs, who had deliberately avoided conspicuous displays of affluence. But supervision by the secret service was much more intensive in Moscow than in Stavropol. Where Aunt Xenia had helped in the Gorbachevs' household in Stavropol, in Moscow official flats and country houses came with staff provided. These chauffeurs, cooks and maids were employed by the KGB, not by the people in whose homes they worked. This branch of the secret police was founded by Stalin, in order to have his functionaries' families constantly guarded and spied upon. The functionaries had grown accustomed to having no need to worry about supplies of scarce consumer goods or food-stuffs, and to chauffeur-driven cars always at the ready outside the door or in the KGB car pool. Their children and grandchildren had never known anything different, and took the system of service and surveillance for granted.

The Gorbachevs had known in Stavropol that the KGB could listen in on their conversations at home and elsewhere. But the supervision had never been as extreme as it was in Moscow. Without referring directly to his own experiences, as General Secretary Gorbachev once said to friends that it was undignified and pointless to supervise the private lives of adults as if they were irresponsible children.

The extent to which holders of high office in the Soviet Union were watched emerges in stories told by two of Gorbachev's friends. Shortly after Gorbachev became a Politburo member, and had moved to the flat in Shchusev Street, he was getting out of his black limousine when he saw an old friend walking by. He went up to him, tapped him on the shoulder, and asked him how he was. 'Fine,' said the friend. 'Good,' Gorbachev replied. 'I'm going home, I'm dead tired.' They shook hands and Gorbachev went into the building. The friend went on his way, but after he had taken a few steps two men came up to him and gripped his arms tightly. One of them asked: 'Who are you? For what reason did you take it upon yourself to address Comrade Gorbachev?' The man tried to explain, but the questions became increasingly threatening. Only after the men had checked and established that he was the District Prosecutor did they let him go with a warning. Another old friend who wanted to say goodbye to Gorbachev before travelling abroad was called to account by Central Committee colleagues. He spoke too often to Gorbachev, and it would have to stop. The friend said that it was Gorbachev's affair if he wished to see old acquaintances. The functionaries looked severely at him, and one of them said: 'That's what you think!'

At first it was not easy for Gorbachev in the Central Committee. In Stavropol he had been the man in charge. Now he found himself a member of an apparatus whose rules he had not yet learned. He could not even choose his personal staff, and had been provided with an assistant without being consulted. This assistant had previously worked for Andrei Kirilenko, who had been a Politburo Candidate in the late fifties and a Central Committee Secretary since 1966, and he made it obvious that he felt superior to his new boss from the provinces. Gorbachev must have had an uneasy feeling of being manipulated by the apparatus.

He occupied a room on the fourth floor of the Central Office Building on Old Square, one floor below the Politburo members, and found it difficult to come to terms with this new way of working, which tied him to his desk. All contact with the outside world was through assistants and the outer office. It was they who decided whether phone calls from friends or acquaintances would be put through to him, and Gorbachev felt screened and isolated in his Central Committee office.

Naturally, as a Central Committee Secretary and Politburo Candidate, Gorbachev was an influential man, but the apparatus made clear to him the limits of his power. His friend Dmitri Golovanov, who worked in broadcasting, asked Gorbachev for a favour. Relations between Golovanov and his chief, the Chairman of the State Committee for Television and Radio, Sergei Lapin, were tense. For this reason Golovanov wanted to be transferred to work as a correspondent abroad, and he asked Gorbachev to mention this to Lapin. Gorbachev was slightly hesitant. He hardly knew the much older Lapin, who had been a Central Committee member for years and ranked as a Minister. Moreover, a personal intervention such as this went against the very rules by which he lived. But he wanted to help his friend, and when he met Lapin at the airport he mentioned Golovanov's request. Lapin called for Golovanov's personal file, and then accused him of having collaborated too closely with Yugoslavian colleagues on a previous assignment. The KGB placed his name on the list of those for whom travel abroad was forbidden.

Lapin apparently informed Gorbachev of this with ill-concealed satisfaction. His relations with other members of the Politburo were more significant to him, and he clearly thought that Gorbachev was of little importance. It would seem that Gorbachev did not forget this incident. After he became General Secretary, Lapin lost his post as chief of radio and television. The era of *glasnost* had already begun, and Lapin's notion of television as strictly an organ of propaganda no longer suited the times.

In his last years in office the ageing Brezhnev lost his grasp of politics. He enjoyed the hymns of praise dedicated to him as father of the people, and had himself decorated with ever newer, ever higher awards. His (perfectly honourable) service as a Political Officer in the Second World War was transformed into a decisive role after several well-known Soviet authors wrote his 'War Memoirs' for him. Army choirs sang about his battle for the 'Little Land', the Kuban bridgehead between the Caucasus and the Black Sea. Now he was visibly growing old. During a televised address he mixed up the pages of his speech, breaking off with a helpless shrug.

But he was still General Secretary and Head of State. No one who wanted to rise in the Party could openly oppose him, and in the battle between those striving to succeed him he could still decisively support his favoured candidate. Those closest to Brezhnev flattered him without restraint, and used their positions to secure huge advantages for themselves. Rumours proliferated in Moscow about the greed of his friends and members of his family. It was said that his daughter Galina furnished herself with luxury items ferried in from abroad by the Moscow State Circus. Diamonds and jewellery had been found at the flat of her lover, whom colleagues at the Bolshoi Theatre called 'Boris the Gypsy'. Her husband, Deputy Minister of the Interior Yuri Churbanov, was widely associated with shady deals and bribery. Such rumours harmed Brezhnev's reputation, and weakened the chances of his inner circle in the power-struggle for succession. That a decision about a new General Secretary would soon have to be made was evident to the entire country, and from 1980 the preparations for this battle kept all the leading men in the Party apparatus busy.

It became clear that the choice would lie between Yuri Andropov and Konstantin Chernenko. The rumours about the private lives of the Brezhnev clan and their uncontrolled greed for paintings, diamonds and limousines could only help Andropov. There is no doubt that Gorbachev felt particularly close to Andropov, who like him rejected the corruption of Brezhnev's circle. But Andropov had no wish to draw Gorbachev into the impending conflict, as, apart from his seat in the Politburo, he had no power-base that could be decisive in the battle. As Central Committee Secretary for Agriculture Gorbachev had had few striking successes, but also no serious failures such as those that had cost some of his predecessors their careers.

After Mikhail Suslov's death in 1982, Gorbachev took over the Central Committee Secretary's responsibility for ideology. He was now in charge of the formulation of the Party's ideological line and the propaganda apparatus that controlled the mass media, for culture and science, and for relations with Communist and Socialist parties abroad. In each of these areas older members of the Central Committee apparatus and the Politburo felt themselves more experienced than Gorbachev, and he had to proceed with circumspection and tact. But he now had the opportunity to secure his position inside the apparatus without powerful men such as the Defence Minister Dmitri Ustinov or the Foreign Minister Andrei Gromyko feeling threatened by him. On the contrary, by his quiet but effective way of working he could recommend himself to them as the best man of the younger generation.

On 10 November 1982 Brezhnev died. For some time it had been rumoured that he was seriously ill and dying in a special sanatorium near Barvikha outside Moscow. Twenty-six hours after his death Soviet television interrupted its programmes and the announcer read the news that the General Secretary had suddenly died.

It is one of the conventions of the Party that the question of a successor to the General Secretary is not openly discussed while the incumbent is still alive. Up to Brezhnev's death the battle for the succession had had to be fought in the wings. There was no tradition and no process for the handing over of power. Tenure of office ended only with death or – as with Khrushchev – with a coup and enforced isolation.

It was important that Brezhnev's post should be filled immediately. Delaying the official announcement of his death by a day gave the Politburo sufficient time to reach its decision. On 12 November the Central Committee elected Yuri Andropov as General Secretary of the Communist Party of the Soviet Union.

Konstantin Chernenko, who for many years had maintained close connections with the organisational apparatus of the Party and its leading functionaries, was the defeated candidate. Ustinov and Gromyko backed Andropov, who naturally also had the support of the KGB apparatus, whose chief he had been for fifteen years. He also had good connections in the Party apparatus for ideology and propaganda. The election showed that Andropov would have to rely on the support of the Politburo, including Chernenko and his circle. His freedom of action was severely limited, and he had to allow the position of second man to go to his rival Chernenko. As Central Committee Secretary he was put in charge of ideology, the post Gorbachev had temporarily occupied. Despite this collective leadership, with its predominantly conservative members, Andropov soon began to introduce a stronger ideological emphasis into politics than had been the case in the days of Brezhnev and his circle.

Yuri Andropov was born in 1914 in the south of the Stavropol region. He started out as a telegraph worker in the Caucasus before becoming a sailor on Volga steamers, graduating from a specialised college for inland navigation and being admitted via the Young Communist League to the Moscow Party College. Like many functionaries of his generation in the years of Stalin's purges, when leading Party members were being arrested and sentenced, he rose quickly to posts that had become vacant. During the war he led partisan groups, and after it he took over Party activities in Karelia, which the Soviet Union had annexed from Finland. For three years he worked in Moscow in the apparatus of the Central Committee, then he was moved to the Foreign Ministry, and from 1954 to 1957 he was Soviet Ambassador to Hungary, being in Budapest when the Hungarian uprising was put down. A year later he was back in the Central Committee, in charge of relations with Communist and Socialist parties abroad. In 1961 he became a member of the Central Committee, and in 1962 one of its Secretaries. From 1967 he was Chairman of the Committee for State Security of the USSR (the KGB), and was KGB chief during the years in which the persecution of dissidents grew harsher. In 1982 he resigned from this post and confined himself to his duties as Central Committee Secretary and Politburo member – perhaps in preparation for the highest office of Party and state. An intermediate period of this kind would in any case have been necessary to spare the Soviet population and the outside world the shock of a KGB chief taking over in the Kremlin.

Andropov's true nature remains unclear to this day. For fifteen years no one in Moscow dared even guess at the personality of the KGB chief. It was said that, although he had never been to the West, he spoke English, and enjoyed whisky, American books and the music of Glenn Miller. But this may have been merely propaganda aimed at Western public opinion. He wrote poetry in the style of the Russian classics, and he apparently protected the Moscow Taganka Theatre when it went beyond the limits of what was tolerated in its criticism of Soviet conditions.

At the Taganka Theatre itself, however, they have another theory about Andropov's motives for helping them. It was said that Yuri Lyubimov, the theatre's director, had rendered Andropov a service which he had not forgotten: he had talked Andropov's son and daughter out of becoming actors.

As KGB chief, Andropov had been widely feared, but once he was in the Politburo the Moscow intelligentsia began to pin their hopes on him. They believed that he was an intellectual, an enlightened functionary, and that was enough after the Brezhnev era to awaken hopes of a change of climate.

In the corridors of the Central Committee it was difficult for Andropov and Gorbachev to continue the long talks of their earlier meetings in Andropov's dacha. On the fifth floor of the building on Old Square Andropov, Gorbachev and Chernenko's offices were next to each other. Gorbachev had the smallest of the three offices. By his chair were three special telephones, secured against bugging, by which high functionaries could immediately be connected with any part of the country. Visitors would wait to be summoned by assistants in a vast reception room.

One of Gorbachev's old student friends visited him in his office in 1983. Gorbachev asked him for a photograph from their student days. He had changed, says his friend. 'He had different eyes, and I felt there was now a barrier between me and the Politburo member.' At this meeting Gorbachev talked about Andropov. There was no one else like him in the Party, no one who was so modest. He did everything himself, said Gorbachev, and his friend felt that this was high praise. Gorbachev's friend knew that in the past Andropov had used his influence to deflect attacks on Gorbachev, but Gorbachev's words seemed to convey more than the gratitude due to a supporter and protector.

Andropov himself clearly saw more than a follower in Gorbachev. He was now seriously ill, and hoped that Gorbachev would be his successor. Their relationship went beyond mutual political interest. Friends of Gorbachev report that towards the end of Andropov's life, in the course of a long talk at his sickbed, the General Secretary had asked Gorbachev to take care of his son Igor and to protect him.

Today Gorbachev's friends say that his relationship to Andropov was not all that close, and that Gorbachev owes less to him than is generally supposed. Perhaps they want to protect him from the suspicion of close connections with Andropov now that former victims of the KGB have been rehabilitated and have become recognised political and moral authorities. Gorbachev was not the only person whose rise had been promoted by Andropov. In April 1983 Andropov had advocated bringing the Party leader of Tomsk, Yegor Ligachev, from Siberia to Moscow as a new Central Committee Secretary. Today Ligachev is Gorbachev's leading conservative opponent in the Politburo. Like Gorbachev, Ligachev did not allow himself to be drawn into the clique of the Brezhnev clan. A committed opponent of alcohol, he had fought for discipline and order in the region over which he had control in western Siberia. For almost twenty years, like Gorbachev, he had been a successful provincial chief without becoming allied to any of the power groups in Moscow. This was important to Andropov, who brought him to Moscow to join the circle of people, who would make the Party and the running of the economy more effective.

Andropov's name is seldom mentioned in speeches or in the press today. He and Brezhnev lived in the same block of flats on the Kutuzovsky Prospekt, and Brezhnev's memorial plaque was removed from its wall overnight when his lifestyle and his policy of stagnation were publicly condemned. Andropov's plaque remains in place, but only on very rare occasions are any flowers left there. The verdict on Andropov has been postponed. Among the high functionaries of recent Soviet history he is still a puzzling figure.

Andropov and Gorbachev were certainly at one in their rejection of the rigid and corrupt Party apparatus. The questions they asked of the Soviet system were not aimed at a merely short-term stabilisation or improvement. They put the development of the

Soviet Party and society in a wider perspective than did their colleagues. For them the structure of the state and society was not a great edifice that needed only a few small corrections in economic and social policy to become perfect. As General Secretary Andropov immediately made it clear in his speeches that he had fundamental changes in mind. Such an ideological tone had not been heard in the Soviet Union since the fall of Khrushchev. Andropov explained that the Soviet Union had reached a historic stage where 'far-reaching qualitative changes in the forces of production and production relations' were unavoidable. He and his closest colleagues wanted to introduce more effective methods of centralised organisation and planning into the economy, but at the same time he spoke of increasing the independence of enterprises in industry and agriculture.

Andropov was interested in a reform model such as had been introduced by János Kádár in Hungary after the uprising had been put down. He had been ambassador in Budapest when Kádár began rebuilding the Communist state from the ruins, and he saw the reforms in Hungary as an attempt to protect the rule of the Party from a new uprising. Delegations were sent from Moscow to study the Hungarian experience, and some returned with the view that such reforms should be tested in the Baltic republics or in Georgia and Armenia. Soviet economists working on reform models knew that in an immense empire such as the Soviet Union change could be brought about only with tremendous difficulty. Even so, they were disappointed that no decisive measures followed the General Secretary's announcements, and that he restricted himself to regional experiments and modest changes to individual economic organisations and enterprises.

Soviet artists and intellectuals were also disappointed. They had hoped that they would be able to examine the conditions of their society more openly and critically, but instead they were restricted by an ideologically-determined cultural policy. In the Brezhnev era the Party and the ministries had often turned a blind eye out of indifference or inertia. Some people attributed the new harsher climate not to Andropov but to Chernenko, who constantly urged 'cultural workers' to create the correct awareness in the minds of Soviet citizens by means of agitation and propaganda, and who wanted to place literature, art and science more strictly under the guidance and control of the Party.

But it was Andropov's attempt to dry out the 'swamp of the Brezhnev era' that determined the atmosphere of all of Soviet life. The police raided Moscow's department stores almost daily to catch people who had left their workplaces early to go shopping. Wine and vodka shops were carefully watched, and anyone discovered there during working hours could count on being reported to his superiors. Officials went from flat to flat establishing who lived there and who spent the night there, and asking for detailed personal records. In post offices boxes appeared with forms for the denunciation of fellow citizens who lived on 'unearned income'. There had been nothing like this in Russia for decades.

Andropov rid the Party and state apparatus of corruption, which pleased Soviet citizens, but now his campaign for order and discipline was affecting their own private lives, creating a climate of mistrust and suspicion. The mere promise of greater freedom of choice for industry and agriculture was not enough to cure Soviet society of its paralysis. In his fifteen months in office Andropov never clearly set out his goals. His policies seemed aimed at a narrow, technocratic reform supported by a new straitjacket of law and order.

Looking back, one can see that Mikhail Gorbachev's visions at this time were somewhat different from Andropov's. Quoting Lenin in his speeches, he emphasised independence and individual initiative. He set out his priorities cautiously, without clearly defining the measures he believed they would require. This gave him no conspicuous political profile at a time when Chernenko's speeches stressed improvements in living conditions rather than Andropov's campaign for discipline. Gorbachev's speeches contained elements of both Andropov's and Chernenko's thinking, and it is noticeable that he avoided conflict with the man who was to be his immediate predecessor as General Secretary.

CHAPTER 6

General Secretary

Andropov may have wanted to introduce more active policies than Brezhnev, but like his predecessor he was an old and sick man, and he was unable to implement the reforms he desired. In May 1983 he took over the Chairmanship of the Defence Council of the USSR, and in June, while still Chairman of the Presidium of the Supreme Soviet, he was elected Head of State. But his public appearances became increasingly rare. Official explanations that he had a cold did little to deceive the public, who knew that Andropov must be seriously ill. In November he was unable to take part in the celebration of the Day of the Revolution – the first time a Soviet leader had failed to appear at this important national event. It was clear that he was dying, and the Politburo prepared itself for a new redistribution of power.

Two months before his death, Andropov tried to resolve the succession crisis in favour of Mikhail Gorbachev. Since October 1983 Andropov had been confined to a hospital bed, from which he tried to govern the country through regular talks with his functionaries and advisers. He hoped to be well enough to give a major speech, which would serve as his legacy, at the December Plenum of the Central Committee. A special speaker's desk for the gravely ill General Secretary had already been built. But it became increasingly clear that Andropov lacked the strength for the task. He therefore prepared his final speech in the form of a proposition with the title: 'On the Responsibility of Central Committee Members to the People'.

On the Saturday before the Plenum Andropov's adviser Arkadi Volsky came to his sickbed to collect the latest corrections. He received a handwritten addition to the papers for the Plenum. As Volsky remembers it today, it read: 'Comrade members of the

115

Central Committee: for reasons known to you I am unable to actively participate today in the leadership of the Politburo Central Committee and the Central Committee of the CPSU. I consider it important to be honest with you: this situation may continue for some time. I would therefore like to ask the Plenum of the Central Committee to consider the matter and to appoint Comrade Mikhail Sergeyevich Gorbachev to the leadership of the Politburo and the Secretariat of the Central Committee.'

Volsky says he took this document to the Central Committee building on Old Square and discussed it with a close colleague. They decided to keep a copy for themselves and to hand the original, via the official channels, to the chief of the General Department (who like Volsky was later expelled from the Party). But at the Plenum two days later, the additional paragraph was missing from the distributed text of Andropov's proposal. Arkadi Volsky says that he was given to understand that he should not interfere in matters which didn't concern him.

Volsky, whom Gorbachev appointed to the Special Committee for Nagorno-Karabakh in 1988, is convinced that Nikolai Tikhonov, then Prime Minister, Party Second Secretary Konstantin Chernenko, and Defence Minister Dmitri Ustinov together saw to it that Andropov's proposal for his successor was suppressed.

On 9 February 1984 Andropov succumbed to a chronic kidney disease and long-standing diabetes.

On 13 February Nikolai Tikhonov, a member of Brezhnev's old guard, proposed Konstantin Chernenko, the 'faithful fighting comrade' of Brezhnev and Andropov, as General Secretary. He praised him as a man who was in touch with all the forces in Soviet society. Chernenko had always cared about the people, shown good will to the Party cadres, played an important role as Ideologue, and taken an active part in the formulation of Soviet foreign and defence policy.

Power relations in the Politburo made the seventy-three-year-old Chernenko appear as the ideal candidate. He promised to 'build on what has been achieved, and to improve it'. He had the trust of old men such as Ustinov and Gromyko, and younger members of the Politburo had no need to fear that his election would for years bar their way to the highest office. The Moscow Party chief Viktor Grishin, only three years younger than Chernenko, saw himself as very much a candidate at the next change of leadership, as did sixty-year-old Grigori Romanov, who had come into the Politburo as Leningrad Party Secretary. Mikhail Gorbachev, the youngest Politburo member of all, was now himself a candidate for the highest office, but he avoided putting himself forward as a rival to Chernenko. As the last speaker, he summed up the arguments in favour of Chernenko's election. Two months later he proposed him as Chairman of the Presidium of the Supreme Soviet, the nominal Head of State.

Gorbachev's relations with Chernenko had never been conspicuously close, but neither were they strained. At the beginning of 1982 the two men had gone together to the Moscow Arts Theatre to the première of a political play in which, with hindsight, one can see a foreshadowing of *perestroika*. The play, *This is How we will Win*, by Mikhail Shatrov, brought scenes from Lenin's last years onto the stage. The actor playing Lenin speaks up for the hopes of the masses against the rule of the bureaucracy, and quotes the 'New Economic Policy', with its loosening of the centralised command economy and its promotion of individual initiative. The play had already aroused controversy before it opened, and had been criticised by the censors of the Ministry of Culture. Gorbachev may have hoped that Chernenko would be sympathetic to the play's message, and indeed Chernenko persuaded Brezhnev and several other Politburo members to see the play. Their visits gave it the official seal of approval and protected it from being withdrawn.

As with Brezhnev and Andropov, Chernenko's age and poor health gave rise to speculation about his successor. Chernenko had never been a good speaker, but now on television Soviet citizens saw an old man, gasping for breath, whom it was impossible to imagine leading the country for long. There was no question of expecting great changes from him. He represented a group which included Ustinov, Gromyko and Tikhonov, now all in their mid-seventies, who no longer had the strength to introduce reforms. When Chernenko had to take breaks from work for reasons of health, it was increasingly Gorbachev who deputised for him, leading the Politburo sessions. Even former Central Committee colleagues who now criticise his policies admit that he did this with extraordinary skill. He saw to it that the sessions rapidly reached decisions without the other Politburo

117

members feeling they were being dictated to. As the youngest member of the Politburo, this required considerable tact.

Gradually it became clear that the starting positions in the forthcoming race for the General Secretary's post were changing. Gorbachev's position seemed to be growing markedly stronger. The triumphant success of his visit to England in December 1984, as the head of a Soviet delegation, proved him to be a man who could successfully represent the Soviet Union in the outside world. When Konstantin Chernenko died on 10 March 1985, after thirteen months in office, it seemed certain that Gorbachev would be his successor.

Naturally he had rivals and opponents in the Politburo and the Central Committee. The sixty-two-year-old Grigori Romanov chose an indirect route: he put forward the seventy-year-old Moscow Party boss Viktor Grishin. In this way he hoped, under another ageing General Secretary, to build up his own power-base for the next election. In a stormy Politburo session Grishin and Gorbachev received the same number of votes. Foreign Minister Andrei Gromyko stepped into the debate. He had rarely spoken so emotionally. The Politburo, he argued, must not again elect one of the old men, among whom he counted himself. They needed a General Secretary who could lead the Soviet Union into the next millennium. The KGB boss Viktor Chebrikov also spoke in support of Gorbachev, linking Grishin with the scandals of the Brezhnev era.

Supporting Grishin were conservatives such as Romanov, who wanted the country to be ruled with an iron hand reminiscent of late Stalinism. Gorbachev's backers were by no means supporters of democratisation, but they saw in him a man with modern policies who sought more effective methods of crisis management. Gromyko praised Gorbachev's Party career, his clear-mindedness and wide experience, his ability to talk to scientists; for him nothing was either black or white, he saw the complexities, but without getting lost in details. He knew where political priorities lay. On 10 March 1985 the Politburo elected Gorbachev as Party leader.

The vote had to be confirmed by the Central Committee, and there was still a certain amount of resistance to the new man. Some of the leading Party functionaries were concerned about the ways in which a dynamic young leader might endanger their influence and privileges. Andrei Gromyko again stepped in for Gorbachev. When his speech was published some days later it was surprisingly different from the usual formulaic addresses published after sessions of the Central Committee, particularly those of the normally dry and emotionless Gromyko. He knew from his work as Foreign Minister, he said, that Gorbachev could assess international developments quickly and intelligently, and always drew the right conclusions in accordance with the wishes of the Party. He added that 'this man has a pleasant smile, but he also has teeth of iron'. The remark sums up what others who had worked with Gorbachev knew about his character and performance. But it also suggests that some members of the Party apparatus did not consider Gorbachev sufficiently resolute to be the new leader. Gromyko was clearly attempting to counter the misgivings of functionaries who considered Gorbachev too ready to compromise.

Unusually, a number of Central Committee members opposed the ruling of the Politburo. The public declaration of the result stated that Gorbachev was elected 'by common consent'. With Andropov and Chernenko, as with all other previous Central Committee resolutions, the word 'unanimous' had been used.

There were probably some members of the Central Committee who felt apprehensive about a young General Secretary who had been a protégé of Andropov. Andropov's campaign against corruption and incompetence had led many of them to fear for their jobs. Under Andropov nearly fifty heads of departments and their deputies had been removed from the Central Committee apparatus. Almost a quarter of the regional Party Secretaries had lost their positions. Nineteen ministers and over eighty Chairmen of state committees had been replaced. Things had calmed down again after Andropov's death. Scarcely a dozen high functionaries had been removed during Chernenko's year in office. The campaign against corruption had virtually come to a halt under Chernenko, who had always been popular in the Party because of his benevolent attitude to the functionaries.

With the third change of leadership in two and a half years, an impatient and power-conscious new generation now had control of the Party. It strengthened its position during the summer of 1985, shunting the supporters of Chernenko and Brezhnev out of the way. The first to fall was Grigori Romanov. He had established his power-base as Party Secretary in Leningrad and broadened it through close ties with the military and the armaments industry. He had been singled out for removal by Andropov, and in Moscow people had whispered for years about his dissipated lifestyle. At his daughter's wedding the guests had eaten off Catherine the Great's dinner service, drunkenly smashing irreplaceable pieces. (Romanov, who still lives in his old Moscow flat, with a large pension, claims that this is a malicious fabrication.) But it is not disputed that at the Party Congress of Hungarian Communists in March 1985 he drew attention to himself by being drunk, and reports of this circulated in Moscow. Now he was replaced as Central Committee Secretary by Yegor Ligachev, who as Andropov's cadre chief had been the purger and cleanser of the Party apparatus.

Romanov had felt that his position was secure because of his connections. That such a powerful man could so quickly lose both his post as Central Committee Secretary and his place in the Politburo shows that Gorbachev was well prepared, and knew exactly what he needed to achieve. He did not want to be the head of a collective leadership like Chernenko, with supporters of the old and the new lines obstructing each other. That would have meant that he could only make minor policy changes, advancing by small steps which would almost certainly come to a halt before his reforms could take hold. Gorbachev needed to create a majority in favour of his policies in the Politburo. His allies, Ligachev, Nikolai Ryzhkov and KGB chief Viktor Chebrikov, also regarded the renewal of the Party and its encrusted apparatus as urgently necessary. They shared Gorbachev's conviction that the pace of economic development and technological modernisation had to be significantly accelerated. In speeches he made in April 1985 to scientists and economic leaders and before the Plenum of the Central Committee Gorbachev named acceleration as the most important element of his new policy. The catchwords *perestroika* and *glasnost*, with which he was to open the battle for the new line, did not yet exist. The guiding concepts were *uskoreniye* (acceleration) and *povorot* (change of direction).

Gorbachev explained to the Central Committee members: 'The pace at which we are advancing in this Five-Year Plan is inadequate. We must increase it, and increase it substantially. This problem must be resolved immediately. No time must be lost.

Gorbachev at the age of six
with his Yevimovich
grandparents

The Gorbachev family
home, where Gorbachev's
mother still lives

Gorbachev (top right) with fellow students in Privolnoye

Gorbachev with Raisa and his mother in Privolnoye, 1989

Gorbachev with fellow students at Moscow University

Raisa as a young mother

Gorbachev, on a visit to the Stavropol region, 1986

Gorbachev and Raisa returning home after the unsuccessful summit
in Iceland, 1986

Raisa in Washington with George Bush, Ronald Reagan and
Gorbachev, December 1987. Raisa is shaking hands with the Soviet
singer Yelena Obraztsova

Gorbachev, Ryzhkov and Ligachev before the Lenin Mausoleum
reviewing the parade on the anniversary of the October
Revolution, 1988

Boris Yeltsin addressing a crowd in Moscow during the 'Congress
of the Peoples' Deputies, May 1989

Gorbachev making his New Year's Day speech on Soviet television, 1991

The socio-economic development of the country, the strengthening of its defence capacity and the improvement of the lives of the Soviet people depend on whether we solve this problem successfully.' He pressed for scientific advances to be immediately introduced into the process of production. He knew from Soviet economists and sociologists the speed with which the technological revolution of the computer age had altered the industrial structures of the West and increased their capacity. If the Soviet Union did not want to fall further behind it would need to remodel its system of economic development and planning so that the findings of scientific research could be carried over into industrial practice.

The Soviet Union had only been able to keep pace with the West in two areas, armaments and space travel. For decades the work of the best Soviet scientists and researchers had been denied to the rest of the economy. If an acceleration in economic growth was to be achieved, argued Gorbachev, technological progress would have to be placed at the centre of the drive for the intensification of the economy. He announced a programme of revolutionary technological change. The planning and direction of the economy was to be reversed. Enterprises would be allowed greater independence in the management of their affairs, and workers would be motivated not only by increased discipline, but also by their own material interests.

The urgent need for such a programme was made clear to Soviet functionaries, and it also expressed the hopes of the scientific-technical intelligentsia. Gorbachev did not, like his predecessors, talk about merely improving the existing system. He wanted more. He had always been a good speaker, and he now impressed the Party with the energy and knowledge with which he attacked the country's economic problems and with his personal commitment to bringing about profound changes.

It was still, however, not apparent just how far-reaching Gorbachev's ideas of the changes the Soviet Union needed really were. He clearly wanted more than just stricter control of economic policy, but the measures he proposed seemed to lie within the framework of Soviet economic and social policy. There was no indication yet of a shift to a Socialist market economy or of the liberalisation necessary for this. Gorbachev knew that he could not expect too much of the Party all at once. He needed to keep the support of the apparatus and the functionaries.

Whether or not Gorbachev already realised that a renewed economic policy alone would not be enough, he must have drawn his own conclusions from the information he had about conditions in the Soviet Union and also about developments in the Socialist states of Eastern Europe that went far beyond mere technocratic reform of the system. In Yegor Ligachev he had a man at his side who had been moulded by traditional ideas of the role of the Party and modes of life in a Socialist society. In the summer of 1985 Gorbachev made Nikolai Ryzhkov Prime Minister. With his experience as a director of heavy industry and Deputy Minister for the construction of heavy and transport machinery, Ryzhkov was an experienced technocrat.

At first the change of direction was most noticeable in foreign policy. Andrei Gromyko, who had so decisively supported Gorbachev's appointment as General Secretary, was given the honourable, but scarcely influential, role of Head of State. For twenty-eight years as Foreign Minister he had determined the foreign policy of the Soviet Union, and he also had considerable influence on domestic policy. Now the Foreign Ministry went to a man with no diplomatic experience – Eduard Shevardnadze, from Georgia.

Perhaps Gromyko was offended that his post was taken over by a man almost twenty years younger than himself. To some observers it appeared that Gorbachev wanted to create his own foreign policy and conduct it through an assistant. Shevardnadze had been a member of the Politburo for seven years, but as far as foreign policy was concerned he was an unknown quantity.

Naturally there was speculation in Moscow about the kind of appointments the new General Secretary would make. The new men were assessed by the old rules, according to their political weight in the apparatus and the power they wielded within the Party. It went unnoticed that Gorbachev was drawing people into his immediate circle for reasons other than the considerations of power politics. The life histories and careers of these men reveal the extent of the break in Soviet policy that Gorbachev now wanted to bring about.

CHAPTER 7

New Men

In the Brezhnev era groups had formed in the Party elite which foreign observers called 'roped teams', because their members pulled each other up the Party hierarchy. Brezhnev surrounded himself with an entourage of old friends and colleagues on whom he could rely and whose lifestyles resembled his own. Gorbachev was never, it would appear, a member of any of these roped teams. In his first decade in Stavropol he had worked with only one man who would later promote him, the Politburo agricultural expert Fyodor Kulakov. As Party Secretary of the Stavropol region he met others who might have helped his career, but he did not form his own power base. When he came to power he remembered the people whose character or abilities had impressed him and who understood his political aims. Some of these he now brought to high office in Moscow.

Gorbachev knew Anatoli Lukyanov from Moscow University. Lukyanov had been his superior in the *Komsomol* Committee at the Law Faculty. Unlike Gorbachev, he remained in Moscow after graduating, and began a successful career in middle-range state and Party posts. He continued his academic work, and in 1980, after seventeen years practising as a lawyer, he obtained a doctorate of law. Since he left university he had been concerned with legal matters of the state and government apparatus, up to 1961 as Chief Adviser to the Commission for Legal Matters at the Council of Ministers, and later as Deputy Head of a department in the Presidium of the Supreme Soviet that co-ordinated the legislative decisions of the highest political bodies of the republics with the laws of the Union. For several years he belonged to the apparatus of the Party Central Committee. From 1977 until the death of Brezhnev he headed the Secretariat of the Presidium of the Supreme Soviet, the highest organ of the Soviet state.

Lukyanov was an important contact in Moscow for Gorbachev, and in 1985 he appointed him to an influential post in the central Party apparatus. As head of the General Department of the Central Committee, Lukyanov in practice headed the standing Secretariat of the Politburo, where important decisions were prepared and the demands and proposals of Politburo members were set down. This was a position of such importance that the General Secretary needed a man experienced in the apparatus and administration on whom he could rely absolutely.

When Gorbachev was elected First Chairman of the Supreme Soviet by the Congress of People's Deputies in 1989, the duties and powers of a 'president' who was only the chairman of a collective body were not clearly defined. Unlike an American President, the holder of the newly created Soviet post cannot govern with a cabinet chosen by himself, and the delegates who had elected Gorbachev were not prepared to accept Lukyanov as his Deputy. Some regarded him as being too closely identified with the old Brezhnev clique. In their opinion the new significance of the Supreme Soviet demanded the election of a man of unquestioned political and moral standing, such as Andrei Sakharov or Boris Yeltsin, as Deputy to the Head of State. They distrusted the functionaries of the old system, and favoured candidates who stood for radical change. Gorbachev on the other hand wanted a man who could deal with the complicated and untried machinery of the reformed state apparatus, and he held fast to his choice of Lukyanov, believing that he needed a reliable colleague at his side rather than a worthy moralist or a dynamic rival. This cost him the trust of some of his supporters, who felt that he was placing himself in the hands of the apparatus, which would delay, or even reverse, his reforms.

Two of Gorbachev's associates from Stavropol rose under him in Moscow. Marat Gramov had been editor of the local Stavropol paper, and Gorbachev had known him since the sixties. He became Chairman of the State Committee for Sport, and later Chairman of the Olympic Committee of the Soviet Union, appointments which were regarded in Moscow as an indication of Gorbachev's loyalty to old friends.

The second man from Stavropol was Vsevolod Murakhovsky, who had been Gorbachev's superior in the Young Communist League and later his subordinate in the Party apparatus. Like Gorbachev, he had close ties with Fyodor Kulakov. As Party chief of Pyatigorsk he had been responsible for the major spas in the Caucasus, where he had cultivated contacts with the top people from Moscow when they came to relax at the sanatoriums. When Gorbachev was called to Moscow in 1978 Murakhovsky was appointed as his successor as First Secretary of the Stavropol region. In 1985 Gorbachev brought him to Moscow and entrusted him with a task of vital importance to the future development of the Soviet Union. Murakhovsky became Deputy Prime Minister and head of the State Committee for Agricultural Industry.

This newly created committee was intended to fundamentally reform agriculture and the food supply industry. It took over these functions from six specialist ministries which until then had jealously guarded their responsibility for various sectors of the agricultural-industrial complex. A rapid improvement in agriculture and food supplies was expected as a result of the dismantling of their bureaucratic apparatuses, but there were tremendous problems of organisation, personnel and politics to be solved if it was to succeed. The resistance in the central administrative bureaucracy, who feared for their jobs, now appeared in the agricultural bureaucracy, who feared a loss of power and influence. In the Politburo itself, where Yegor Ligachev was responsible for agricultural policy, there was open distrust of reforms that could weaken central control. Ligachev had lost influence in the Party now that he was no longer Ideology Secretary. As Central Committee Agricultural Secretary he was faced with almost insuperable problems, but he was sufficiently experienced to use the power of the Party apparatus to slow down agricultural reforms.

Faced with this opposition, Murakhovsky had difficulty in achieving results, and the population noticed no improvements in food supply. Murakhovsky was a good but not outstanding functionary, a decent man who had always been loyal to Gorbachev, but he was not able to overcome the Moscow apparatus.

★

A third man from Stavropol, Alexander Nikonov, is now Director of the All Union Academy of Agriculture in Moscow. Though Gorbachev contributed to his rise, Nikonov was not a follower of Gorbachev, nor was he brought to Moscow by him. In fact he came to the capital from Stavropol two months earlier than Gorbachev, who sometimes joked that Nikonov had dragged him along. Nikonov is one of the most important agricultural experts in the Soviet Union, an independent thinker who expresses his opinions vehemently. When he talks of the poor living conditions of the farmers, or the mistakes of the agricultural functionaries, his anger is obvious.

Nikonov was born in 1918. His ancestors were farmers, but his father became a metalworker in Petersburg, where his friends included Nikolai Bukharin, whom after the Revolution Lenin called the 'darling of the Party'. Alexander Nikonov was born in Latgale, a region between Russia and Latvia that fell to the Latvian republic when it won its independence. His father sent him to a Latvian school and saw to it that he went to the university in Riga. He therefore grew up as a Russian in an independent Latvia in the interwar years, in a region where Latvians, Estonians, Jews and Russians lived together amicably. It was a terrible experience for him when, after the Hitler-Stalin pact, thousands of Latvians were deported to Siberia.

Alexander Nikonov distinguished himself as an officer in the Second World War, after which he returned to Latvia and was given the task of organising agricultural co-operatives. For two years this seemed to him a way to improve conditions on the land, he says, until enforced collectivisation began, 95 per cent of Latvian farmers were driven into *kolkhozes*, and a new wave of deportations hit the republic.

In the period when Khrushchev wanted to make the lives of farmers easier Nikonov became Agricultural Minister of the Latvian republic. But he could not conceal his criticism of Khrushchev's methods. After serious disagreements with the First Party Secretary of Latvia, Arvid Pelshe, he had to leave Latvia. He took the first post that was offered, heading a new agricultural research institute near Stavropol. He did not like the warm southern climate, but he felt that in a newly founded institute he might be able to achieve something important. Besides, the institute belonged to the highly respected Agricultural College of Stavropol. Nikonov says that on his first visit to Stavropol a young man came up to him and said: 'Good morning. I've heard of you. My name is Gorbachev.'

Twenty-seven years later Nikonov vividly remembers how pleasantly surprised he was by this first meeting, above all by the fact that the young Party functionary he had met was so 'democratic' in his behaviour. Since then relations between the two men have remained friendly. In Stavropol Gorbachev could speak openly with Nikonov about the problems of agriculture and agricultural policy, and came to trust his advice. At the time of their first meeting Gorbachev had just been entrusted by the Party with the difficult task of carrying out Khrushchev's latest agricultural reform. Nikonov says that Gorbachev was opposed to combining the small *kolkhozes* into larger units and having the farmers move from villages into agro-towns, which, he felt, could only further damage the farmers' self-confidence and their willingness to work. Gorbachev had to live with the conflict between the central agricultural policy and his knowledge of the real situation, and Nikonov's experience and independent thinking were a great help to him in those years. And it was under Nikonov – by then Director of the Agricultural College – that Gorbachev studied and obtained his diploma in Stavropol.

In the seventies Nikonov was twice invited to move to the Agricultural Institute of the Academy of Sciences in Moscow, but he turned this promotion down. Gorbachev supported him, pointing out that Nikonov was needed in Stavropol. In 1978 Nikonov was again called to Moscow. He visited Gorbachev, who was holidaying in Piatigorsk in the Caucasus, and asked him whether he should take over the Department of Economics at the Agricultural Academy. ' "Tell me what I should do," I asked Gorbachev. He thought a while and said: "Take over the department. I think something is going to change there." ' So Alexander Nikonov went to Moscow in August 1978, two months before Gorbachev himself left Stavropol to become Secretary for Agriculture in the Central Committee.

As Director of the Academy in recent years Nikonov has spoken in favour of the reform of Soviet agricultural policy. He also fought for the rehabilitation of important agronomists and biologists who became victims of Stalin's Terror for criticising the methods of collectivisation and proposing alternative models, or whose genetic and biological research Stalin considered hostile to the Party. In this struggle Nikonov had to call on his friend in the Kremlin for help. For example, Gorbachev had to intervene personally with the KGB in 1987 before the agronomist and philosopher Alexander Chayanov's name could again be mentioned. In the Supreme Soviet Nikonov was among the pioneers for new legal provisions for the farmers' ownership of land. He did not, as his opponents maintain, fight for the abolition of the *kolkhozes*, but for real co-operatives that would manage their affairs independently of the orders of the state and Party and where the farmers could be masters of their own land. The outcome of these disputes, the new law regarding property, is a compromise, Nikonov believes, but is nevertheless a step towards a future in which farmers will be able to cultivate and bequeath their own land, even if they are not masters of it to the extent of being able to sell it.

At seventy-four, and after many disappointments, Nikonov is full of hope for Gorbachev's Russia: 'For the first time since Lenin the country is lucky again in its leader. But the system is so overladen with dogmatism, intolerance, the fear of responsibility and work, that Gorbachev's task is unbelievably huge.'

A new moral beginning and a new climate of independence among the farmers are more important to Nikonov than all Gorbachev's changes to the law and technological improvements. Nikonov's expertise and his philosophical and moral commitment have greatly influenced Gorbachev's thinking. It is significant that, as a young Party functionary in Stavropol, Gorbachev sought such a friend and adviser.

The two most important politicians Gorbachev has brought to Moscow are Eduard Shevardnadze, who in a few brief years has carried through the new foreign policy of the Soviet Union that has changed the world, and Alexander Yakovlev, who has contributed more to the spiritual and political opening up of Soviet society than any of the other people around Gorbachev, perhaps even more than Gorbachev himself.

Foreign Minister Shevardnadze is a long-standing friend of Gorbachev's. They were functionaries in adjoining regions, Gorbachev to the north of the Caucasus, Shevardnadze in Georgia, which lies to the south. In the seventies the Gorbachevs were often guests of the Shevardnadzes in Georgia.

Eduard Shevardnadze was born in 1928, the son of a teacher in a small town in western Georgia. He is only three years older than Gorbachev, but when the two men met for the first time he already had an unusual career behind him. At nineteen he was an instructor in the Tbilisi *Komsomol* Town Committee, a functionary on the lowest level. In Moscow his acquaintances tell a story about this early phase of his political life that makes him seem a young man of remarkable independence for that time.

As an instructor Shevardnadze had to help with the children's organisation, the Young Pioneers. He met a Young Pioneer leader named Nanulya, and proposed to her, but she turned him down. Her parents had been politically persecuted during the Stalin purges of the late thirties, and marriage to her would destroy Eduard's political career before it had even begun, she thought. This was in no way an exaggerated fear. Anyone whose parents had been victims of the purges could hope at best for employment on the lower levels of the apparatus during Stalin's lifetime. With every change of job or flat, in fact at virtually every step of their lives, Soviet citizens had to record the arrests and sentences of their relatives on questionnaires. Many personal and family ties broke down under this pressure, and it was taken for granted that one dropped friends who had been compromised. If their husbands were arrested, women got divorces on the grounds that it was unbearable to live with an enemy of the people. Nanulya had lived with the consequences of her family tragedy, and like millions of others had had to get used to the fact that she would be burdened by it all her life.

She knew that Shevardnadze had been selected to attend the *Komsomol* College in Moscow, an important stepping-stone for a political career. When she told him of her family's political taint, she imagined that their relationship would end. But a few days later he phoned her. Everything was all right, he said, he could find work as a teacher. At that time teaching was regarded as a demeaning profession for a young man.

Eduard Shevardnadze did not go to the *Komsomol* College in the capital, but his marriage did remarkably little harm to his political career. He was accepted into the Party at the age of twenty, and at first his career ran a similar course to Mikhail

Gorbachev's. But between 1954 and 1956 he is alleged to have worked for the KGB in Georgia, although his Moscow friends stress that this was during the Khrushchev years, when the rehabilitation of Stalin's victims was under way. After less than two years he returned to the *Komsomol* apparatus, from which he moved over into the Georgian Party organisation.

Shevardnadze had studied history at a college of education in Georgia, a subject that in those years, along with law and philosophy, was considered a good starting point for a Party career. In 1964 he became First Deputy Interior Minister of Georgia, and a year later Interior Minister.

The reports an Interior Minister of Georgia would have come across at that time must have provided an education of a strange kind. Georgia was proverbially known as a land governed by nepotism and contacts, where corruption and connections permeated the entire network of the Party, government and economic apparatuses, to the very top. In his seven-year tenure of office as Interior Minister Shevardnadze must have kept free of such entanglements, because when, in 1972, Georgia's First Party Secretary Vassili Mshavadnadze sank in a swamp of corruption and was removed, Moscow appointed Shevardnadze as his successor. Everything suggests that Yuri Andropov, as Moscow KGB chief and a leading opponent of the corrupt clan system, was instrumental in Shevardnadze's promotion.

Gorbachev and Shevardnadze were now First Party Secretaries of neighbouring regions. In the Party structure the Stavropol region and the Republic of Georgia are on the same level. They are also approximately the same size, and despite the differences in their populations and traditions they had similar problems. Shevardnadze, like Gorbachev, introduced agricultural reforms that offered more self-administration and material inducements to the *kolkhozes*. In the towns he tried to hand over responsibility for industry and supplies to newly formed organisations that could plan and decide with greater independence. Like Gorbachev, he was a good speaker who knew how to get his ideas across. In his speeches to the Georgians he cleverly combined his personal style and *Komsomol* education with the traditional language of his people, which inclined to pathos.

In his battle against corruption, for example, he reminded the Georgians of the heroic songs of their past; the Georgians were no longer tillers, heroes and poets, but had degenerated into speculators, black marketeers and thieves. The Georgian middlemen who sold grapes, melons and peaches at high prices in the markets of Moscow and other major cities had their freedom to travel restricted. Shevardnadze made himself unpopular with Party functionaries once when, at a vote, they unanimously raised their hands as usual. He commented drily that it was not the raised hands that needed to be counted, but the expensive foreign watches on the wrists. The word spread as far as Moscow that Shevardnadze had personally prevented a pitched battle between Georgians and Armenians in Tbilisi when, during a football match between a Georgian and an Armenian team, the referee's decision enraged the Georgian spectators. Shevardnadze himself left his box and went into the arena to try to calm and separate the fighters. The next day excited fans blockaded the airport in an attempt to paralyse air traffic and prevent the referee getting away.

The brawling in the football stadium was a result of old tensions between Georgia and Armenia. More serious national disputes have frequently disrupted Georgia. Native Georgians make up only about two thirds of the republic's population, and the western part of Georgia, with its tourist resorts on the Black Sea coast, is an autonomous Abkhazian republic. In the mountains live Ossetians, Chechens, Svanetis and many other peoples, who speak their own languages and bitterly defend their independence. Added to these are Armenians, Azerbaidjanis and, in the bigger towns, Russians and Ukrainians. Some of the tensions are between individual peoples, others between larger national groups and the leadership claims of the characteristically Russian Soviet Union.

In Georgia there had been mass protests by Abkhazis, who because of the immigration of Georgians and Armenians now only made up 15 per cent of the population in their own autonomous republic. In Tbilisi in 1978 several thousand Georgian students demonstrated against the imposition of Russian alongside Georgian as the republic's official language. Shevardnadze managed to calm the student demonstrators outside the Party Committee building, and prevented acts of violence by the demonstrators and the police. Then he negotiated with the central apparatus in Moscow, and succeeded in having the law declaring Russian as Georgia's second national language repealed.

Gorbachev must have known what Eduard and Nanulya Shevardnadze thought of Stalin's Terror. At the end of the Brezhnev era, when Stalin's rule was once again not permitted to be treated in art and literature, Shevardnadze protected the work of the director Tengiz Abuladze, whose film *Repentance* shatteringly settles scores with Stalin's and Beria's dictatorship. At the time the film was made Stalin's reputation as a war leader was being resuscitated in Moscow, and Shevardnadze ran the risk of being reprimanded or punished by the Moscow leaders. Just how much of a risk he had taken was only apparent years later in the period of *glasnost*, when the film was released. Georgian film directors say today that Shevardnadze not only gave permission for their films to be made, he also defended them against the countless problems created by censorship and the Party authorities.

Shevardnadze also spoke out openly for a revival of Georgian culture. He and his wife shared a love of literature and art with the Gorbachevs, and Shevardnadze was also interested in Raisa Gorbachev's research into life on the land. In 1971 he set up an Institute of Public Opinion at the Central Committee of the Communist Party in Georgia, three years after Raisa's doctoral supervisor, Professor G. V. Osipov, had founded the Institute for Concrete Social Research at the Academy of Sciences in Moscow. Gorbachev and Shevardnadze were linked by mutual interests and problems, as well as by their basic political attitudes.

For all his independent thinking, Shevardnadze was a man of the Party and of his time. As Interior Minister he was chief of a police apparatus whose methods were no better than those in the rest of the Soviet Union. And he had to render homage to the leaders in Moscow as fulsomely as did other Party functionaries. He praised General Secretaries Brezhnev and Chernenko as 'prodigious authorities' and flattered the leadership by saying that for the Georgians the sun rose not in the east, but in the north. Some of his fellow Georgians suspected him of being a puppet of Moscow.

At the same time that Gorbachev came to Moscow as Secretary of the Central Committee, Shevardnadze was appointed candidate of the Politburo, although he remained in Georgia as First Secretary. He was a member of the Presidium of the Supreme Soviet

of his republic, belonged to the Military Council of the Transcaucasian Armed Forces and was Major General of the Police of
the Military Council of the Transcaucasian District of the KGB.

Few people in Moscow knew who Shevardnadze was when,
on 2 July 1985, Gorbachev introduced him to the Supreme Soviet
as Foreign Minister, successor to Andrei Gromyko, who had been
the longest-serving Foreign Minister in the world.

Alexander Yakovlev, now closely associated with Gorbachev's
reforms and the 'new thinking', had been appointed as Russian
Ambassador to Canada in 1973, after he had lost his position as
Executive Head of the Propaganda Department of the Central
Committee following an ideological dispute.

The post of Ambassador to Canada was a kind of political
exile. In 1973 Gorbachev had closely followed the events that
interrupted Yakovlev's Party career, when he had turned against
a number of Soviet writers and publicists who romanticised the
world of the Russian village.

In the spring of 1983 Gorbachev, as Secretary for Agriculture,
visited Canada to study its methods of food production. He would
have been briefed by the Party apparatus about the Ambassador
in Ottawa, but he must have known that he was receiving at best
a one-sided report. Shortly before his departure, Gorbachev met
an old friend, a journalist, who knew Yakovlev from the time
when he had been responsible for radio and television in the
Propaganda Department of the Central Committee. The journalist was an admirer of Yakovlev, calling him 'genuine *muzhik* from
Yaroslavl', with a good heart and brilliant mind. He also told
Gorbachev that the 'exiled' Ambassador in Ottawa had his own
ideas about what was happening in the Soviet Union and the
world. Gorbachev, he thought, would get on well with Yakovlev.

Alexander Yakovlev was born in 1923 near the city of Yaroslavl, the eighth child of a family of farmers. He was decorated
in the war, in which he lost a leg. He was accepted into the
Communist Party in 1944, and after the war he studied history
at a college of education. His Party career advanced with unusual
rapidity. At thirty he was appointed Deputy Head in the field of
science and culture in the Central Committee of the Party. This
was at the onset of the new era after Stalin's death, when reshuffles

in the Party apparatus were creating places for rising men. Three years later Yakovlev continued his history studies at the Party Academy for Social Sciences, and he was one of the very few Soviet students to be allowed to see the world beyond the frontier. In 1959 he was sent to Columbia University in New York as part of an exchange programme. Among the academics there he got to know Henry Kissinger, of whom he said twenty-five years later that he had seemed a serious and sincere man, and that he had liked him.

It must have been a highly stimulating time for him, even if what he published about the USA on his return to the Soviet Union suggested that nothing about America had pleased him – one of his books was entitled *The Intellectual Misery of the Apologists for the Cold War*. In articles such as 'The USA: From a Great Country to a Sick Country', or 'Stages on the Way to War and Betrayal: The Secret Documents of the Pentagon', one hardly finds a positive word about the society and political system of the USA. His book *From Truman to Reagan* depicts the USA as a nation in which fraud and demagogy reign, where organised crime is stronger than the law, and where the lie has become the ruling principle. He describes the American mass media and mass culture as glorifying cruelty, justifying the use of force and sexualising art. Judgements of this kind are rife in Yakovlev's publications up to the mid-eighties.

Although these writings are clearly products of the Cold War, they are also coloured by his own experience. If in his essay 'Pax Americana', Yakovlev calls America 'the land of lonely people and communal fear', his judgements are not dissimilar to those of American sociologists of the early sixties.

After his return from the USA Yakovlev's rise in the Central Committee apparatus continued smoothly. His American experience was useful in the Propaganda Department, especially in the radio and television section. While he was working in the Central Committee he obtained a doctorate in history, and in 1968 he became a Professor at the Academy of Social Sciences of the Central Committee. His academic subject then, as before, was America. He rose to Deputy Head of the Propaganda Department and, in 1971, to Executive Head of Department. His chief was the Party Ideologue Mikhail Suslov, who clamped down hard on any deviation from the Party line.

A clash with Suslov in 1973 abruptly ended Yakovlev's career in the Central Committee apparatus. At that time the *Komsomol* magazine *Molodaya Gvardiya* devoted itself to Russian nationalist thinking, which naturally harmonised with the conservative line of the Party leadership. Since the Second World War this national tradition had become central to Soviet ideology. The war was now called the 'Great Patriotic War', in which the Russian people's courage and readiness to make sacrifices had saved the Soviet Union and won victory. For Brezhnev, this victory was a justification of Soviet policy. Publicists and writers contrasted an idealised Russia with the corrupt Western society and its 'cosmopolitan' (i.e. Jewish) influence. They celebrated the peasant traditions of the Russian village, the strong character of the simple Russian, and firm leadership. Not all of these writers were mere hacks producing propaganda for the Party. Some were genuinely seeking old values which would give support and order to people's lives. But most simply used the old formulae as a means of papering over the cracks in the spiritual structure of the Soviet state and society.

On 15 November 1972 an article by Alexander Yakovlev entitled 'Against Anti-Heroism' appeared in the newspaper of the Writers' Union, *Literaturnaya Gazeta*. He sharply attacked the rising tendency in literature and philosophy towards 'reactionary romanticism', in which the patriarchal world of the peasant was praised as a desirable counterbalance to city culture. He reproached writers for idealising the stagnation of daily life in the Russian village, for setting allegedly ancient Russian roots against 'intellectualism', and for propagating Russian chauvinism. Among the champions of this tendency he included Alexander Solzhenitsyn. Yakovlev recalled the reality of Tsarist Russia, with its poverty, backwardness and reactionary social policies.

The article unleashed a storm of controversy among Moscow intellectuals, and conservative publicists and writers immediately prepared a counter-attack. Mikhail Sholokhov, who had won the Nobel Prize for his novel *Quiet Flows the Don*, an epic about the battle for collectivisation in the Cossack villages, was chosen to take their complaints to the Party Ideologue, Mikhail Suslov. Towards the end of his life Sholokhov had become increasingly reactionary, hating every Western influence and despising Moscow intellectuals. He was also an antisemite, and had requested that writers be forbidden to use pseudonyms, the only purpose of which was to conceal their Jewish names. Suslov's views on the role of the Russian tradition in Soviet history and politics were certainly closer to those of Sholokhov than to the arguments of Yakovlev. He certainly did not want the head of the Propaganda Department to show such traces of independent thought.

During the reshuffles of the Politburo and apparatus that took place in 1973, the controversy about Russian tradition and Russian nationalism continued. In the non-Russian republics, such as the Baltic states, nationalism was opposed. Pyotr Shelest, the Party First Secretary in the Ukraine, was dismissed and then removed from the Politburo for failing to suppress Ukrainian nationalism. Russianness was regarded as the unifying force of the empire and of Soviet patriotism. Yakovlev's article had questioned this attitude, and he was reproached for wanting to bring about a split in the Russian intelligentsia.

For this reason he was moved from the ideological apparatus of the Party to the Foreign Ministry in 1973, and sent as Ambassador to Canada. This was not, however, an unimportant post. In Ottawa Yakovlev, as an American expert, could report to Moscow developments in the neighbouring USA. The Ambassador to Canada is less burdened with protocol and official diplomatic duties than Moscow's man in Washington, and from his Canadian observation post Yakovlev wrote analyses which served as background to the formulation of Soviet-American policy.

Yakovlev did well in Canada. He became friendly with Canada's Prime Minister Pierre Trudeau, an intellectual outsider in Canadian politics and a critic of the USA and its society. Yakovlev's intelligence and dry charm even made him a popular participant in television talk shows. After ten years of service he had become the doyen of the Diplomatic Corps when, in the spring of 1983, the visit to Canada of the youngest Politburo member was announced. Gorbachev had to bear the heavy burden of the Soviet Union's confused agricultural policy, and Canada, whose wheat the Soviet Union now needed in order to make bread for its citizens, was an important subject of study for him. But Gorbachev was interested in far more than the production methods of capitalist organised agriculture. In Alexander Yakovlev he found a man with whom he could talk as intensively about

American world policy and society as he could about the problems of their own country. 'Love at first sight' was how a mutual friend described the meeting in Ottawa between Gorbachev and Yakovlev.

Gorbachev's visit to Canada was a great success, as much because of his carefully measured speeches before the Canadian Parliament as for his relaxed manner, which impressed television watchers. The American magazine *Newsweek* compared his performance to that of an American Presidential candidate. The visit gave Gorbachev a taste of international success, and made him more confident in his dealings with the West. Other Soviet leaders on visits abroad had felt and behaved as if they were in enemy territory, but in Canada Gorbachev discovered that he could win friends and make a good impression abroad, and this became an important factor in his future foreign policy. Yakovlev's briefings had contributed to his success, and Gorbachev had been impressed by this as well as by his talks with the Ambassador about world problems.

Gorbachev returned from Canada to Moscow in May. On 28 October 1983 the Soviet news agency TASS reported that the former Ambassador to Canada, Alexander Yakovlev, had been appointed Director of the Institute of World Economy and International Relations in Moscow. Gorbachev had argued for the return of Yakovlev after his ten-year exile.

The Institute for World Economy and International Relations – IMEMO – is one of the three main 'think tanks' of Soviet policy, along with Professor Georgi Arbatov's USA-Canada Institute and the Institute for the Economy of the Socialist World System, under Professor Oleg Bogomolov. In these institutes, attached to the Academy of Sciences, fundamental problems of Soviet domestic and foreign policy are studied and reappraised for the highest Party and government officials. Several thousand scientific experts examine policies of armament and disarmament, political trends in other countries, changes in the world balance of power and economic problems. Since the end of the seventies, IMEMO had increasingly concentrated on research into the economy of the Soviet Union itself. It had warned that the output of Soviet agriculture and industry was too low to sustain the arms race with America. Its critical analyses had aroused the displeasure of higher Party and government officials, and its position had weakened. After the death of the previous Director the post remained empty for over a year before Alexander Yakovlev was appointed. Under Yakovlev a new orientation of Soviet foreign policy was formulated. From him came the initiative that freed Soviet policy from its single-minded fixation on its opponent, America, and produced the concept of the 'common house of Europe'.

Alexander Yakovlev was Director of IMEMO for two years. During this period work began on an early draft of *perestroika*, which Yakovlev considered urgently necessary. In 1984 he accompanied Gorbachev on a state visit to Britain. Gorbachev impressed even Margaret Thatcher as a man 'with whom one could do business', and the British press fêted him as the new red star in the east. The astonished Western world had discovered a Soviet leader with a new style, a dynamic man, quite unlike his senile predecessors, who already seemed to stand for a new Soviet Union. Gorbachev was excellently prepared for his visit, and in Britain he found a platform from which he could engage in the transatlantic dispute over Ronald Reagan's Strategic Defense Initiative, the so-called 'star wars', which seemed to herald a new technological arms race in space – an arms race of which the Soviet economy was incapable. Once again Alexander Yakovlev had proved himself a good adviser.

In 1985, when Mikhail Gorbachev became General Secretary, Yakovlev returned to the Central Committee apparatus, becoming the chief of the Department for Culture and Propaganda. This was a key position, from which the guidelines of the new policy could be spread throughout the Party and the mass media. In a time of radical change it was vital that the new thinking should be carried through and made ideologically secure in the apparatus by a man who had Gorbachev's trust and knew his intentions. In quick succession Yakovlev was promoted to Central Committee Secretary for Propaganda, Culture and Ideology, candidate of the Politburo, and six months later, in July 1987, to full member of the highest body of the Party.

It was a constant struggle for Yakovlev to get the Party apparatus to accept the ideas he shared with Gorbachev, often in the face of determined opposition from Yegor Ligachev and other conservatives. He needed to be a clever tactician, with no organisational weaknesses or ideological uncertainties.

In his speeches, he claimed that the spiritual horizon of philosophers and sociologists had become so narrow that they could only make a limited contribution to research in human problems. 'When a person begins asking himself the eternal questions about the meaning of life, of moral choice or about the ethical basis of his behaviour,' said Yakovlev, 'then he no longer turns to professional moral philosophers.' For him Marxism-Leninism was a unified ideological system, enclosed in itself, but one can sense in some of his speeches doubt as to whether ideological answers are sufficient to the real needs of human beings in a changing world.

Alexander Yakovlev was anything but a careerist, and he had little interest in the privileges available to him as a member of the Party elite. He still lives in the four-room flat assigned to him in 1967, and he has never owned a car. It appears that he has made no compromises in order to rise to the leading position he now holds. Sometimes he speaks about the state of his country and the Party more like a political scientist than a Politburo member: 'When, as Marx expresses it, we went from the realm of ideas to the realm of fact, we discovered we could not master reality. We still live in the realm of ideas, and this means we still live in the realm of illusions.' These are unusual words for a man from the Propaganda Department of the Party.

Representatives of the democratic left wanted to win over Yakovlev as their spokesman, and even considered nominating him to oppose Gorbachev in the election for General Secretary. During the Twenty-eighth Party Congress, conservatives attempted to discredit him as an enemy of Marxism. Yakovlev said that this was the last Party Congress in which he would participate. He would only be prepared to play a political role in the Presidential Council, and held the view that a member of this council should not belong to the Politburo. He made an exception, for a limited period, for Gorbachev.

Before the delegates at the Congress, who were deeply entangled in the battles that had begun between the factions, he spoke with the confidence and serenity of a man detached from party politics. But he also warned the democratic left against leaving the Party. That would only strengthen the conservative wing, which, though doomed, should not be underestimated. 'If you leave the Party, what then?' he asked the delegates. 'You will not be able to create a party of your own that can compete with the existing one. This party has a history of a hundred years, there are loyalties and nostalgia here, which by the way are noble feelings. A split does not solve the problem. Our party must find renewal in the dispute and become completely different, psychologically, morally and politically. It hurts when your head gets banged against a wall, but there's no other way. Comrades, we must continue to fight.'

But there were limits to what he could endure in this dispute, which exposed him not only to political reproaches, but also to personal slander. Yakovlev knew that the old, corrupt or conservative functionaries needed to be eliminated, but he warned the excited young delegates against settling personal scores. He himself had undergone a transformation since having to handle the rehabilitation of leading cadres destroyed by Stalin. 'I don't know if you can understand the moral crisis I found myself in when I became Chairman of the Rehabilitation Commission. This was not good for me personally. I developed a feeling of deep pity for all those who had lived before us and had held leading positions. They had really all been victims. Today it is easy for us to accuse them. But perhaps, comrade democrats, the time has come to call a halt and progress.'

On the current state of Soviet politics Yakovlev says: 'Socialism has not yet been built. What we have is the feudal rule of organisational departments. We should take a practical approach and not feed people with lies. When I listen to our debates I think, as a veteran of ideology: Good God, how we've crippled the consciousness of the people. What is ideology? I am firmly convinced it's the social experience of every single individual, which gives him the ability to choose and decide. As for theory, there is a great deal we don't understand yet. Look at today's battles, and you'll see we've only taken the first few steps. In my bookcase there is a 250-page manuscript, an analysis of Marxism as I understand it. I believe this criticism of mine is actually a defence of Marxism. Everyone says Marx created a theory of the human being. But he did not create such a theory, and I believe he did not even try to. He created a theory of class struggle, a brilliant doctrine, but one that we need to reject.'

A delegate asked about Lenin. He had a high opinion of him, said Yakovlev: 'But I don't find all his books enlightened. It seems to me his most significant characteristic as a politician was his ability to change his point of view according to circumstances.'

He warned the left reformers in the Sverdlov Hall against excessive ardour: 'Everything has its proper time in politics. One can't ignore public opinion, the feelings of the people. I always took myself for a romanticist, but now I understand that we live in a conservative country, even if I never suspected just how conservative it is. It has been trampled flat by Stalinism.'

It was Gorbachev's wish that Alexander Yakovlev should be a member of the new Politburo. But Yakovlev declined – as did Shevardnadze. They understood that Gorbachev wanted to avoid splitting the Party to keep a grip on the gigantic apparatus, but it must have seemed to them that the Politburo had rightly been devalued and that in future it could no longer determine the fate of the Soviet Union. Their refusals must have been disappointing for Gorbachev. Raisa Gorbachev spoke about it with some bitterness, as if Yakovlev had defected. But Yakovlev, like the social scientist he was, had soberly analysed the situation and come to a decision. He was the first political leader in the history of the Soviet Union to voluntarily give up his place in the Party leadership.

There is hardly anyone in Gorbachev's circle who better illustrates the developments that have led to *glasnost* and *perestroika* than the philosopher Ivan Frolov. Gorbachev first made him editor of the Party organ for theory, *Communist*, and in autumn 1989 editor of the Central Party paper *Pravda*. Frolov was one of the four assistants Gorbachev brought to the General Secretariat of the Party. Remarkably, three of them had lived in Prague between 1965 and 1968, when those debates began about the reform of Communism that ended with the suppression of the 'Prague Spring'.

At that time a number of younger Soviet sociologists, historians and philosophers had been sent to Prague to collaborate on the newspaper *Problems of Peace and Socialism*. The paper was the organ of the *Kominform*, which had been created as the common institution of the Communist Parties of the world, as a replacement for the dissolved Communist International. In Prague the Soviet academics came up against critical problems of Communist development as they worked and debated with eurocommunists

141

and reform Communists. Today many of them are heads of academic institutes or delegates to the Supreme Soviet. 'Prague was our university,' says Ivan Frolov today. 'There we had the opportunity for international contacts that were very rare in Moscow. And there a cadre of people was formed who began to think about the new problems.' It is no coincidence that Gorbachev chose three of his four closest collaborators from this group. The talks he had with his Czech friend Zdeněk Mlynář in 1967 would have drawn his attention to the 'Praguers' in Moscow.

Ivan Frolov began studying philosophy and biology at Moscow University in the fifties. He was a highly gifted young scientist, and during the Thaw he was drawn into the scientific and political controversy about genetic research. The general trend of his research was unambiguously directed against the teachings of the agrarian biologist Trofim Lysenko, who had been declared an incontrovertible authority by both Stalin and Khrushchev. Because Frolov's work took account of the findings of modern Western genetics, he was not awarded his doctorate. Frolov tells how a well-meaning older scientist suggested he should not take such risks. 'Why are you creating unpleasantness for yourself?' he said. 'Just throw away the critical pages.'

Frolov was at first not prepared to do this, but eventually he realised that he would have to comply with such suggestions. 'I never considered reasonable compromise out of the question, provided basic principles were not harmed,' he says today. 'So I let some of the criticism of Lysenko stand, and the rest I cut.' In those days scientists had to appease the authorities if they wanted to go on working. Older scientists who still retained an eye for talent began to promote and protect him. But as late as 1968, when he wanted to revise his old dissertation, Frolov's wife begged him not to destroy his life with a work that could not even be published.

In Czechoslovakia in 1965 Frolov became head of the scientific board of the magazine *Problems of Peace and Socialism*. His next three years in Prague were to turn him, and many of his colleagues who were to surface twenty years later in Moscow as reformers, from a scientist into a politician.

In 1968 Frolov returned to Moscow and became editor of the magazine *Questions of Philosophy*. There he formed a circle of natural scientists, philosophers and writers who debated ecological problems in their new political and ideological dimension. In the Soviet Union, where until then such questions had never been dealt with scientifically, it was difficult and dangerous to take a global view of environmental problems. The official line was that while the Socialist use of atomic energy represented progress, in the hands of imperialists atomic weapons were a threat to humanity. The environment was only threatened under capitalism, and man's place in society was already adequately and conclusively defined in Marxist-Leninist ideology. Anyone who took a different view of these questions was suspected of attempting to undermine the foundations of the Soviet system.

'We only wanted to look at the new problems of ecology, of humanity and humanism,' says Frolov. 'A glance at the magazine's list of contents is sufficient to show how close our themes were to today's problems. Many of our authors prepared the way for *perestroika*.'

The debates taken up by *Questions of Philosophy* were suppressed, but its fierce criticism of Party functionaries led to no direct personal consequences for Ivan Frolov. The stagnation of the Brezhnev years had its good side, Frolov says ironically. 'The Brezhnev era was a kind of porridge, a sticky heap where decisions were sometimes made, and sometimes not.'

During this period Frolov was able to publish academic articles, but his books did not appear in Russian. He was, however, not a dissident, and did not publish illegally in the West. He found editors at the Moscow Progress Publishing House, which published Russian books in foreign languages and sold them abroad, who supported his work. 'Because my books were not in Russian they didn't end up on the desks of the ideologues who surrounded Suslov and Brezhnev,' Frolov says today.

I asked him which thinkers had influenced him before he became a close adviser of Gorbachev's. 'For me one of the most interesting philosophers is Erich Fromm,' he says. 'I always had much more in common with him than with "ultramarxists" such as Academy member Mitin, with whom I often disagreed. I always said to myself, "What does it matter to me that we're both in the same party and that he swears by Marx and Lenin?" Erich Fromm and Jürgen Habermas are closer to me. As a convinced Marxist I get much more from them than from a dogmatician. Marx and his works are at the pinnacle of human culture.

Under Stalin Marxism was reduced to platitudes and entered the textbooks like that. And that's why today's youth have no faith in Marxism. But even in my youth that kind of Marxism repelled me, and that was why I began to study authentic Marxism. That made me a convinced Marxist, which helped me to stand up against the dogmatic ideologues. I was convinced that I was the true Marxist, and not them.'

Outside the Soviet Union Frolov attracted attention as an interesting thinker even if, in the final period of Brezhnev's rule, scientists of his calibre had no opportunity to publish and openly discuss their thoughts at home. But many of them knew each other, and they could exchange their ideas in trusted circles. Frolov also took an interest in economics. The economic situation in Russia was so bad that economists could no longer be forbidden from thinking aloud. Among Frolov's friends was the economist Leonid Abalkin, who is today Deputy Prime Minister, and who already before the end of the Brezhnev era was working on fundamental reforms of the Soviet economic system. It was among such independently thinking economists, sociologists and philosophers that Mikhail Gorbachev looked for advisers and collaborators when he came to Moscow. They were specialists, and had access to information that was concealed from other Soviet citizens. They had learned to see through the limitations of the system and to form their own opinions. But they had also learned to keep to the rules of the game, and not to reveal their conclusions. Gorbachev wanted to make use of their knowledge and experience when he took over the leadership.

When Gorbachev became General Secretary of the Party in 1985, he made Frolov one of his assistants. Frolov concentrated on problems relating to the protection of the environment and the use of atomic energy, but his work was not confined to technological and practical problems. As always he was aware of the relationship of man to nature and of the individual's place in the social and philosophical system. Such questions touch directly on ideology, and therefore on the foundation of Party and state in the Soviet Union. Gorbachev would not have chosen Frolov as his assistant if he had not known of his philosophical approach to world problems.

How much influence Frolov had on Gorbachev's ideas is hard to evaluate. Frolov himself is reticent about his part in the formation of the new thinking. In January 1990 he said to a correspondent of the newspaper *Moskovskii Komsomolets*: 'The entire history of philosophy shows that philosophers have made the priority of common human values their main concern. As long as philosophy exists, its attention will be focused on the human being. Everything new has already been thought of. The concept of "new thinking" applies to Joliot-Curie, to Russell, to Einstein. The manifestos of Russell and Einstein declare that we all need to understand that we belong to the genus human being, and to forget everything else. If we don't take account of that we won't survive. We have to remember first of all that we're human beings, and as human beings we have to learn to think in a new way. It's a brilliant insight, the direction Mikhail Sergeyevich has taken is very interesting. He's said that fifteen years ago he read publications on global human and environmental problems. At first he rejected Lenin's view that the problems of society take precedence over the class interests of the proletariat. Then he thought hard about whether this formulation fitted the present time. And then he went further, because in Lenin one doesn't find the priority of common human values. Gorbachev himself introduced this concept. But as a conscientious, academically educated man he always went back to Lenin. He himself arrived at this formulation which is at the heart of the new political thinking. This has absolutely nothing to do with me. I took part in the process of discussion and pointed out problems, but that's all. That's the philosopher's job. The role of a politician of Gorbachev's stature who also happens to be able to think philosophically is a different matter.'

CHAPTER 8

New Thinking

The scale of the new thinking introduced into Soviet politics by Gorbachev was not discernible in the speeches of his first years. But the Soviet people must nevertheless have sensed something, because no leader had spoken so directly to them for a quarter of a century. Gorbachev knew how effectively he could speak, and made great use of this ability. He was the driving force behind reform. The Soviet people certainly understood this by the time of his speech in 1985 to functionaries at the Smolny Institute of Leningrad, where Lenin had spoken before him. In this speech Gorbachev spoke of the great changes that were necessary if the Soviet Union was to become a modern country. He spoke of the immense effort the whole country would need to make, of a massive mobilisation of creative forces, and of the need to work in a new way. After a decade of senile leadership, the Soviet people now had the strong, dynamic leader they longed for.

Gorbachev also went among the people, and asked them what their problems were. 'Either we talk openly or our talking has no purpose at all,' he said on a visit to a Moscow car factory. Workers had become used to telling high functionaries on visits carefully regulated by protocol that everything was fine. Now the Party chief himself was asking them to tell him the truth about their work and conditions. In a Moscow hospital Gorbachev asked the nurses if their wages were sufficient to live on, and did not appear surprised to be told that they were not. People seeing this on television were amazed. Before Gorbachev no political leader had ever been interested in the reality of their daily lives. Nor had any of them understood how to use television effectively.

In 1982 a friend had pointed out to Gorbachev how important a relaxed, persuasive and confident public manner was, especially on television. The dacha provided for him as a Politburo member was equipped with an old 35-millimetre cine-projector, with which his predecessors had been able to watch American films that were not shown in Soviet cinemas. Gorbachev's friend Dmitri Golovanov, who worked in television, transferred recordings of Gorbachev's speeches to 35-millimetre film, and Gorbachev and Raisa watched these recordings over and over, discussing what he should avoid and how he could put himself across better. Ultimately this was to help him to persuade Soviet citizens of the necessity for his new policies. Gorbachev's public popularity increased his authority within the Politburo. At the Twenty-seventh Party Congress he was to set out his new programme for the future, and he needed the support of leading Party members. The Party was still bound to a programme that had been agreed in 1961, and much of which was plainly absurd: by 1970 the Soviet Union would have overtaken America in the per-capita production of industrial and consumer goods: by 1980 the Soviet Union would be so rich that all its people's demands and expectations would be met. Such claims still stood in the Party programme in 1985. The Party needed realistic new guidelines that would give hope for the future. Gorbachev's programme described Soviet problems realistically, and dispensed with magnificent promises.

Even so, it was clear that the programme was a compromise. The conservatives in the Party refused to abandon their old political formulations. They still saw the world as divided into two hostile camps, and felt that the Soviet Union was the most progressive country in the world. The heading of the first part of the programme expressed these ideological illusions: 'The Transition from Capitalism to Socialism and Communism – Essence of the Present Epoch'. The second part was called: 'The Tasks of the CPSU for the Perfection of Socialism and the Progressive Transition to Communism'. This was a long way from Gorbachev's wish for radical, even revolutionary change. The Party programme on which the collective leadership had agreed proceeded from the old idea that the 'objective' laws of the development of society would of themselves lead the Soviet Union from Socialism to Communism. All that was required was the acceleration of socio-economic development.

Gorbachev was more successful with the Party's economic

strategy, in which scientific-technical advances and a structural alteration of social production were emphasised as the main levers for an increase in production. In his speech he stressed that the Soviet Union would need to push forward to 'Socialist self-management', in other words a break with the command economy and greater powers for economic organisations and enterprises. He also spoke of the 'technological reconstruction' of the economy, resorting to the usual Party rhetoric when he described greater efficiency as the way to the attainment of the Party's defined aims by the third millennium.

The second man in the Party, Yegor Ligachev, made it clear where the limits of change lay for him: 'We're talking of the Socialist self-management of the people. This has nothing to do with the anarcho-syndicalist variant of self-management that is set up in opposition to the Socialist state, that is based on group ownership and represents naked group interests. Socialist self-management is founded on social ownership and combines state, collective and personal interests.' Gorbachev had to accept these restrictions to the debate, which made a more open discussion of new concepts of a Socialist market economy, such as Gorbachev's economists had proposed, impossible. He was not aiming for an anarcho-syndicalist system, but if he wanted to revive the country's social and economic forces he had to avoid a dogmatic argument with the conservatives. The dispute over the third programme the Communist Party of the Soviet Union had ever set itself ended in a kind of ideological shadow-boxing. Gorbachev could quote more Lenin in support of his ideas than his opponents, but his most important objective was to get through a Party programme that would not block the way to change.

This meant that in preparation for the Congress, and at the Congress itself, the old leadership had to be treated with care. The future must not seem to be a break with the past. The mistakes of the era from Brezhnev to Chernenko were considered, but not severely condemned. They were treated as forgivable sins from a time that had not quite freed itself from the personality cult. Only one person seemed eager to begin settling accounts. This was Boris Yeltsin, whom Gorbachev had brought from Sverdlovsk to the capital and made chief of the Party apparatus. Some thought of him as Gorbachev's closest confidant, his spearhead or, more in keeping with Yeltsin's style, his crowbar.

Yeltsin, who had himself been First Secretary of an important region, reproached other provincial Party chiefs for having presented themselves as miracle workers and created political vacuums for themselves in which they were protected from all criticism. He attacked them as opportunists who thought principally of their own comfort and advancement.

Yeltsin had already found the theme on which, in the years to come, he would base his opposition to Gorbachev: the privileges of the high functionaries. At the Twenty-seventh Party Congress, however, it still seemed as if he was only saying what Gorbachev thought, but more emphatically. In his sharp criticism of the deplorable state of inner-Party affairs, Yeltsin demanded an improvement in the structure and the work of the Party apparatus. The Party needed to win back the role of political leadership which it had lost by its constant interference with the economic and administrative leadership. Yeltsin saw the Party as the clamp that held together the often opposed interests of the country's regions and groups. Here he seemed quite close to Yegor Ligachev, who also wanted to subject the Party cadres to severe criticism and control. Only by a careful comparison of their speeches does one notice the differences between them. Ligachev was opposed to those sections of the press which had begun to criticise the privileges of high functionaries, while Yeltsin openly referred to them.

At the Party Congress Gorbachev gave the impression that he was closer to Yeltsin's position than to that of Ligachev, although he did not openly take sides. When the Congress ended it endorsed Gorbachev's 'political report', but the Party programme and statute did not read like the breakthrough to a new policy. No basic reforms through which Soviet policy might more quickly approach Gorbachev's aims were announced. The delegates had agreed to his policy of an acceleration of technological and economic development, but what was adopted was a programme that corresponded to the power relations of the Congress. When several delegates wanted to call the new programme the 'Gorbachev programme' he rejected the suggestion as a relapse into the personality cult. This may have appeared a modest retreat into the mutuality of collective leadership, but was in fact a clever move: Gorbachev did not want to be too closely associated with a programme that he regarded as far too restricted to overcome the country's real problems.

Gorbachev knew that more was required than reining in and cleansing the Party and more effective leadership of the Soviet economy. But he had to take the resistance of his colleagues in the leadership into account, and did not reveal the true extent of his intended reforms. He was still at a learning stage as Party leader, and did not yet have a fully-fledged programme that could be convincingly defended against the objections of his conservative opponents. His own political ideas would only become clearer to him in the course of his conflict with the ponderous Party apparatus. The more closely he examined practical methods of change, the more clearly he saw that limited technocratic improvements in the system would not be enough to solve the extreme crisis of the Soviet economy and society.

His first declared aim had been economic reform, and to achieve it he had tried to fight the resistance of the apparatus with the forces of the apparatus. Now he realised that he would need to mobilise society itself against the apparatus. Yegor Ligachev had been afraid of this development, and tried to halt it, but Gorbachev deliberately set free those forces whose criticisms he knew from analyses and personal experience. Since the beginning of the eighties he had read many objective scientific descriptions of Soviet living conditions. Like the authors of these reports, Gorbachev believed that solutions to the complicated problems of Soviet society could only be found if the real conditions were factually and ruthlessly examined. From the beginning of 1986 Gorbachev publicly asked for an open dialogue, that with the catchword *glasnost* was to become the lever with which society would be roused from its long paralysis.

There were many journalists in the Soviet press who longed for such a signal. Respected commentators such as Alexander Bovin and Fyodor Burlaski were only waiting for their cue. They had made their names during Khrushchev's Thaw, and in the twenty years that followed they had been obliged to compromise, but had not lost their authority. Now they could more openly write what they thought. Young journalists throughout the country, who had unwillingly accepted their role as controlled formers of opinion, could now report abuses about which they had previously had to keep silent.

Their freedom was still limited, but even the exposure of local abuses hinted at the crisis which pervaded the entire system. The criticism of bureaucrats was a simple and popular beginning which suited the intentions of the leadership. Corruption and the careless squandering of national property could now be exposed under the new conditions of greater openness. Previously criticism had only been allowed from above, but now the entire hierarchical system had been stood on its head. The numerous revelations of the wrongdoings of managers and bureaucrats pointed to a deep and fundamental rottenness at the core of the system.

But journalists were not able to draw this obvious conclusion, and could only single out individual cases. Supervision of the press, radio and television was still in the hands of the old media functionaries. What could be printed or could appear on the screen was subject to strict political control. For this reason, in the early phase of *glasnost*, novels, films and plays gave a more complete portrait of Soviet reality than the press. They could depict the spiritual warping of the Soviet people, whom official censorship had denied not only the works of great Russian writers, but also those human values that had once given meaning and stability to life, and could show the material and spiritual impoverishment of conditions in the villages. Some went further, examining social power relations.

Among these was the play *Braking in the Sky*, which ran for several weeks at the Moscow Theatre of Satire. In the play General Secretary Gorbachev has just visited a provincial town, where he has, as usual, spoken with the people and the Party functionaries. As the play opens the last pictures of his departure are still being shown on the television screens in the committee room of the local Party Committee. But the First Party Secretary has already summoned his colleagues. He has decided to punish everyone who spoke openly in reply to Gorbachev's questions about abuses and problems. He threatens those who attempt to justify their criticisms with the loss of their already modest privileges. He summons the public prosecutor and the judge and initiates proceedings against those who want to oppose him. But he has forgotten that the television cameras which recorded Gorbachev's farewell address are still set up in the committee room. When he discovers that their reels of film contain not only Gorbachev's departure, but his own attempts to bend his colleagues in the Party, administration and industry to his will, the First Secretary panics. The film is already on its way to Moscow with the reporters from state television. He puts pressure on the airport chief, threatening to expose abuses at the airport if the plane is not called back. But the pilots do not understand this order, and refuse to obey it. The wife of one of them is brought to the airport and has to tell her husband over the radio that they will not get the three-room flat they have been waiting for for years if he disobeys instructions. The plane turns back, the First Secretary has won time, and is already on the phone to Moscow. His connections in the capital's Party apparatus will see to it that no one finds out what happened.

The play's audiences – and among them during the first performances there were often Gorbachev supporters from the Central Committee – quickly understood that it was not just one single Party Secretary who was being exposed here. In the play the Party chief did not even have a name. He stood for the Party itself, which ruled and regulated everything. While it had the power to do this abuses could neither be rectified nor prevented. The real forces in the country could not develop while provincial barons and the central Party apparatus could manipulate the law to suit their own ends.

Without legal security there can be no spirit of individual initiative. The economy cannot be renewed if it is not directed by economic thinking, but has to obey the instructions of Party authorities which subject it to political or personal demands. Even ministries are unable to function if the highest Party organ, the Politburo, sees its role as making decisions on the improvement of the quality of video cassettes or the production of umbrellas, as it did until the mid-eighties. The branches of the Party apparatus intervened in daily decisions in all areas of life. Many functionaries saw this as the foundation of the Party's strength. Conservative political leaders were completely unconcerned about the privileges to which the middle cadres clung. What mattered most to them was the stability and order of the state, which the power of the Party upheld. They feared that more open discussion of social and economic questions could lead to the fundamental question of what actually legitimised the Party's rule. If the true state of

Soviet life was made visible, profound changes would be unavoidable.

Criticism of the bureaucracy of the state and economy was followed by protest against the intelligentsia and the media still being kept under control. Now the role of the Party and the functionaries was being openly questioned. According to Lenin, 'The Party rules, the state administers.' But what would remain to the Party if it gave up the key positions of administration? In Moscow the reformers were already beginning to suggest that the Party should limit itself to setting general goals and steering the country through political education and encouragement. Control over practical decisions would then, as set out in the Constitution, lie with the organs of government, with the Soviets, the local, city and republic parliaments and with the Supreme Soviet of the Union.

Until now parliament's role had been to unanimously endorse what the Party organisation had decided the day before. The apparatus selected the delegates according to a fixed quota of workers, farmers and intellectuals, with additional specifications of age and sex. Appointed for their political reliability and only called to a few sessions a year, the delegates were unable to do any real work. They regarded themselves as mere instruments of the Party apparatus that appointed or dismissed them. There was no feedback to the population, who at the ballot boxes simply endorsed the only candidate. The supposedly elected parliament was no counterbalance to the Party apparatus, which alone took decisions and had no need to fear either opposition or contradiction.

The reformers in Moscow felt encouraged by Gorbachev to look for counteracting forces to the Party apparatus in society itself. Gorbachev let it be known in his speeches that he needed a different Party, that Soviet society could only be renewed once the complacency of the functionaries had been shattered and they became more accountable to the population. Gorbachev believed that he could engineer this process. His opponents, on the other hand, feared that an easing of the centrally directed system and more open debate about the country's real problems could lead to the disintegration of the system of rule. Neither they nor Gorbachev had fully understood how fragile the state and society in the Soviet Union had become. For decades the country's problems had been concealed by propaganda and rigid Party control.

The conservatives were still convinced that they could solve the crisis by introducing measures for improved management and stricter discipline. Gorbachev had better information at his disposal, and had thought more deeply, but he could not impose his will on the Party apparatus and change it from the inside on his own. For this he needed the support of the population, and especially the intelligentsia. His proposed reforms were held up or emasculated by the middle and lower ranks of Party and government bureaucrats.

From autumn 1986 Gorbachev began to draw together a group of the most important economists in the Soviet Union, assigning them the task of outlining a programme for radical reform. From the economist Abel Aganbegyan came the concept that first of all Soviet economic development needed to be accelerated. An increase in the production of material goods would motivate the leaders of enterprises and the workers to work better, faster and more imaginatively. This would further increase the rate of development, but everything depended on whether during the first phase the population believed that the policy would succeed, and after the failure of past economic programmes and promises people had long ago become suspicious of change and resigned to the existing conditions. Aganbegyan's programme, despite its liberalising elements, was essentially conservative. It was based on the theory that more output would lead to higher earnings and higher earnings to more output. But the Soviet citizens in the empty shops already had more money in their pockets than they could spend. As long as there was nothing to buy, payment for output was no incentive for harder and better work. The bureaucracy of the state and the economy also prevented individual initiative and achievement from being appropriately rewarded, and instead of a rise in production there was actually a decline.

'Gorbachev is quick on the uptake, and he changes his views according to the reality,' says the economist Gavril Popov. At the end of 1986 Popov was called by Gorbachev to discuss economic policy. He summarises Gorbachev's view of the situation: the policy of acceleration was marking time, and a successful reform of the economy could not rely simply on technocratic and organisational changes, but needed a broader foundation of changes in the political system.

On Gorbachev's instructions leading economists such as Oleg Bogomolov, Leonid Abalkin, Popov, Aganbegyan and Anchishkin assembled. Together they developed the outlines of a radical reform of the economy that would put an end to the omnipotence of the State Central Planning Committee, 'Gosplan', which had long gone beyond simply planning economic development in favour of giving ministries and enterprises direct and detailed instructions. This had brought it into conflict with enterprises, the ministries, the Party apparatus and the economic organs of the republics. But they were all now united in their resistance to a comprehensive reform that would threaten their established power bases.

The economists knew this only too well. They knew the old joke about Gosplan: at the end of the military parade on Red Square, when all the gigantic rockets have rolled past, a small group of civilians with briefcases marches by. A foreigner asks what this means. 'That's our Gosplan, a weapon of tremendous destructive capability,' comes the reply. Gosplan now joined forces with the economic and state apparatuses against radical reform. Had the new programme been realised, Gavril Popov says today, Soviet citizens would not be faced with empty shelves in the food stores. And Professor Oleg Bogomolov believes that Gorbachev's greatest mistake was not to press the programme in the strongest possible terms at the Central Committee sessions, the most important of which, in June 1987, had been given the theme: 'The tasks of the Party for a fundamental restructuring of the running of the economy'.

CHAPTER 9

Perestroika

From the beginning of 1987 Mikhail Gorbachev stated more clearly that technocratic reforms and the acceleration and rationalisation of planning and economic processes could not alone lead Soviet society out of its stagnation. He spoke for the first time about 'radical reform', and of the need for qualitative changes in the economic system of the Soviet Union. In the months leading up to the June session of the Central Committee Gorbachev consulted with economists who believed that the dismantling of central and local bureaucracy and the introduction of market-economy elements were essential steps in the restructuring of the Soviet economy.

Some of these economists had collaborated in the sixties with the market-economy orientated economist Professor Liberman and on the reforms that the Prime Minister of that time, Alexei Kosygin, had tried to introduce. These attempted reforms had failed because they had been too limited and because the resistance of the bureaucratic apparatus isolated individual projects and stifled them. Now these economists hoped that Gorbachev's programme would achieve a breakthrough. In the previous two years a revolutionary restructuring had been discussed in a general way. Now a package of reform measures whose components were already defined and built into a timetable was presented. At its plenary session the Central Committee agreed that the next Five-Year Plan would begin to work with new economic structures. Gorbachev's advisers saw the reforms as an unambiguous step towards a 'Socialist market economy'.

This term, however, did not appear in the papers available to the Central Committee or in the notes given to its members. At best, when this basic principle of the planned new economic mechanism was concerned, all that was coyly mentioned was 'the relation of money to goods'. For most of the functionaries, as for most of the state bureaucracy, the concept of a market economy was still unacceptable, even when qualified by the adjective 'Socialist'. The idea of a policy of 'Socialist pluralism' made them uneasy, as it would end their monopoly on information and the formation of opinion. An economy ruled by market forces rather than by the political apparatus would take from them much of their power, and could even threaten their privileges and social status. To many it was clear that these dangers still threatened even when it was only 'the relation of money to goods' that was being discussed.

Public criticism of the way in which the Party and the state were run became increasingly bold. The people regarded the bureaucracy as the main cause of the paralysis of the Soviet economy. For the typical Soviet citizen the term 'bureaucrats' included not only the functionaries in the administrative departments, the ministries and the Party apparatus, but also the heads of ordinary food stores. The citizens assumed that lower-level bureaucrats procured a few extra provisions for themselves, while those at higher levels enjoyed privileges such as dachas, official cars and imported goods. Mikhail Gorbachev too regarded the bureaucratic apparatus which had proliferated over the past sixty years as the major obstacle to reform in the Soviet Union.

The bureaucracy was in need of radical restructuring, to a degree that would have been unacceptable to most of the Party apparatus and its leaders. Even Gorbachev repeatedly stressed that his reforms were intended only to lead to improvements within the existing system. Perhaps his reassurances were meant to calm those for whom the process of restructuring was moving too fast and too far, but it is also possible that at this time he had not yet decided whether he only wanted to modify the system in certain areas, or to aim for more fundamental changes.

In any case, Gorbachev's statements during this period were not without contradictions. Speaking to journalists shortly after the Central Committee plenum, he again narrowed the range of envisaged reforms. Proposals to abandon the system of a centrally planned economy had not been adopted. Gorbachev seemed to indicate that he agreed with the majority of Central Committee members in rejecting moves in this direction: 'We have not entered into this, and we would never agree to it, because we want to strengthen Socialism and not replace it with another system.' When he said that the reforms would not go beyond the boundaries of Socialism, the kind of Socialism he envisaged was open to question. But it was clear that in his view the Communist Party needed to retain its leading role, and that the reform process would take place through it.

These and other comments made advocates of far-reaching reform begin to suspect that Gorbachev did not intend to make sweeping changes to the system, but merely wanted to improve the very mechanism that in their opinions had prevented economic progress. But the Soviet intelligentsia continued to place their hope in Gorbachev and his policy of *glasnost*.

Gorbachev must have been aware of the paradox of a policy which attempted to dismantle bureaucratic and central power, but which could only make these changes with the help of the central bureaucracy itself. Four weeks after the Central Committee plenum, Gorbachev said that the country's elite style of leadership had made it impossible for the people to influence policy. On a visit to Murmansk, in the far north of the Soviet Union, he said that the inflated administrative apparatus had to be simplified, and that this dismantling of the bureaucracy would be done with a sense of responsibility, and would take care of every individual affected.

But he recognised that the prevailing conditions were drastic: 'For decades the management of the economy and society has been based on centralisation and on administrative and command methods. This has led to a great inflation of the apparatuses of state and economic administration, as well as the apparatus of social organisation and also to an extent the Party apparatus. At present 18 million people work in administration. That is 15 per cent of the entire working population.'

A few days later, speaking to a group of Leningrad Party cadres, he called bureaucracy the most dangerous enemy of revolutionary restructuring. Naturally he took account of the likely resistance of his audience. He was familiar with the ponderousness and inertia of the apparatus, but he needed its support if he was to carry through his policies.

In 1986 he had said that although the people wanted change, between them and the leadership stood the apparatus of ministries and the Party, which did not want to give up its power and privileges. He put this point more strongly in the autumn of 1987: 'People often ask if there is political opposition to *perestroika*. There is no political opposition among the Soviet people. The workers are completely in favour of *perestroika*. They are pushing us forward. We constantly feel we're being urged not to turn back and not to slow down the pace.'

Gorbachev's projection of his own hopes onto the workers was completely in accordance with Communist theory, which sees the stronghold of progressive political reasoning and the driving force for change in the working class. In actual fact the debate about fundamental reform of the economy was over the heads of the majority of the Soviet population. Most workers were of the opinion that *perestroika* meant, first of all, an improvement in their standard of living. They felt that the profits of their hard work had been squandered by the administration, the bureaucracy. The top people had enriched themselves and obtained privileges and robbed ordinary workers of the fruits of their labour. Higher wages, better food supplies, workers' flats and more free time were their main expectations. They criticised the bureaucratic management, but expressed little desire for reforms that could bring with them increased pressure to produce, job uncertainty and rising prices. The unions, held in low esteem by the workers, now tried to seize on these social demands in order to present themselves as the genuine representatives of the workers' interests.

Gorbachev's speeches during these years reveal how narrow was the area in which he could work on reform. In the spring of 1987, in an article in the theoretical Party magazine *Communist*, Alexander Yakovlev examined the connections between the power of the bureaucracy, rigid ideological dogmatism and the forms of ownership in society. He wrote: 'Bureaucracy relies on dogmatism, just as dogmatism relies on bureaucracy. Bureaucrats, like dogmatists, can only exist by harming the interests of society. They exploit their affiliation to the state apparatus, endowing it with mythical omnipotence. Hence the attempts to nationalise everything and anything and to attribute every success and every achievement to the administration.' Yakovlev saw state ownership (equated with social ownership), which enabled the bureaucrats to extend their influence, as the main cause of economic stagnation. Bureaucratic managers declared that anything which curtailed their managerial rights was a residue of capitalism.

As an example, Yakovlev mentioned the *kolkhozes*, which were no longer genuine co-operative property. The article set out the main causes of stagnation and the fundamental changes that would be necessary in the process of *perestroika*. Gorbachev must have read the article before it was published.

He was also aware of the resistance, partly ideological, partly emotional, from the Politburo and, even more, from the upper functionaries of the Party, state and economy. At that time Yegor Ligachev was still the second man in the Party leadership, and until he was voted out of the Politburo and retired in the summer of 1990, he was the spokesman for the apparatus. At sixty-nine he was the oldest member of the Politburo, a stocky man with rimless glasses and grey hair. A basically friendly man, at the speaker's desk he turned into a power-conscious functionary, repeatedly drilling ideological principles into his listeners.

In the reform debate of 1987 Ligachev stressed that the new course was not aimed at Western-style liberalisation, but at the reinforcement of 'Socialist' democracy. In this he also saw a strengthening of the people's autonomy, but he insisted that the reform process would have to take place under the Party's leadership. For him the restoration of peasants' property was an assault on Socialist dogma, a first step on the road to the introduction of a different political and social system. Market-economy principles seemed to him to threaten the Party's claim to leadership. He believed that the Soviet Union had essentially kept to Lenin's guidelines, and that after a number of improvements the Socialist system would – more or less in its present form – overtake capitalism. Ligachev never set out or published his economic and socio-political ideas as a unified theory. Perhaps this would have been superfluous, as the Party and state apparatus accepted his ideas as virtually self-evident.

It was not only diehard conservatives who feared far-reaching criticism of the Soviet system. Anatoli Lukyanov, whose organisational talent and intelligence Gorbachev had valued since their student days and who was a trusted colleague, was among those who in 1987 tried to limit the scope of research into the causes of stagnation, restricting criticism of the historical development of the economy. Without mentioning Stalin, he claimed that the methods used in the construction of industry and the collectivisation of agriculture had been essential for the building of Socialism and victory over fascism.

Soviet historians and economists had already gone a great deal further in the public debate. They described the enforced collectivisation, which had cost millions of peasant lives, as the original cause of the decline of Soviet agriculture. And they recognised Stalin's enforced industrialisation as the origin of the centralised command economy whose inertia had brought about the current problems of the Soviet economy.

More and more Soviet writers began to express doubts about the historical inevitability of the course of Soviet history. Alexander Bovin, one of the most headstrong and intelligent Soviet journalists, was among the first to point out that in the twenties there had been alternatives to the centralised command economy. For Bovin, as for other intellectuals, what mattered was to keep an open forum in the current debate on reform models for Socialism. If in the twenties, before Stalin, it had been possible to discuss different models and paths for the Party and society, that justified discussion in the current situation that went beyond the limits set by functionaries like Ligachev and even at times by Gorbachev. Bovin felt that the development of the Soviet Union differed so completely from what had been planned in Lenin's lifetime that contemporary Soviet society was not in a position to develop the possibilities of Socialism. A historically outdated form of Socialism would therefore have to be replaced by another. If *perestroika* failed it would appear that nothing could reverse the stagnation in the Soviet Union and other Socialist countries, and capitalism would increasingly come to be regarded as an alternative.

Soviet scientists and journalists continued to attack the country's bureaucratic command economy, with its disastrous combination of the concentration of power with the fear of taking any kind of responsibility. Since the Revolution a gigantic and ponderous apparatus had been created that crushed the productive forces of Soviet society.

An almost religious faith in organisation, wrote Nikolai Shmelev, had produced apathy, corruption, waste, envy and alienation. Shmelyov and others demanded the rapid removal of power from the administrative apparatus of the state and the economy. Preventing this was the apparatus's unshakeable belief in its own infallibility.

Critics of the system could cite the words of Lenin himself, who in the last years of his life had attacked the bureaucracy in the severest possible manner, calling it 'the enemy within'. Quoting Lenin was a familiar Soviet method of avoiding criticism, but Party functionaries had grown so accustomed to the tactic that it no longer had much effect. Naturally they knew that criticism of the bureaucracy implicitly meant criticism of the Party itself, which had after all created the bureaucratic institutions. The bureaucratic command economy underpinned the political power of the Party functionaries, and economic reformers also took up the cause of political democratisation. They felt that they represented the avant-garde of Gorbachev's reforms, but were ready to accept his limits to the dispute as a necessary compromise for the time being.

In the summer of 1987 Otto Lakis, the deputy editor of the magazine *Communist*, commented that, despite all previous resolutions to reduce it, the administrative apparatus had continued to proliferate. He believed however that this trend was about to be reversed. At this time Moscow intellectuals, scientists, writers and journalists saw Gorbachev as embodying all their hopes for the future. He was clearly aiming for a far-reaching reform of society, involving political democratisation and spreading economic reform on a wider front. It had become easier to justify politico-economic reform to the Party, as the leadership and functionaries had been aware since the Brezhnev years that the established economic mechanism had long ago reached the limits of its effectiveness, and that its immobility stood in the way of all further progress.

Without a new economic programme those socio-political improvements that could free the population from its indifference and torpor, and enable the Soviet Union to compete economically and militarily with the USA and other capitalist countries, could not be achieved. It was therefore possible for Gorbachev to win the Party's support for a more or less consistent politico-economic programme. But the programme soon came up against the delaying action of the bureaucratic apparatuses of the economy, the state and the Party. The social reform that would create the required conditions for a successful economic reform was still urgently needed.

Gorbachev had made little progress since January 1987 with his attempt to gain Party approval for such a reform programme. In the autumn he resumed the battle, but before this there had been an incident which had made his friends and supporters uneasy. Gorbachev had gone for a holiday to the government dacha at Pitsunda on the Black Sea, and was absent from the capital for an unusually long time, gathering his thoughts and writing his book *Perestroika and the New Thinking*. But hardly had he left the capital before his rivals in the leadership team began making their views public.

Yegor Ligachev and the KGB chief Viktor Chebrikov, both Politburo members, made it clear in speeches and interviews that they set strict limits to discussion of the crimes and mistakes of the Stalin era and wanted to slow down the pace of restructuring. Headlines in the West puzzled over Gorbachev's apparent loss of power. In Moscow too the supporters of *perestroika* were uneasy at the increased coverage of the conservative leaders in the media. Some felt that the General Secretary had made a grave tactical error by taking a holiday at such an important stage in the battle.

When Gorbachev returned from his working holiday, he gave a speech in Murmansk in which he announced changes to the Party apparatus and the removal of old-style functionaries who opposed reform, and showed that his power had not diminished. He had outmanoeuvred his conservative opponents by moderating his more radical formulations and seeming to offer them a compromise. The majority of the Soviet population, who hoped for a better life from *perestroika*, and also Gorbachev's intellectual followers, now felt confident that the programme of reform would continue.

These compromises with the right went too far for one of the Soviet leaders, the First Secretary of the Moscow Party organisation, Boris Yeltsin. Gorbachev had brought him to Moscow from the industrial city of Sverdlovsk in the Urals. Tall, bullish, with silver-grey hair, Yeltsin is an imposing figure. He talks slowly, and leaves his listeners time to think when he makes a polemical point. He registers exactly how his audience is reacting and can immediately adapt to their mood. He has a tendency to strike attitudes, but this only increases the impression he gives of energy and dynamism.

He was one of the most firmly committed to Gorbachev's reform policies, and was in the vanguard of the fight against corruption and nepotism. At the Twenty-seventh Party Congress in the spring of 1986, he criticised the Party and state apparatus with notable severity, and demanded changes in its structure and selection. He reproached his colleagues with irresponsibility and a lack of discipline, with giving themselves the airs of bosses, and with being unable to accept criticism. He spoke of opportunists, handy with the Party rulebook, who tried to thwart every radical change, and particularly attacked the privileges and benefits of the ruling caste, demanding the uprooting of the bureaucracy and with it social injustice and the abuse of privilege. Already he had struck the populist note on which his popularity was to be increasingly based. He emphasised, however, in the usual manner of Party functionaries, that the Party was the only power that could bring about change, and the only authority which could guarantee that the common cause would be served.

Although Yeltsin criticised high Party functionaries for projecting themselves as miracle workers, his own style of leadership revealed how much he himself was tied to a political tradition in which the Party Secretary intervened personally in all aspects of his district's life. Even before he came into conflict with the Party apparatus and then with Gorbachev himself, observers in Moscow, while being well disposed to him, had noted critically that Yeltsin had a tendency to do things on his own, and sometimes to give rather theatrical performances. In his early days in Moscow he appeared at the food store Gastronom No. 1 and tried to buy beef. When he was told they had none he revealed the fact that he was First Party Secretary of Moscow, and asked where the meat was that he knew had been delivered that morning. As usual, it had been kept in cold storage, to be sold later, at a surcharge, to people with connections.

Acts of this sort made Yeltsin popular with the people. His critics, however, objected that the problem of supplies in Moscow was not going to be solved by such stunts. Yeltsin, they said, was still behaving like a Party boss in Sverdlovsk, and had not understood that Moscow, with its 9 million inhabitants, was a state in itself, with complicated political structures and a network of inter-related interests and dependencies.

As Moscow Party Secretary Yeltsin found himself opposed to a number of Party organisations whose interests in no way coincided with the dismantling of bureaucratic posts and privileges. These included the Party organisations in the big ministries and administrations, in the central social organisations, and in the industry and trade apparatuses of the city. It was hard for Yeltsin to break through the closed front of this experienced network, and he could do little more than make occasional surprise reshuffles in administrative posts. Yeltsin was at his best in direct contact with the public, and gave the impression of being frustrated in his attempts to reform the apparatus.

In some respects there were striking similarities between Yeltsin and Gorbachev. The speeches of both avoided the usual hot air of ideology and Party propaganda. Both had risen in the apparatus, apparently fitting in and not seeming to harbour personal ambitions, yet secretly unhappy about the condition of the Party and the lifestyle of their colleagues. Both had learned that long-term political goals could only be achieved by compromise, although Yeltsin, more frequently than Gorbachev, was inclined to hasten tactical decisions by personal intervention. Both had chosen a simple lifestyle for themselves and their families, rejecting some of the usual privileges. All this had created the impression that Gorbachev and Yeltsin were close friends and colleagues. When Yeltsin went further in his criticisms than Gorbachev, Moscow citizens considered it a co-ordinated tactical move, in which Yeltsin led the attack while Gorbachev secured the conquered territory.

But it became clear in October 1987 that, despite certain similarities in their objectives, there were profound differences between Gorbachev and Yeltsin. Yeltsin was no longer prepared to take the line of compromise by which Gorbachev wanted to bring reform forward. Against the advice of Gorbachev, he sought direct confrontation with Yegor Ligachev in the Central Committee, with an unusually direct speech for this body of the Party.

Yeltsin began with an attack on the privileges of the top functionaries. There had to be an end to the spoils system, especially while supplies to the population were not improving. *Perestroika* would make no progress until this army of bureaucrats and hacks had been defeated. He quoted letters from citizens asking for Soviet troops to be withdrawn from Afghanistan, then he turned to the Central Committee: 'It is time, comrades, to stop talking and start acting. It is time to use power. And we have the power. It has been entrusted to us by the people. But if we sink into the swamp and fail to use it to defend the interests of the people, then perestroika will remain without effect.'

Yeltsin then made a direct attack on Ligachev, accusing him of shouting at him and playing the schoolmaster. Instead of practical comradely help, he said, all he got were lectures and gruff reprimands. He then criticised Raisa Gorbachev. She interrupted his work with telephone calls, instructions and requests. He would not permit such interference. This was a popular reproach: for some time the Soviet public and the Party had been wondering what role Raisa actually played, and with what right. A personal attack such as this, before the Central Committee, was highly unusual. It indicated that the relations between Gorbachev and Yeltsin had deteriorated dramatically.

Yeltsin's outburst put Gorbachev in a difficult position. The Central Committee meeting had been meant to vote on the speech that Gorbachev intended to give on the Day of the Revolution about the state of Soviet politics and the break with the Stalinist past. Now Yeltsin had brought about a split in the Central Committee, inadvertently strengthening the opponents of reform. Twenty-four speakers, among them nine Politburo members, spoke against Yeltsin, criticising his 'political adventuring' and his supposed ultra-left radicalism. Some reproached him for having avoided criticism by his custom of working alone. Gorbachev, in common with other speakers, mentioned Yeltsin's previous successes, but declared that he lacked the strength and insight required to lead the Party organisation of Moscow. He called Yeltsin's speech politically immature, confusing and contradictory. Yeltsin had put his own ambition above the interests of the Party, and ascribed his own weakness and mistakes to others.

It seemed to be the end of Yeltsin's Party career. In an abrupt reversal, he admitted the mistakes with which he had been reproached, and said they had been caused by his ambition. He took back his criticism of the implementation of perestroika, and acknowledged that he had lost face as a political leader and a

Communist and wronged the Moscow Party apparatus, the Politburo and Mikhail Gorbachev. Whatever the differences between
him and Gorbachev, when Yeltsin ran up against the closed front
of Central Committee members who had no desire to accept the
dismantling of their own positions and privileges, he weakened
Gorbachev's position in the conflict with the conservatives. But
his outburst also laid the foundations of his future popularity.

Yeltsin's speech was not printed after the Central Committee
meeting, but a fairly accurate version of it was soon circulating.
The Party press published the speeches of Yeltsin's opponents,
but it was possible to reconstruct from them the general direction
of Yeltsin's speech. In many of Moscow's underground stations
anonymous notices appeared on the walls, backing Yeltsin and
supporting his criticisms. At some stations young people risked
handing out leaflets in support of Yeltsin. Word spread of a
planned demonstration on Trubnaya Square, but the time was
not yet ripe for that: forty or fifty people stood about in the
extreme cold singly or in small groups, trying to look uninvolved,
while round the corner trucks full of police lay in wait. No one
yet dared speak out openly in Yeltsin's cause.

Basically, Yeltsin had not cut a convincing figure in the Central
Committee. He had misjudged the attitude of the overwhelming
majority, and had produced the opposite effect to that he
intended, provoking Gorbachev and putting him in a difficult
position. After his condemnation by his opponents, he had exhibi-
ted a degree of self-criticism, real or assumed, that went beyond
the usual model within the Party. But this did him no harm with
the Soviet population, who shared his dissatisfaction with the
slow pace of progress and found in Yeltsin a spokesman for
their anger and frustration. After leaving the Politburo, Yeltsin
appealed to Gorbachev to rehabilitate him during his lifetime. He
had been forced into the role of martyr by the Party apparatus,
and Gorbachev certainly considered him politically dead. But
Gorbachev recognised the mood of the people. Yeltsin was not
completely discredited, although he lost his post as Party chief in
Moscow, and he was unexpectedly appointed Deputy Minister
for Construction, giving him an organisational base from which
to begin his fight to return to the centre of power.

The Yeltsin controversy overshadowed the retirement at this
Central Committee plenum of Geydar Aliyev from Azerbaidjan.

He had risen to the Politburo under Brezhnev, and for Gorbachev's supporters he exemplified the privilege, nepotism and corruption of that era. Gorbachev had taken the opportunity to rid himself of Aliyev not by accusing or condemning him, but by letting him retire to Azerbaidjan for health reasons, with honours and a special high pension.

Gorbachev's major programmatic speech before 6,000 members of the Party elite was to be given in the great Kremlin Palace on the seventieth anniversary of the Revolution, in November 1987. The speech needed the consent of the Politburo and the Central Committee, but the recommendations and drafts of his advisers went substantially beyond what the majority of the Politburo considered acceptable.

A few days before the anniversary speech, to an audience of foreign delegates which included not only Communists but Social Democrats, Greens and representatives of other progressive groups, Gorbachev had been outspoken in his criticism of former Soviet foreign policy, and had declared that one could no longer view the world as a battleground between two opposed ideological systems.

At the celebratory meeting in the Kremlin Palace, however, Gorbachev's speech revealed the compromises he had made with the conservatives. He described the historical development of the Soviet Union and the current state of its domestic, economic and foreign policy. He acknowledged the repression of the thirties, but condemned those who had broken the law under Stalin as real criminals. He spoke of Stalin's victims as 'many thousands of Party members and those outside the Party' at a time when Soviet publications put their numbers in millions. In some respects Gorbachev's address was less of a break with the past than that with which Nikita Khrushchev had begun the first phase of destalinisation more than thirty years earlier. This was disappointing for many Soviet intellectuals, and Andrei Sakharov complained publicly that Gorbachev had not told the whole terrible truth about Stalin's crimes. But Gorbachev's speech had not been intended to put an end to criticism of Stalin. In an interview Alexander Yakovlev let the intellectuals know that Gorbachev's words were not to be taken as a binding directive. The General Secretary was simply operating with extreme caution in an area which his conservative opponents had made particularly dangerous.

In his comments on the situation of the Soviet Union Gorbachev stressed that a reform of society was urgently necessary, giving the democratisation of society as a whole priority over a radical reform of the economy, which he described as the second of the two key problems of *perestroika*. The economy he envisaged would combine centralism and self-administration in the best possible way – again a compromise. On the one hand Gorbachev was making an unexpectedly optimistic assessment of the progress of reform, but on the other he was letting it be known that the coming years would be difficult. He admitted that the resistance of the conservatives would increase, and revealed how well informed he was about the mood of the country by mentioning the collectives, which were not to make public their resistance to economic reform and democratisation until a year later. He also warned against both the forces of dogmatism and conservatism and those for whom *perestroika* was not producing results quickly enough.

As might be expected, neither the conservatives nor the radicals were particularly pleased with this speech. The reform wing wanted a greater show of determination and a timetable of measures for changing society. Gorbachev's statements on foreign policy were more readily accepted. He anticipated a new, more mutually dependent relationship between states, capitalist and Socialist. The future would no longer be shaped by class conflicts, but by the common interests of humanity.

Gorbachev, who was revising Lenin's theory of imperialism without referring to it, was mindful of the conservative wing of the Party and the army when he declared that the defence capacity of the Soviet Union must remain high enough to preclude the military superiority of 'imperialism' over socialism. This was an invitation for the army to rethink its policy. Previously it had aimed for superiority, but now it had to accept the concept of parity, of equal strength. Once again Gorbachev was keeping reform in motion without asking too much of conservative forces or pushing them into confrontation.

Gorbachev was in a strong position in the debate on foreign policy and disarmament. His first trips abroad had given the Soviet population the feeling that their General Secretary could meet and talk with Western leaders with confidence and as an equal. Television, which relayed pictures of his visits to London, Paris and Reykjavik, had also naturally shown Raisa, and Soviet women noticed with satisfaction and even pride that, in dress and appearance, she held her own with the wives of Western leaders. Gorbachev's new, less confrontational foreign policy contributed greatly to strengthening his position. The Soviet population now hoped, for the first time in many years, that a lasting peace could be secured. They saw indications that the government might be ready to withdraw its troops from Afghanistan, and they were optimistic that the negotiations on arms limitation or disarmament would reduce the pressure on the economy and contribute to an improvement in the standard of living. At summit conferences Gorbachev regained the ground he had lost at home both to the conservatives and to radical reformers such as Yeltsin.

Gorbachev's meeting with Ronald Reagan in the White House in December 1987 appeared almost like a peace celebration to Soviet television watchers. What the Americans called 'Gorbymania' also came over on screen. Gorbachev's immersion in the masses, his car stopping so that he could shake hands with enthusiastically friendly Americans, carried as much weight as the signing of the agreement to reduce medium-range missiles and the indications that the Soviets and the Americans were reaching agreement on how to end the war in Afghanistan. This made no small contribution to Gorbachev's standing in the Soviet Union.

The INF agreement laid down for the first time the conditions for the destruction of an entire range of nuclear weapons. Although the Soviet military had to accept the fact that the numerical superiority of their medium-range missiles was being sacrificed, at the same time the West was losing the only missiles it possessed that could reach targets in the Soviet Union from European (mostly German) territory.

It was later revealed that in Washington Gorbachev had succeeded in carrying through his plans for disarmament despite the objections of the military, whose older leaders had at first refused to countenance any reduction of Soviet strength. While economic reforms made only slow progress and hardly brought any practical improvements, while democratisation resulted only in friction and rejection among state and Party functionaries, successes in foreign policy were clearly recognisable. The international reputation of the Soviet Union had grown with Gorbachev's prestige and popularity. He knew that he needed his successes in foreign policy if he was to hold his own in the struggle for power in the Party.

In the West, as in the Soviet Union, it is customary to regard this conflict in the Kremlin as a specifically Soviet phenomenon. But since the mid-eighties what had been taking place in the collective leadership could be compared with the struggles for position which are commonplace in coalition governments in the West. Communist terminology obscures such similarities by insisting on the unity of the leadership and the entire Party. In fact, in the mid-eighties the Soviet leadership team included members who took very different positions on state policy. All were conscious of the necessity of winning the support of larger groups in the Party, the administrative apparatus, among intellectuals and in the population, which resulted in a degree of accountability rare in Soviet politics.

Gorbachev increasingly filled influential posts in the Party leadership with his own supporters, but did not punish or expose those who were forced out. Nor did they lose their privileges or their luxury flats. This made the process of change easier for Gorbachev, but by the spring of 1988 he had still not achieved a broad enough power base to be able to take decisions quickly and alone, confident of the support of the Party.

In the spring of 1989, ninety-eight members and candidates of the Central Committee resigned, declaring that they were too old to do justice to the tasks ahead in a time of rapid change. This enabled Gorbachev to reduce the number of conservatives in the Central Committee by twenty-four, but he still did not have a majority for reform among the 251 members of the new Central Committee. At the beginning of 1990 the Politburo was still predominantly made up of men who viewed rapid change with distrust – even if, like Ligachev, they had fought on Gorbachev's side in the battle against corruption in the Party apparatus.

This had already become apparent in 1988, in the battle over the country's future political direction that peaked in the so-called 'newspaper feud' between *Sovietskaya Rossiya*, the Party organ of the Russian Federation, and *Pravda*, the organ of the Central Committee. On 13 March a letter from an unknown university teacher from Leningrad, Nina Andreyeva, appeared in *Sovietskaya*

Rossiya. She professed her faith in the rigid principles of traditional Marxism-Leninism, and branded the opening of pluralist, if still limited, political debate as an attack on the leading role of the Party. For months *Sovietskaya Rossiya* had been publishing articles that were neostalinist, antisemitic and hostile to *glasnost.* Copies of the Andreyeva letter were distributed in Moscow and other cities, and placed in the letterboxes of functionaries and intellectuals.

It was clear that the letter was not simply a spontaneous expression of one individual's outrage, but a carefully prepared document against the whole policy of *perestroika.* Its author deplored the break with the Stalinist past, demanded a positive assessment of the role and personality of Stalin and rejected the demand that surviving Stalinists should show remorse. She castigated an emerging 'left liberal Socialism' that set itself up as a bearer of a humanism free of class conflict, and reproached neo-liberals and Trotskyites with betraying the working class and the Russian nation. Antisemitic undertones were unmistakable. Nina Andreyeva flattered the national pride of Great Russians, but at the same time she attacked those who declared that the enforced collectivisation and the destruction of the peasantry was misguided and evil.

Many Moscow intellectuals doubted whether Nina Andreyeva was the sole author of the letter. They believed that it must have been added to or edited by Yegor Ligachev or his colleagues. But in fact the letter was largely the work of the old teacher, who still retains her fanatical admiration of Stalin and her dogmatic Marxism-Leninism. Ligachev and his staff did not write the letter, and are even said to have cut sections that were aimed too clearly at Gorbachev and his demands for democratisation. But it was evident that Ligachev essentially approved of the contents of the letter. Its Russian nationalist tone, combined with its defence of Stalin and the leading role of the Party, resembled the statements of the conservative politicians surrounding him.

The letter appeared as Gorbachev was leaving for a visit to Belgrade, which gave the conservative forces time to give it the appearance of an official document. For a few days the letter was used in Party organisations and in the army as evidence of a new turn in Soviet policy. The situation was dangerous for Gorbachev. At the worst, a disconcerted Party apparatus could be converted to a conservative policy. At best the Party would be locked into a new struggle over its direction.

Gorbachev returned from Yugoslavia five days after the publication of the letter, and it was two weeks before he refuted it at a meeting of the Politburo. *Pravda* published a response on which Alexander Yakovlev and his colleagues had worked, with Gorbachev's assent. The Andreyeva letter was described as a statement of a conservative and dogmatic attitude that opposed any attempt at reform. The forces that had used the letter as an ideological manifesto against *perestroika* were reproached with jingoism and a fatalistic interpretation of history. Anyone who defended Stalin in this way also approved the use of Stalinist methods against developments leading to democracy, which relied on the freedom of thought and speech. The article did not say which were the forces in the Party that wanted to halt the reform process, nor did it name names. Its reprimands were directed against the editors of *Sovietskaya Rossiya*. By publishing the letter they had irresponsibly backed an attempt to revise the decisions of the Party.

The editors of *Sovietskaya Rossiya* printed the article from *Pravda* without comment, admitting ten days later that printing the letter without taking up an editorial position had been a mistake. But their self-criticism did not go far: the editors clearly felt that there was an approximate balance of power between the conservatives and Gorbachev's supporters, and that there was no need for them to admit to fundamental mistakes.

With the *Pravda* article, however, Gorbachev made it clear to the Party functionaries and the population that there would be no turning back, even if the battle for *perestroika* was hard, and would get harder. This was a necessary signal to the Party functionaries in the provinces. Gorbachev needed their support in the election of candidates to the Nineteenth Party Conference, at which profound and long-term changes in Soviet society and its political structures were to be initiated. The majority of the functionaries only followed the new line unwillingly, and Gorbachev could not allow them to get the impression that their resistance would find support in high places.

The process of destalinisation continued, despite the confusion created by the Nina Andreyeva letter. Newspapers described the crimes of the period, showed photographs of mass graves, gave the numbers of Stalin's victims, which far exceeded the 'thousands' cited by Gorbachev in the autumn. Communist leaders whom Stalin had dismissed and 'liquidated' were rehabilitated. In many cases this rehabilitation recognised the death sentences as illegal, but made no statement about the correctness of the victims' positions. Nikolai Bukharin, however, was more comprehensively rehabilitated. The New Economic Policy of the twenties which he had founded in theory was again taken up and debated as the precursor of current reforms. Every case of rehabilitation was a moral condemnation of Stalin's policy of enforced co-ordination, strengthening the right to debate alternative kinds of Socialism and therefore permitting the development of a plurality of opinion in the modern Soviet Union.

But the situation remained unclear. The basic organisations of the apparatus nominated the delegates to the Nineteenth Party Conference, and it seemed that a definite majority of the delegates sent to Moscow would be conservatives. Gorbachev optimistically announced that the conference would give *perestroika* a new impetus, and he succeeded in winning the Politburo's acceptance of ten points which made the general direction of his policies the guideline for the forthcoming conference. This was a considerable victory.

It had become evident that Gorbachev's critics from the right and the left differed substantially in their political behaviour. The reform wing was inclined to attack Gorbachev's decisions, and even Gorbachev himself. Among the conservatives, on the other hand, the old habit prevailed of accepting Politburo decisions without contradiction, and of not criticising the top Party leadership. This meant that the conservative representatives from the Party apparatus and the provinces who were made uneasy by change would follow the line approved by the Politburo and the Central Committee – perhaps reluctantly, but without voting against the decisions of the leadership.

The ten points had been largely written by Gorbachev himself, and elaborated by trusted colleagues. They had clearly been set down quickly, and some sections appeared to have been added later, apparently in order to placate the conservative majority. Most Central Committee members maintain that Boris Yeltsin hardly saw the ten points before the conference, and he certainly expressed no opinion on them. But after their acceptance by the Politburo they were considered as approved by the leaders of the

Party apparatus, and therefore already accepted by the majority of the delegates.

Gorbachev's calculations worked. It was noticeable that most delegates to the Party Conference agreed to the programme of social change without enthusiasm. Those speakers who set limits to *glasnost* and who wanted to slow the pace of *perestroika* received the loudest applause. Even Viktor Afanasiev, the conservative editor of *Pravda*, asked the delegates why they were so hostile to the press and to *glasnost*.

General Gromov, Commander in Chief in Afghanistan, gave one of the reasons in his speech: 'No one, not one person in this country, has the right to destroy the belief of the young that service is a duty, and that military service is not lived through for nothing.' Others like him justified the war in Afghanistan and the sacrifices of the soldiers. They refused to accept the allegedly nihilistic criticism of the war in the press, which they considered had been instigated by those elements in the country which planned to destroy the people's faith in the past and their trust in the older generation.

The writer Yuri Bondarev warned dramatically of an ideological amorality, which would bring with it spiritual ruin. The attempt 'to do without leadership, to do without guidance in any area', said Vladimir Karpov, the new First Secretary of the Writers' Union, was a kind of idealism that would lead to anarchy. There were some courageous and brilliant speeches in defence of *glasnost*, but Gorbachev's true position remained unclear. The speakers he interrupted most sharply and impatiently were invariably those who spoke out most decisively for more openness and democracy. He let the more conservative speeches of members of the apparatus pass.

Most of the speakers had something alarming to report from their region. Of the farmers it was said that since the Brezhnev era they had been living in a kind of serfdom. They had borne the burden of collectivisation and industrialisation. The state had taken everything from them, and now it was time to give them something back so the supply crisis could be eased, one delegate shouted. The Health Minister admitted that infant mortality in the Soviet Union was higher than in many Third World countries. The Chairman of the Committee for Education acknowledged that half the country's schools were without heating, running water or sewerage, and the nursery schools could not provide places for one and a half million children. The First Secretary of the Young Communist League reported that it had not been possible to overcome distrust and indifference towards the new line. Many young people thought of it as a mere churning out of revolutionary phrases. Speakers attributed the workers' lack of enthusiasm for the reforms to the fact that the shops were still empty and the prices rising.

A few delegates spoke as if economic reform had already failed. The economist Leonid Abalkin, whom Gorbachev considered an expert and whom he was later to make Deputy Prime Minister, doubted whether there had really been a turn in economic policy and whether the leadership actually understood the problems.

But, in their accustomed fashion, the delegates unanimously accepted the points put forward by Gorbachev. They declared radical economic reform necessary because the country stood on the brink of an economic crisis. They voted for further measures for a far-reaching democratisation of the Party, with functionaries to be elected by secret ballots, not just selected by the Party apparatus. They supported the creation of a Socialist state in which not only were citizens answerable to the state, but the state to the citizens, and where the administration of justice was based on the law and not on the instructions of Party Secretaries. They accepted that independent social organisations and unions could voice their interests and take part in the political debate.

It is hard to say whether any of the delegates fully recognised the significance of point six, which proposed the full restitution of the powers of the Soviets of People's Deputies. According to the constitution, the Soviets are parliaments. But for decades they had been mere mock parliaments, whose members were selected by the Party leadership and who therefore felt accountable to the Party rather than the people. The organs of the executive would now once again be subordinate to these Soviets and their delegates. This would give the elected parliaments of the Soviet Union a stronger role, and would place them on an independent, equal footing with the Party and its power apparatus.

Probably neither the delegates nor even the high functionaries were aware of the effects this would have on the role of the Party. They had long been accustomed to Party rule not being diminished by these gestures towards democracy, and were visibly astonished when Gorbachev asked for their consent to a change for which they were unprepared. Gorbachev's proposal implied that in future certain Party and government functions would be amalgamated. For example, the Party Secretary of a district would also be the Chairman of that district's Soviet. On the surface, this seemed to represent a strengthening of the Party Secretaries. But as he had to put himself up for election to the district Soviet, he therefore ran the risk, if defeated, of losing his Party post.

Perhaps this did not seem a serious risk to the delegates, who had never seen the electoral defeat of a Party candidate in their lives. But they were speechless when Gorbachev proposed that this principle of amalgamation should extend to the two highest offices of the Party and state. The General Secretary of the Party would also be the State President after a Congress of People's Deputies had been elected, and would have powers substantially greater than those formerly possessed by Chairmen of the Presidium of the Supreme Soviet in their predominantly symbolic roles. Some delegates saw Gorbachev's proposal as a move to appropriate total power, comparable to Stalin's. They had not realised the shifts of power that would come about as a result of Gorbachev's proposed changes. The leader of the Party and state would have more power at his disposal in his state office than in his Party role. The principle of secret elections contested by several candidates would weaken the Party apparatus. Open elections to the Soviets, even if no other political parties were permitted, would lead to parliamentary organs of control that would no longer be dependent on the apparatuses of Party and government. Gorbachev himself, with powers that corresponded to those of the American President, could shift the focus of his activity from the Party to the government apparatus if the Party functionaries resisted his changes. An Italian Communist who attended the Conference as a guest summed up her reaction: 'Gorbachev is fed up with these Party functionaries. He wants to dissolve the organisation by way of elections.'

The strengthening of the future role of a Chairman of the Supreme Soviet, which seemed tailored for Gorbachev himself, alarmed his supporters on the reform wing. They doubted whether this concentration of power was a step towards democratisation. Gorbachev even reproached his advisor Leonid Abalkin with not understanding the reform of the system, because the future Deputy Prime Minister had serious misgivings about whether Soviet society could actually be democratised under the existing organisations and by maintaining one-party rule.

The outcome of the Party Conference was ambiguous. The resolutions that the delegates accepted were not made public until four days later, after a Politburo meeting at which they were probably edited or revised. Gorbachev's demand for a concentration of power in the Chairman of the Supreme Soviet was watered down. How this resolution could be realised was not to be debated until 21 June, at a plenary session of the Central Committee at which Gorbachev himself, as Chairman of the Commission, would work out the necessary measures for the realisation of the reforms. As he had often done in the past, Gorbachev had taken a step back in order to advance. The *glasnost* debate, which was again taken up in the Politburo after the Conference, produced a formula that was practically a charter for more openness in the media: 'No one has a monopoly on the truth, and there is also to be no monopoly on openness.' The Communist Party had never before conceded this.

Gorbachev's summing-up urged the delegates to renounce the 'blind faith in a bright future', and formulated his aims in restructuring: 'A new, human face of Socialism'. This was the very goal that had been proclaimed twenty years earlier in Prague, before the Soviet Union and its allies sent in the tanks.

CHAPTER 10

Opponents

The inactive majority of Party functionaries were naturally unable to keep up with the reformers who surrounded Gorbachev. But change in Soviet society was now moving even faster than the Party. As a result of the greater openness in the media, dissatisfaction was no longer confined to muttered complaints from Soviet citizens queueing for food. Increasingly, in letters to the papers, workers risked criticising the managers of their enterprise or their city administration and complained about the food shortages, which had worsened since the beginning of *perestroika*. 'Now we've got *perestroika*, but where are the sausages?' works committees asked in broadcasts on Soviet television. Those who had gained most from the changes so far had been scientists and writers whom *glasnost* had given the right to free speech.

But the openness of debate had also encouraged varied groups of the population to band together to represent their own interests. This had not been allowed by the KGB and the Party in the past. Now so-called 'informal unions' were created. According to the press, by the beginning of 1988 thirty to forty thousand such groups had already been formed throughout the country.

Many of them were made up of young people. Their subculture had previously been suppressed, but now rock groups and fan clubs met in attics and cellars. The lyrics of foreign and Russian rock songs satisfied their unfocused rebellion against adult life. These groups also served as an alternative to the Communist Youth League, which had previously monopolised their leisure time.

Other groups were concerned with social issues. One of the first of these called itself 'Compassion'. It was officially admitted that 40 million people in the Soviet Union lived below the poverty line, and the young founders of Compassion felt that the care provided for the poorest members of society by the state needed to be supplemented by the charity of other citizens. Their care for the old and the sick won the support of the administration, enterprises and the *Komsomol*. They were considered politically harmless, but the fact that they had banded together voluntarily and independently broke the monopoly of the Party, which alone had formerly been allowed to organise social work.

Other groups quickly aroused the suspicion of the authorities, particularly the environmentalists, who blockaded building sites, tried to save historic buildings from demolition, and protested against nuclear power stations. They were often supported by well-known scientists and writers who had previously submitted petitions against the destruction of the environment to the Politburo, without going public. Ecology groups who put the strategy of passive resistance to the test were quite new in Soviet society.

There were also groups which worked voluntarily at weekends rebuilding ruined churches, and some of these were connected to a new movement that under the name 'Pamyat' – memory – aimed to revive the national heritage of Russian culture. Pamyat quickly gained support, but the demonstrations of its most radical wing showed that not every relaxation of centralised control would necessarily lead to a liberalisation of Soviet society. In the Pamyat rallying cries the old catchphrases of Russian chauvinism reappeared, and beneath them could be detected traditional Russian antisemitism. In the altered political climate Pamyat was tolerated, and some Party functionaries appeared to seek allies among the nationalist conservative forces for the battle against *glasnost* and *perestroika*.

Opposing forces also gathered. From Moscow to the provinces committees of the 'Memorial' alliance were formed, which wanted to keep alive quite different memories from those of Pamyat. They spoke out for a public reappraisal of the tyranny of Stalinism, for the rehabilitation of its victims and the building of memorials.

In many enterprises and cities political clubs for the support of *perestroika* were formed, at which the changes were discussed and the most active supporters of democratisation met. These groups were tolerated as 'informal associations'. New political parties were still forbidden, and oppositional groups carefully avoided the word 'party'. In Moscow a group called the Democratic Union came forward with a demand for a multi-party system, free unions and the national republics' right to demonstrate on Pushkin Square for self-determination. The Soviet authorities regarded these activities with less patience than those of the more informal groups. In 1989 demonstrations by the Democratic Union were forbidden and broken up by the police. But such intervention was usually followed by punishments that were mild in comparison to the brutal repression of former times: a few days in prison or a fine. As a result there were always demonstrators prepared to demand multi-party democracies in the city centres of Moscow and Leningrad. The political leadership had no wish to return to a climate of persecution or suppression, which would have stifled all attempts at democratisation.

Away from the cities of the Russian Republic the 'informal groups' had already set in motion quite different movements, of which the Party leadership in Moscow was unaware. In Armenia, for example, a network of groups, led by highly respected scientists and artists, had formed to protest against the destruction of the environment. Their struggle against the chemical and nuclear industries had turned into a battle for the survival of their country. This combination of ecological and nationalist demands lent the movement a dynamism that the informal groups in the capital lacked. Old nationalist demands in Transcaucasia reawoke, and a violent conflict broke out with its neighbour Azerbaidjan. Moscow tried to keep the conflict secret, resorting to the old measure of a news blackout, but an unofficial network of communications now extended throughout the Soviet Union, and the Party's monopoly on information no longer existed. Armenian information services and organisations distributed televised records of demonstrations to foreign news correspondents. The Supreme Soviet of the Armenian Republic and a large section of the Party organisation there showed solidarity with the national movement. The once monolithic Party had disintegrated into separate blocs.

In the three Baltic republics developments were outwardly less dramatic. But since 1986 far-reaching plans aimed at giving the republics economic independence within the Soviet Union had been intensively worked on, with the public support of the Party leadership and the government. This took place under the banner of support for *perestroika*, whose aims for economic modernisation could be more easily realised in Estonia, Latvia and Lithuania than in less developed regions of the Soviet Union. It seemed that the three Baltic states could show the way to *perestroika*, and Moscow saw no reason to cut short the debates on the improvement of the economic system.

But in the Baltic republics the demand for economic self-determination was merely the common denominator of many forces: persecuted groups which demanded national independence and secession from the Soviet Union; the newly formed Greens, who wanted to protect the natural resources and environment of their country from Moscow's ministries of industry; Communists who considered that the Party could only be saved if it boldly spoke out for national interests. Some leading Communist functionaries gained new popularity in their republics by placing themselves at the head of nationalist movements and emphatically representing the wishes of the population to Moscow. But soon they were no longer able to control the nationalist movements which, with the press and television of their republics at their disposal, could drown out the propaganda from Moscow headquarters.

The Communist Party's claim to leadership of the Soviet Union is laid down in Article 6 of the Constitution, which reads: 'The leading and guiding force of Soviet society, of its state and social organisations, the heart of its political system, is the CPSU.' The article states that the Party determines the line on domestic and foreign policy, thus ensuring it an absolute monopoly on power that places it above any government. But in the border republics this claim to leadership had already been undermined, and the path to a multi-party system was already being taken.

Elections for the Congress of People's Deputies began early in 1989. For the first time in over sixty years Party headquarters did not nominate the candidates, and the people would decide who was to represent them in the highest legislative body of the Soviet Union. The Party Conference the previous summer had built a range of security measures into the election process by which it intended to keep control of the selection of candidates. Other parties were not allowed to put themselves up for election. But although there were no opposition parties, stormy meetings revealed that in the eyes of the people the Party had lost its right to nominate candidates. Especially in the cities, the candidates most critical of the Party's rule nearly always prevailed. In many places the election commissions met with resistance if they attempted to manipulate the selection process.

Even in provincial cities thousands of protesting citizens gathered if, for example, the Party Secretaries removed a journalist from the list. To their astonishment the functionaries discovered that a large section of the Soviet population was vigorously insisting on its new democratic rights. Russians are traditionally thought to believe in authority and to be patient. Most of their history, apart from the short interlude after the Revolution, has been moulded by the Tsars, by Stalin's dictatorship and by the Party's monopoly of power. Now an almost anarchic desire for resistance erupted against the authorities.

To keep control of selection, the Party laid down in the electoral law that 750 out of the 2,250 Deputies would not need to stand for regular election, but would be nominated by social organisations. But even this means of steering failed. In the Film Makers' and Writers' Unions radicals and critics of the Party were nominated. In the Academy of Sciences the administration was unable to gain support for its proposed list of conservative candidates. After the administration of the Academy removed Andrei Sakharov from its list, young academics forced a new selection and succeeded in getting him and a number of others from the reform wing into the Congress of People's Deputies. In many social organisations critical delegates, whose chances in the electoral districts would often have been slender, were sent straight to the Congress of People's Deputies.

The Party apparatus believed that it at least was safe from such surprises. It had the right to select and appoint a hundred delegates who would not need to stand for election. This included Gorbachev. Thus the places of the Party leadership were guaranteed in the Congress, but by no means all the high functionaries found themselves on this list of a hundred. Some prominent conservative Party Secretaries of districts and cities were missing, and had to stand for election. Many were unconcerned, as they were confident of their power in their home regions. Gorbachev had taken the opportunity to force these opponents of reform to show that the people were behind them. Almost four hundred of them managed to appear as the only candidate on the ballot sheet of their district.

In most electoral districts, however, two or more candidates fought out the election. Never before had the Party apparatus, the bureaucracy and the system been so severely assailed as at the meetings held in the spring of 1989. Shortages became the main theme. A Professor of the Party Academy of Social Sciences informed voters that they would have to stand in long queues for meagre quantities of food that even cats would refuse to eat, while leading Party members would be supplied by special shops with sausages and organically grown vegetables. A general defended the space programme with the argument that the unpopular anti-alcohol campaign had been more expensive. A television commentator called the 18 million bureaucrats of the ministries and the administration useless eaters who prevented development, clung to their jobs and could not be pushed out even by Gorbachev.

No one had seriously expected the candidates' criticisms and promises to win over the voters. On the evening before the elections most Soviet observers believed that the voters would overwhelmingly choose those candidates who declared themselves moderate supporters of the Party and of *perestroika*.

The result in the most significant electoral district in the Soviet Union, Moscow itself, came like a thunderbolt. Boris Yeltsin had stood against the director of a car factory, a respected and successful Party member. The Party had done everything possible to prevent Yeltsin from winning. Proceedings had been initiated in the Central Committee to examine statements of Yeltsin's which were allegedly damaging to the Party, and which could lead to his expulsion. Leading Party members publicly attacked Yeltsin, calling him an unsuccessful Party Secretary and a superficial demagogue.

These attempts to crush a popular and outspoken critic were dangerous, and the Party leadership had overestimated its power. Their criticism of Yeltsin enabled him to appear as a martyr persecuted by the apparatus. In the days before the election mass meetings showed that a large number of voters were eager to declare their support for the candidate the Party was trying to eliminate. They organised groups of observers in the polling stations to see to it that votes for Yeltsin were not destroyed or invalidated.

6.7 million people were eligible to vote in the electoral district of Moscow that Yeltsin contested. He received 89.4 per cent of the votes cast.

Party functionaries received the shock of their lives. Yuri Solovev, First Regional Secretary of Leningrad and Politburo candidate, had no opposing candidate to beat and still lost. All but 15 per cent of the voters had simply crossed out his name. Reports of the catastrophe that had befallen many Party Secretaries only slowly reached Moscow, and were at first received with incredulity. In Estonia virtually the only candidates to succeed were those who had the support of the nationalist movement. In every major city in the Soviet Union the winning candidate was a severe critic of the apparatus and the government. In the rural districts, however, the apparatus had once again succeeded in manipulating the elections, and most of the Party's candidates prevailed.

Statistically, the newly elected Congress of People's Deputies was a congress of Communists. 88 per cent of the elected delegates were Party members, a substantially higher percentage than in 1981. But many of them were quite different Communists from their predecessors. The number of critical intellectuals from the worlds of culture and science had substantially increased. These people had become Party members in the course of their careers, but not *apparatchiks*. They were determined to make the Congress of People's Deputies the great tribunal for the debate on the future of the country.

Deep into the night Soviet citizens followed the battle of words being fought on their television screens by their elected representatives. During the day work in the ministries came to a virtual standstill while the sessions were broadcast. Industrial enterprises reported a fall in production because the workers were watching the Congress of Deputies. Lectures and classes had to be cancelled. The entire country was transfixed by this outburst of democratic debate.

The Congress's debate on economic policy had been eagerly awaited, but the foundations of the system were being tackled from every side. One delegate, a well-known weightlifter, dared to attack the power of the KGB and ask for the secret police to be placed under the control of people's representatives. There was open debate on who was responsible for outrages in Azerbaidjan and the bloody suppression of demonstrators in Georgia.

One Deputy proposed dismantling the Lenin Mausoleum and finally burying Lenin next to his mother, as he himself had wanted. The writer Chingiz Aitmatov described the idea of world revolution as barbaric. There were no longer any resounding speeches to be heard about the progress of the Soviet Union or the end goal of Communism. The conservative deputies tried to justify the army's 'international struggle' in Afghanistan, but even they did not contradict a small group of Politburo members who condemned the invasion as 'illegal'. The conservative majority in the congress seemed listless and disorientated, unable to do more than feebly caution the more radical delegates against criticising every aspect of the existing system.

Mikhail Gorbachev had to try to restrain and direct this confused group of 2,250 delegates, many of whom felt compelled to air the grievances of their voters and their long-bottled-up complaints about the country's politics. As the old Communist rule forbidding the formation of rival parties was still in force, the substance of the new delegates' positions had not been previously cleared with anyone. There was no anticipating how they would vote. The voting mechanism itself reflected the old days of unanimous endorsements of the leadership's views. At first, as Chairman of the Congress, Gorbachev had to attempt to count the votes with his index finger. Eventually counting centres for individual blocks of the immense hall were connected by phone to the presidium. It was obvious in the hall and on television that only Gorbachev was capable of directing this superparliament and channelling the enthusiasm for debate.

The image of a single man attempting to direct 2,250 delegates awoke distrust as well as admiration. Resistance came not from the long-serving functionaries, who almost out of habit still followed the lead of the General Secretary, but from the reformers, who made up a third of the delegates. They feared that the new parliamentary body would be incapacitated by its powerful Chairman. Many of them understood that, in view of the immense problems facing the country, Gorbachev needed power to get his reforms through. But if Gorbachev wanted to be both General Secretary and Head of State they felt that the democratisation process itself was threatened.

Emerging as the most important speaker was the man Gorbachev had brought back from internal exile, Andrei Sakharov. No one could accuse him of ambition or a craving for power. The nuclear physicist, the father of the Russian hydrogen bomb, was already a respected moral authority among his colleagues before he took his stand against the state with his demand for an end to military nuclear research. He had courageously stood up for human rights and democracy when this was still mortally dangerous in the Soviet Union, and for this he had been harassed, persecuted and banished to the provincial city of Gorki. For years his voice had only been faintly heard in Moscow, but courageous friends had seen to it that the world did not forget the man who had been one of the first to speak out against the destruction of the environment, and who even from his illegal isolation in Gorki demanded human rights for the oppressed.

Heinrich Böll wrote of him: 'He gives the impression of being dreamy, sometimes almost absent, but he is awake, always present, amiable and – this only *seems* a paradox – a humble fighter whose relentlessness is his strength. I'm tempted to call him a marvel, and it may be his apparent inexplicability that angers the Soviet rulers, that makes them malicious. They don't understand him, don't understand that someone who could relax and enjoy his fame as a scientist of genius, who, crowned with laurels, could enjoy his honours, should selflessly fight for something that, though laid down in almost every constitution in the world, is only fully realised in a few states – human rights. It is difficult, almost impossible, to explain to a fully established functionary, equipped with all the insignia and material trappings of power, that someone wants something *for others*, not for himself.'

The most powerful functionary in the Soviet Union, however, understood who Sakharov was. There can hardly have been an act of deeper symbolic significance in Gorbachev's life than picking up the telephone in December 1986 and recalling Andrei Sakharov from exile. Over a hundred other dissidents were released from penal camps and prisons at this time, but Gorbachev felt that a mere administrative act by the police authorities would not do justice to the stature of a man who would now resume his place at the forefront of the intellectual life of the Soviet Union.

The outward circumstances of this telephone conversation seem almost farcical. On the evening of 15 December 1986, several telecommunications workers appeared in Andrei Sakharov's guarded flat in Gorki and, without explanation, began to install a phone. Eighteen hours later, at about three o'clock in the afternoon, this telephone rang for the first time. Andrei Sakharov relates: 'A woman at the exchange said, "Mikhail Gorbachev will talk to you." Naturally I was quite surprised. Then I heard him say: "This is Gorbachev." "Yes," I replied. "Good afternoon." He informed me that the Presidium of the Supreme Soviet had decided that I could return to Moscow. Then he continued: "I hear that you have a flat in Moscow, so there should be no problem there. I hope you will resume your patriotic activity." I thanked him for my release, but said I was very sad because of the murder – and that is the word I used – of my friend Anatoli Marchenko in a prison hospital. He didn't take the matter up, but said he had received my letter of 15 January, in which I had appealed to him for the release of all prisoners of conscience in our country. He said: "We have made enquiries about all the names in your letter and freed many of them. Others however come into a special category." To this I replied that no special category had been mentioned in my letter. It dealt exclusively with prisoners of conscience, in other words with people who had been imprisoned solely because of their convictions and who had never used violence in defence of their beliefs. He was clearly listening, but made no comment. Then, so it seems to me, I ended the conversation. I don't know why. I believe we could have continued.'

It was a remarkable decision to personally phone Andrei Sakharov and release him. Never before had a General Secretary phoned a dissident. Many functionaries felt that Gorbachev's act could be explained by Sakharov's worldwide reputation. Even in the West some were inclined to see this dramatic release as a public-relations exercise. But the gesture was too large to be written off as a merely tactical move. Gorbachev knew Sakharov's 'Reflections on Progress, Peaceful Co-existence and Intellectual Freedom', which his wife Yelena Bonner had read out at the presentation of Sakharov's Nobel Peace Prize. He also knew of his views on world ecology and his demands for the democratisation of society.

Gorbachev, say former colleagues, felt an inner affinity with Sakharov, and believed that his contribution was vital to the great debate on change in Soviet society. The decision to recall Sakharov says a great deal about Gorbachev's qualities both as a man and a politician.

It was almost a year before Andrei Sakharov had fully recovered from the persecution to which he had been subjected, found his footing in the new political conditions, and begun to speak publicly again. The West was suspicious about his support for Gorbachev's reforms, but in no way had Sakharov become the mouthpiece of official policy. He was however convinced that Gorbachev's policies were moving in a direction that could lead to more democracy and human rights. But he was too much of an idealist to accept the policy of compromise with which Gorbachev was steering towards his goals. He asked for the reform policy to be brought into effect more rapidly and logically. His unconditional adherence to his principles made him a striking figure in the Congress of People's Deputies. The sixty-seven-year-old professor who walked to the speaker's desk a little distractedly, but obviously determined to enter into debate with Chairman and General Secretary Gorbachev, seemed to be the only opponent who matched Gorbachev's stature. Occasionally Gorbachev, wanting to move the Congress on to practical matters, grew impatient with him, but there was clearly a mutual respect and understanding between them that was stronger than their differences.

For many conservative delegates, however, Andrei Sakharov became the main enemy. When one speaker attacked Sakharov with particular venom and half the hall applauded, Gorbachev turned to his deputy Anatoli Lukyanov. He had forgotten to switch off his microphone, and many of the delegates heard his words: 'This has to be seen. They call this democracy.' Some delegates heckled Sakharov's speeches, some of them crying: 'Zuckerman! Zuckerman!' – as if the name Sakharov, derived from the Russian word *sachar* (sugar), marked him as a member of the 'Jewish cosmopolitan world conspiracy'.

The moderate liberal delegate Ira Andreyeva gives her account: 'The worst and at the same time most important moment of the Congress sessions came for me when they didn't want to let poor Sakharov speak. At the end of the session some of us ran over to the great man, to console him. I turned and saw that Gorbachev was still sitting alone at the presidium table. On the huge stage of the Congress Hall he seemed so small, so tired, almost exhausted. I felt a catch in my throat. This, after all, was the man who had made the whole Congress possible, without whom our meetings could never have taken place. I went to the stage and he looked up. I said, "Mikhail Sergeyevich, I want to thank you on behalf of the Moscow Group of Deputies." He didn't seem to hear what I was saying. He said in a sad voice: "Don't you understand what has happened? Don't you have any pity for the old man? I know that kind of delegate inside out." He seemed quite distressed at the way Sakharov had been treated.'

Two days before Sakharov's death, the two men clashed in the Congress of People's Deputies. Gorbachev had hurriedly wound up a point of order. He said to the delegates: 'That's all. Can we now deal with questions?' He then called up Sakharov, addressing him as 'Andrei Dmitryevich', in the respectful and intimate manner. There was uproar in the hall. Gorbachev raised his hand for quiet and said to Sakharov: 'New proposals.' Sakharov wanted an alteration in the draft on the law on ownership of enterprises and land. An objection had been raised that the draft was not in accordance with the Constitution. For this reason this essential piece of economic legislation was not being dealt with in the current session. Sakharov now wanted to change the wording of the text sufficiently to avoid conflict with the Constitution, so it could be approved more quickly. Gorbachev listened with scarcely concealed impatience. Then he said: 'I have the impression that you yourself don't know how your proposal could be realised, and we don't either.'

It was quite simple, Sakharov started to object, but Gorbachev had no more time. He interrupted Sakharov a few times with brief comments. Sakharov wanted to show him some of the telegrams and letters he had received supporting his position. 'Come and see me and I'll show you three portfolios with thousands of telegrams,' said Gorbachev, declining. 'I have 60,000 telegrams,' Sakharov replied. Gorbachev raised his hand: 'That's all. Let us stop putting each other under pressure, manipulating public opinion and leaning on it. That is something we will not do.' There was laughter in the hall. Sakharov laid his letters and telegrams on the table before Gorbachev and left the tribune. It was the last exchange between the two.

Gorbachev was the master of the sessions, but the entire population of the Soviet Union could see on television how confidently the Deputies of the People's Congress, and later the small body of the Supreme Soviet elected in their districts, performed. This was very different from the brief meetings of the Party Central Committee, which took place behind closed doors and of which only dry reports and extracts of speeches appeared in the newspapers. At the Congress it was Gorbachev and the Deputies who decided. The members of the Politburo, normally clearly set apart as the leaders of the country, were hardly visible, and only rarely spoke. At first special places had been reserved for them on the stage, and then in a kind of box of honour. Some delegates objected to this. Full of new self-confidence, a Deputy went to the speaker's desk and calmed the critics: it made absolutely no difference where the Politburo members sat, as they had in any case no role to play at the People's Congress. Finally the Politburo members sat in the hall with all the Deputies. Before the eyes of the Soviet public, power had shifted from the Party to the elected Congress of People's Deputies and the Supreme Soviet. Hardly anyone doubted that Gorbachev had wanted this transference of power, and had brought it about by his tactically astute politics.

But the elected Deputies also made Gorbachev himself feel their new power. They subjected him to an hour of questioning, during which he even had to give information about his holiday dacha, before electing him, against minimal opposition, Chairman of the Supreme Soviet, in other words *de facto* President of the Soviet Union. Gorbachev bore this unaccustomed trial with composure, but he sounded a little irritable when he assured the Deputies that, although he accepted such questioning as part of the democratic process, they were not to imagine that he had not noticed what some of them were aiming at. He then raised an index finger and said: 'Gorbachev sees everything!' The Congress of People's Deputies laughed.

The delegates also devoted plenty of time to the debate on the candidates Gorbachev had chosen for high state and government posts. Even Anatoli Lukyanov, whom Gorbachev had known since his student days, was only elected after a long and bitter debate. The designated Prime Minister Nikolai Ryzhkov had to justify his previous activity in the government apparatus for hours, before a large majority finally confirmed his appointment. Some new ministerial candidates were rejected, and Gorbachev had to use every means of parliamentary procedure to ensure that Defence Minister Dmitri Yazov could keep his office.

In the course of the disputes the alliances among the deputies became clearer. After over seventy years something like an official opposition again came into being in the Soviet Union, although of course it could not yet call itself even a parliamentary group. Around Boris Yeltsin and Andrei Sakharov there formed the 'interregional group'. Its four hundred delegates felt that they represented the advance guard of *perestroika* in a predominantly conservative congress. Most of them thought of themselves as Gorbachev's allies, who only wanted to push forward his policies more rapidly than the majority. But even among them were many who had been made impatient by Gorbachev's tactics. Up to this point he had had to fight the resistance only of the conservative Party apparatus. Now the democratisation he himself had brought about had created a new opposition on the reform wing of Soviet politics.

Gorbachev clearly foresaw the problems that would arise for him, but he considered them an unavoidable part of the move towards greater democracy. Perhaps he had imagined democracy as less problematic and complicated than it was proving. At any rate, signs of impatience and even intolerance increased during the debates.

Gorbachev had, however, won his fight for the leadership of the Soviet Union. He was now both Chairman of the Supreme Soviet and General Secretary, a position from which, it would seem, he could effectively see through his reform policy in the Party and the state. Yet Gorbachev's powers were not clearly defined, and could not be unconditionally converted into executive force. Moreover, he himself had limited his own power. Increased pluralism of opinion and democracy were decisive elements of his plan for the reformation of the Soviet Union. He could not rule like a dictator if these forces were to evolve. Formerly, the Party apparatus and the secret police had held the country together by force. Now, inside and outside the Party, various political groups had come into being. In many republics the nationalist movements had more power than the Party organisations and the old state apparatus. The relaxation of domestic policy, and the resulting growth in national, regional and local movements, threatened the Soviet Union with disintegration.

Even in the great Russian Republic, the heartland of the Soviet Union, the democratisation process had altered political consciousness. Gorbachev was leading the Central Committee, step by step, towards political pluralism. In this transitional phase from a one-party to a multi-party system, the political landscape had become confusing. There seemed to be no groupings within the Party on which Gorbachev could rely with certainty. In parliament and the Central Committee there were only informal groupings. Most of them publicly declared themselves in favour of Gorbachev's policies, but by this they all seemed to understand something different.

Before the elections for the Supreme Soviet of the Russian Republic in April 1990, Soviet sociologists attempted to analyse the new political forces that were taking shape in society.

The first group they identified as the 'Westerners'. They favoured a multi-party system, or an unclearly defined political pluralism, and took their bearings from Western European and American culture. In their view only a liberalising economic policy, with competition, a free market and private ownership of the means of production and of the land, could bring any hope of economic improvement. The sociologists classified 15 per cent of Muscovites as 'Westerners', but found that among people under thirty more than a third favoured such a radical restructuring of the Soviet Union.

The second group they called the 'left populists'. They wanted 'Socialism with a human face', a more humane society with greater rights for the individual. Many of their views accorded with those of the 'Westerners', but they wanted to set narrower limits to economic reform and private ownership. 17 per cent of Muscovites fell into this category.

The 'right populists' made up 25 per cent of those questioned, but only 17 per cent of young people. They criticised the state of the Soviet Union and the rule of bureaucrats, and distrusted the intellectuals, who, they felt, had won too much power in the media. For them the main problems of society were corruption, the black market and pornography. Sociologically the 'right populists' could be classified as workers and lower and middle ranking officials.

On the extreme right of the spectrum were the 'national patriots', with 5 per cent support, very few of whom were young.

Above all they wanted a strong state. For them, it seemed, the autocracy of the Tsars and the dictatorship of Stalin merged into a mystical idea of the Soviet Union, which had to be protected equally from liberal influences and from capitalism.

The sociologists described the largest group of those questioned as 'state supporters'. 27 per cent of Muscovites were uncritical of the Party and the state. They hoped for improvements, but did not necessarily want more democracy and liberalisation. The memory of victory in the Second World War confirmed their faith in a Soviet Union capable, in their eyes, of improvement even under the existing rule.

Here, in the once monolithic Party state, one can see the seeds of a Western European spectrum of political parties. But Soviet conditions have not yet allowed these vague movements to coalesce into organised groups. Even defining them as 'right' or 'left' in Western terms poses obvious problems. This confusion is increased by the fact that in all camps the leading spokesmen are Communists. For decades the most active people in the country had joined the Party. Now they became aware that in reality they represented various parties that were far more than mere factions. But while factions and parties were officially forbidden, candidates could present themselves both as Communists and opponents of the Party.

On such uncertain ground it was difficult for Gorbachev to find a reliable political base. He had the support of most of those on the reform wing, or 'left', but they were not uncritical of his policies, and their ideas were often contradictory. They pressed for more democracy, but at the same time urged Gorbachev, as Head of State and Party, to use his power to break the resistance of the opponents of reform. The 'right' also expected strong-arm politics from Gorbachev, but they wanted him to put the brakes on reform and limit the critical debate. As the whole country could clearly see the need for change, and as Gorbachev was the only man who could bring this change about, he attracted the support of opposing forces. He could not simultaneously fulfil all their expectations, and there was no tradition of balance and compromise in Russian politics. Gorbachev also had the problem that he wanted to govern by the rules of parliamentary democracy before he had brought such a system into being.

Gorbachev is the dominant figure of Soviet politics not only because of the offices he holds, but also because of the strength of his personality. But the new political groupings that are forming are looking for their own spokesmen, and for the first time men are appearing who regard themselves as Gorbachev's rivals. Among them is Boris Yeltsin, who quite openly claims this role.

After Gorbachev, Boris Yeltsin is the greatest political talent in the country, but he is more of a populist leader of the opposition than a man of far-reaching political ideas. He sees himself as a future leader of the Soviet Union. In the spring of 1990 he was elected as President of the Russian Federation, giving him an authority second only to Gorbachev. And his stunning electoral victory in Moscow established him as the people's tribune, who could win against the apparatus. Supported by a large number of intellectual helpers, he has become Gorbachev's harshest and most outspoken critic.

'Of course one can't go at full speed from the beginning,' he said in February 1990. 'I know change needs to come a step at a time, but I reproach Gorbachev for his constant compromises and half measures. In five years of *perestroika* no comprehensive programme has been worked out. We're building a house by putting in a window here or there, tiling a bit of the roof, and we still haven't built the foundations. The economic policy doesn't look very different from what was attempted under Khrushchev and Kosygin. And now the statistics show that there's no growth and that production is decreasing.' Yeltsin accused Gorbachev of having watered down his strategy for tactical reasons. His attempts to secure the support of all groupings in the Party for his policies had led to paralysis. 'If you keep Yegor Ligachev in the Politburo then you're giving the conservative forces time to consolidate and signalling to them that they're still in power,' says Yeltsin. 'After the Nineteenth Party Conference or after the last Plenum was the ideal time to get rid of Ligachev. Something binds Gorbachev to Ligachev. While Ligachev remains in the Politburo most Party Secretaries will think they have support at the top. And these are the people who are preventing the transition to a market economy.'

But here Yeltsin seems to have misjudged Gorbachev's calculations. He calls Gorbachev a general of *perestroika* without soldiers, and lists the many members of the Central Committee who are conservatives or supporters of conservative policy. Yeltsin himself had hardly been able to convince anyone in the Central Committee, and only a minority in the Congress of People's Deputies, and unlike Gorbachev had no remedy and no power with which to decisively change the Central Committee and the Politburo.

In January 1990, at the Central Committee Plenum, he was the only one to vote against the Party's new platform, and his political ideas remain unclear. For example, he claims that Gorbachev neglected developments in the Baltic republics for five years, and only went to Lithuania when the independence movement had become strong. He says that Gorbachev sent in the army too late in the Transcaucasian conflict, and that his policy of compromise triggered the revolts in which the populations of major industrial cities removed the local Party leaders. These are not the arguments of a democratic populist, but of a man who wants to uphold order from the centre. This recalls the arbitrary, volatile Moscow Party Secretary Yeltsin, who fired functionaries and officials but failed to control the Party apparatus.

Yeltsin expected Gorbachev to break the power of the Party apparatus, to permit opposing factions and parties and to put through a market-economy programme, despite the fact that in the committees a large majority of delegates opposed such reforms. 'I respected his intelligence and his courage, and I supported him when he began *perestroika*,' says Yeltsin. 'But he's changed since he came to Moscow from Stavropol. He used to be a modest man who lived simply. Now he can't bear criticism, he only hears what he wants to hear. At the November Plenum of the Central Committee he completely lost his self-control. He stood up, pushed his chair abruptly to one side and shouted: "Do you want the General Secretary's chair? Take it!" On other occasions he doesn't listen, but shouts.'

Others have observed these signs of impatience in Gorbachev, but attribute them to his being overburdened and exhausted. Yeltsin, who on the one hand accuses Gorbachev of a wavering policy of compromise, on the other imputes to him a dictatorial hunger for power that threatens democratisation. Yeltsin points out that he himself does without the privileges of the apparatus. His wife goes to the same shops as other Muscovites. He was unable to get medication for his grandson. But that, he says, is better than a life of double standards. When he talks about privilege he occasionally hints that Gorbachev has had four new country houses built, but does not give any evidence to support these accusations.

The dacha Gorbachev uses in Razdory near Moscow is certainly neither newly built nor his property. Somewhere in the Baltic states Gorbachev has another dacha, says Yeltsin, and he also uses a government dacha on the Black Sea at Pitsunda. Only one of Yeltsin's allegations has any substance at all. A new country house was built in Foros in the Crimea, not far from Brezhnev's dacha. Raisa Gorbachev wanted a summer house there, says Yeltsin, and it was built at great cost. In fact this is not Gorbachev's house, but the Central Committee dacha.

Gorbachev's Presidential salary is 4,200 roubles, and he receives no salary as General Secretary. Even if he did not need to pay the new tax of sixty per cent on his Presidential salary, his income would be extremely low by Western standards, although it is high in comparison to the average income of Soviet citizens.

When Yeltsin rebukes Gorbachev for privilege he likes to bring in the name of Raisa. He says that she is ambitious and has a strong influence over her husband. On one occasion he warned Gorbachev that the people could not understand why his wife accompanied him on official visits abroad. 'If these visits are criticised,' Gorbachev replied brusquely, 'then the cultural level needs to be raised.'

For whatever reason, Yeltsin has transformed himself from Gorbachev's ally into one of his most bitter opponents. If Gorbachev is not removed from office by a rebellion from below, prophesied Yeltsin, then the conservatives will seize back power. He is disappointed at the slowness of development. 'In Eastern Europe the people achieved more in a few weeks than we have in five years,' he says. His speeches contain elements of demagoguery, and he appeals to that part of the population which is disappointed by the progress of the new economic policy. Here he has won support from both the left reformers and the centre right. Part of his popularity is undoubtedly due to his rejection of the privileges other Party functionaries accept as their due. And many ordinary Russians are convinced by his demands for decisive, effective leadership that could quickly put an end to the shortages of supplies.

But some intellectuals who helped to plan the new economic

policy, and who had become disillusioned because Gorbachev had not carried it through, also went over to Yeltsin. They share Yeltsin's conviction that reform can only be achieved by restructuring the system, but even they are not sure how far he really wants to go. He needs the votes not only of those who want radical change, but also of those who fear a market economy. Yeltsin too, it seems, needs to be a politician of compromises.

Gorbachev has chosen another way. He uses the structures of Party and state to change them from within. This is a difficult balancing act, in which tactical and strategic compromises are unavoidable. One of the most politically astute of the liberal People's Deputies, Sergei Stankevich, believes that there are advantages and disadvantages if, like Gorbachev, one remains a part of the Party apparatus yet tries to fundamentally reform it. Gorbachev has been able to prevent the apparatus from turning openly and decisively against his policies. 'He grew up in the apparatus, and the apparatus feels it,' says Stankevich. 'He shows the people in the Party that he's one of them, and uses the ritual formulae they're used to. He has one foot in the apparatus, and from there he can begin radical reforms without a revolt immediately breaking out. With the other foot he's outside the apparatus, and he now has to shift his weight onto this foot if he wants to complete the reforms. But the apparatus is mistrustful, and the moment it feels itself really threatened – and radical reforms are, after all, a real danger to it – the organising functionaries change their attitude. The conservative forces are still trying to keep Gorbachev on their side. The future depends on whether Gorbachev is sufficiently determined to carry his reforms through against them.'

In this situation Yegor Ligachev could be either Gorbachev's ally or his opponent. Ligachev, like Gorbachev and Yeltsin, came to Moscow from the provinces with a spotless record. Yuri Andropov, then General Secretary, had entrusted him with the department that dealt with the Party's organisational work. Ligachev and Gorbachev had known each other since the end of the sixties, when Ligachev had headed the Commission for Youth in the Supreme Soviet, which Gorbachev took over from him in 1974. They had come to know each other through working together in Supreme Soviet and Party committees.

In Gorbachev's first years as General Secretary, when he rid the Party apparatus of corruption and incompetence, Ligachev was his most important supporter. Ligachev likes to imply that Gorbachev's election as General Secretary would have been impossible without him, and that they introduced *perestroika* together. At first he was the second man in the leadership, the head of the Secretariat of the Central Committee, responsible for the Party cadres and ideology. He backed Gorbachev when the policy of acceleration was introduced. But his ideas of the changes needed in the Soviet Union were always narrower than Gorbachev's. *Glasnost*, the new freedom of the media, struck him as a dangerous threat to the ideology of the Party. He opposed the increasingly outspoken criticism of Soviet history in newspapers and magazines. He objected with outrage to the representation of the Soviet people as slaves who had been fed lies for decades.

Ligachev's feelings struck a chord with many who had been made insecure by the new appraisal of history and society. They felt themselves personally injured by the massive criticism of the past. Under Stalin's leadership during the war they had defended and saved the homeland, and during the Brezhnev years they had uncomplainingly endured harsh conditions. The revision of the historical picture seemed to them a devaluation of their lives' achievements. Ligachev also spoke for the Party functionaries when he pointed out on their behalf that the average wage of those employed by the Party was only 200 roubles, which placed them twenty-sixth on the country's wage scale. When Ligachev spoke before groups of Party members he often won more applause than Gorbachev.

Ligachev believes it is an unassailable fact that the Party must remain the supreme authority in the country, answerable only to its own leadership. Political pluralism would threaten not only the Party's position, but also the very cohesion of the Soviet Union. For him reforms could not go beyond the modernisation of the one-party system. He felt that the stability of the system was threatened by *glasnost* and *perestroika*, by freedom of debate and economic reform.

Ligachev is not a good public speaker. He has the manner of a Party Secretary used to obeying his leader, like the old-fashioned Soviet Communist he is. But he is no reactionary opponent of economic modernisation. In the first years of *perestroika* he spoke out decisively with Gorbachev for a technocratic reform of the economy that would make it possible to catch up with the West. But there were always clear limits to his ideas. Rationalisation and technological progress would modernise the Soviet economy without leading to an information society. Modernisation was to be based on social awareness, as formed by Russian and Soviet history.

Ligachev was not slow in building a bridge between conservative Communists and Russian nationalists. 'The Party must firmly demand an explanation if the national shrines are neglected,' he said at the beginning of 1986. 'History, the Revolution and its monuments are a strong means of educating the people. And we must educate them in such a way that they protect the national spirit that lives on in historical and cultural monuments, in stone and bronze, in the uniqueness of the names of cities, streets and villages.'

While the catchword of the new policy was 'acceleration' Ligachev stood firmly at Gorbachev's side. But when it became clear that Gorbachev wanted more than just modernisation and a limited relaxation of the central command economy, Ligachev voiced misgivings. 'I never flew round the Statue of Liberty,' he said, alluding to Boris Yeltsin. 'I believe that we are marching to Communism.' Half-private small enterprises, restaurants and businesses seemed to him the first step on the road to capitalism, even if they were justified by Lenin's co-operative theories. It was easy to denigrate some of the new entrepreneurs as speculators who were taking advantage of the difficult situation, and Ligachev's criticism of them was popular.

That farmers might be allowed to own and cultivate their own land meant for Ligachev the beginning of the destruction of *kolkhozes* and state farms. The entire economy needed to be built on social ownership if the Soviet system was not to be destroyed. In the late summer of 1989 Ligachev came back from a trip to East Germany and Czechoslovakia with glad tidings: fundamental changes were not necessary in Soviet agriculture, because he had seen in the Czechoslovakian and East German co-operatives and state farms how successfully Socialist progress was being made in the collective economic system.

In an economic reform aimed at a Socialist market economy Ligachev saw the danger of a logical progression to new forms of enterprise that would evade central control and finally lead to the establishment of private property.

Ligachev's views have a large following among the Soviet people, as well as among Party functionaries in the ministries who see their jobs threatened. Some of the managers of industry are also afraid of the demands that would be made by a liberalisation of the economy. Pensioners and many workers believe that prices will rise after the reforms and that their already small incomes will be even less adequate. In a time of rapid change they were looking for stability, which Ligachev represented for them.

Actually, Ligachev had little need to fear a multi-party system. He could have been the leader of such newly formed groups as the 'United Front of the Working Population' and the 'Bloc of the Patriotic Movement', which like him held traditional Communist and Russian values. However, although Ligachev had been manoeuvred out of his strongest posts in the Party apparatus, he had never – unlike Yeltsin – openly opposed Gorbachev. For a long time he played down and blurred the differences between his and Gorbachev's ideas. He remained a man of the apparatus, for whom the appearance of unity needed to be preserved, as open opposition meant the first step to the formation of factions in the Party leadership and finally to the admission of opposition parties in society. This was just what Ligachev did not want, so he had to be satisfied with a share of the Party monopoly of power. As a conservative Communist, he relied on the inertia of the apparatus, but in the meantime even the apparatus had come to understand that without reform it would be unable to survive.

Gorbachev has introduced the Party to reform step by step. The renunciation of the Party's political monopoly, which had seemed unthinkable a year earlier, was accepted by the Central Committee in February 1990. Apparently Gorbachev had simply reformulated the Party's claim to leadership. In future it would fight for its position as the ruling party, he explained, but it would do so within the framework of the democratic process. It would give up its legal and political advantages and defend its programme in debate and in collaboration with other social and political forces. This was not the announcement of a multi-party system which had been demanded the weekend before in Moscow by 200,000 demonstrators, but it was nevertheless a turning away from the claim to leadership on which the Communist Party had based its power for seventy years.

The overwhelmingly conservative members of the Central Committee accepted that profound changes had already taken place in society. In practice there was already a multi-party system in the Soviet Union, Prime Minister Nikolai Ryzhkov explained, and the Communist Party could not ignore this fact, but would have to live with it. Less than a year earlier Gorbachev had still called debate on a multi-party system 'mischief'. Now the formation of new political groupings had convinced him that the Communist Party would lose its credibility if it were to oppose this development, as only a return to a police state could prevent the new awakening of society.

Gorbachev advanced step by step, only changing his ideas to ensure their acceptance by a majority of the Party. At times this made him appear hesitant and inconsistent. His closest collaborators, however, were working towards a strengthening of the system of government, whereby Gorbachev as President could tackle the economic and political problems of the Union more energetically. Gorbachev, as so often, revealed nothing, but his former assistant Ivan Frolov, since autumn 1989 Chief Editor of the Party paper *Pravda*, announced on 9 February 1990 that the Supreme Soviet was debating the introduction of a genuine presidential system, and that a majority of the 2,250 members of the Congress of People's Deputies would vote for this change to the Constitution. Then the Congress could either elect a transitional President of the Soviet Union or set a date for general and direct elections, at which for the first time in history the Soviet people could select their President. In either case the country would soon have the strong President it urgently needed in a crisis that threatened its cohesion.

By apparent hesitation and clever compromise Gorbachev had reached a stage where it seemed that the impossible had been achieved: he remained the leader of a Communist Party whose monopoly of power he had abolished, and was on his way to being the first elected President of the Soviet Union, who would no longer need to share his power with the Party apparatus.

CHAPTER 11

At Home and Abroad

Outside Russia, Gorbachev was already considered a politician of world historical importance. He had achieved much more than simply leading Soviet foreign policy away from its former rigidity and isolation. On his trips abroad he had cut a dazzling figure, and in the opinion polls of virtually every country he was far ahead of America's President Ronald Reagan as the world's most popular politician. His personality and manner had greatly diminished the distrust of the Soviet Union which had grown during the Cold War. For the first time the world was willing to believe a Soviet leader who declared that a nuclear war was no longer wageable, that peaceful co-existence meant more than merely a chance for the Soviet Union to catch its breath, and that the new political thinking had as its aim a genuine, long-term collaboration in the solving of global problems that threatened all of mankind. All over the world, people who had longed for an end to the arms race felt that their hopes had been realised.

This breakthrough onto the world political scene had been achieved by a man from a small village who had spent over twenty years of his life ruling a province far from Moscow. When he first appeared in the capitals of the West, people knew nothing about the roots of his political thinking. He was regarded suspiciously as the representative of a new generation of Soviet politicians whose skill at public relations simply concealed the old aims. What Gorbachev really wanted was often better understood by the people of the countries he visited than by their political leaders.

Gorbachev had first gone abroad in 1966 to study East Germany's agricultural policy. To his hosts he seemed an inquisitive man full of questions for workers and farmers. But he had not especially impressed them. They saw him as a man of moderate importance, possibly a future leader of the Young Communist League.

Hardly anyone took much notice of his first visit to the West. In 1975, as First Party Secretary of Stavropol, Gorbachev had visited West Germany and taken part in the German Communist Party Congress in Stuttgart, held to mark the thirtieth anniversary of the victory over Hitler. He had not been a conspicuous figure, but had taken as close a look at his first Western city as the short time permitted. What seems to have stayed most clearly in his memory is a conversation with the owner of a petrol station. To this day he refers to it in his talks with visitors from West Germany.

'Near Frankfurt I talked to a petrol station owner. He said to me: "Stalin said Hitlers come and go, but the German people remain. But then, at the end of the war, the Soviet Union split the German people." ' In his talks with the President of West Germany, Richard von Weizsäcker, Gorbachev added that the Western powers had been the first to support a separate state in Germany. And any realistic politician had to adapt to the existence of two German states.

On Gorbachev's second trip to the West, to Canada in 1983, his partners in discussion were no longer petrol station owners but the leaders of the economy. This time he came as a member of the Supreme Soviet and the Politburo and as Agricultural Secretary of the Central Committee. At first the North American press regarded him as merely a junior member of the Soviet leadership, but the Canadians discovered a lively, curious and open-minded man who could express himself in an almost American way, but without becoming too casual. His visit was not of outstanding political importance, but his experience in Canada taught Gorbachev that he could make an impression good enough to overcome years of hostile propaganda against the Soviet Union.

Gorbachev's performance in Canada also impressed the veteran Foreign Minister Andrei Gromyko, who as 'grim Grom' had created quite a different style of foreign policy. Gromyko was in favour of letting Gorbachev gather his own experience of foreign affairs, and Gorbachev was glad to be given the opportunity of seeing the world through his own eyes.

This distinguished him from the older leaders of the country. Gromyko had dutifully endured rather than enjoyed his hundreds of trips abroad. Mikhail Suslov spoke for most of the ageing Party leadership when he tried to talk Stalin's daughter out of travelling to India for her husband's funeral: 'What makes you want to go abroad? My family and I have never had any desire to travel abroad. It's totally uninteresting.' For most Soviet leaders the rest of the world was hostile territory, about which the best source of information was the reports of embassies and the secret service. If there had to be trips abroad, then they were to be carried out according to strictly regulated protocol, and limited to official speeches and meetings.

Gorbachev broke away from this practice. In June 1984 he took the opportunity to travel to Italy, representing the Soviet Union at the funeral of the Italian Communist Party chief Enrico Berlinguer. Italy's Communist functionaries, who for years had been attacked by Moscow as dubious eurocommunists, noticed to their surprise that this Soviet guest had no desire to lecture them. On the contrary, he talked to them about the internal problems of the Soviet Union itself, and evidently had less interest in binding Italian Communists to Moscow's line than in learning from the undogmatic thinking of a strong Communist Party in a capitalist country.

In December 1984 Gorbachev went to London. Although he came as the head of a delegation of the Supreme Soviet, this soon became virtually a state visit. It was known in London that Chernenko was ailing, and that Gorbachev could soon be the leader of the Soviet Union. But such political considerations paled before the impression Gorbachev made on his British hosts. In London careful preparations had been made to ensure that Gorbachev's visit would not be disturbed by human rights demonstrations, but from the moment he arrived it was clear that Gorbachev was a self-assured and confident man, who would not allow his visit to be restricted by protocol and security measures. He wanted to see, hear and discuss. He was witty and charming, but could also give a cool, carefully considered reply if human rights were mentioned. Even then, he did not lecture his audience in the style Westerners had come to expect from visiting Soviet leaders.

The Times wrote: 'The friendliness and humour of Mr Gorbachev and his wife's charm have made a great impression on their hosts.' It had in fact been a clever and unusual step to take Raisa to London, and it was certainly not the custom in Moscow at that time. Even protocol was unclear about how to treat the wife of a Politburo member and head of a delegation. When the delegation left Moscow Raisa had been nowhere in sight. She was already on the plane. Even when the Ilyushin landed in London she did not get out with the members of the delegation, but waited until the greetings were over and the official visitors had been driven away. On a state visit to Paris a year later things were already a little different: once again no one in Moscow saw Raisa board the plane, but in Paris she came down its steps with her husband. She was not to appear openly at both the departure and the arrival until 1985, on the way to the Summit Conference in Geneva.

Evidently there was disagreement in the Politburo about where the wife of the General Secretary could be seen and where she could not. For state visits abroad, Gorbachev could easily deflect criticism by referring to international protocol. But on trips within the Soviet Union functionaries and ordinary people occasionally asked themselves whether Raisa's presence was necessary, and what office the wife of the General Secretary actually held.

Such considerations did not bother the media in the West. Raisa was well dressed and attractive, and seemed to take an interest in everything she saw. She asked Margaret Thatcher where she had bought her earrings, and the next day went to Cartier in Bond Street and bought a similar pair. They cost several hundred pounds, which a man from protocol paid. In Moscow the rumour spread that Raisa had a gold American Express card, and had spent a fortune shopping in London. In reality she bought very little, and on her return she told the House of Models in Moscow, who had fitted her out for the trip, that she preferred being dressed by her Moscow dressmakers to buying clothes in the West.

But there can be no doubt that the fashions and lifestyle of the West fascinated her. This became even clearer in March 1985, when she described Pierre Cardin's *haute couture* clothes as 'works of art'.

Almost as much as Mikhail Gorbachev's style, this unexpected image of a Soviet woman began to change the ideas of Western observers. Perhaps the Soviet Union was different after all from what the West had believed.

At Chernenko's funeral, foreign guests of state noticed in conversation with Gorbachev that the Soviet Union now had a leader of quite a new kind. Previously, on such occasions, Foreign Minister Gromyko would slip his Head of State notes on foreign policy to be repeated verbatim, and would himself speak on particularly difficult matters. Now Gorbachev spoke off the cuff. Foreign experts noticed with admiration that Gorbachev almost always spoke without the notes which in most countries are customarily prepared by the Foreign Minister and his officials for answering questions on complex problems. Gorbachev not only had an excellent memory, he had undoubtedly studied the relevant issues closely. For his trips to the Summit Conferences in Geneva, Reykjavik and Washington, Gorbachev made a particularly important innovation. Leading Soviet scientists, writers and experts on foreign and economic policy accompanied him, and were always prepared to give information on new policies to journalists, who could usually find out very little from their brief talks with the main participants. They were so open and approachable that they outshone even the PR-conscious Americans. This brought Gorbachev's ideas far more attention in the West than could have been achieved by official press conferences. In restaurants and hotel rooms Gorbachev's experts carried on discussions on subjects ranging from the economic problems of the Soviet Union to the damage to the environment, and let it be known that the cost of the arms race was too heavy a burden for the development of their country. This gave them added credibility when they spoke about the new political thinking that would free world politics from ever-increasing military spending.

Here the full import of the Soviet Union's new direction in foreign policy became clear: if a nuclear war was no longer considered wageable, then foreign policy no longer needed to make the balance of the military blocs the main issue, and an end to the arms race was conceivable. If ideological factors were not to dominate the formulation of foreign policy, the relations between states could be normalised and economic exchange promoted. Formerly it had been an axiom of Soviet foreign policy that imperialist capitalist states, by their very nature, continually and fundamentally threatened world peace.

From the new perspective peaceful co-existence could now become a long-term co-operation between East and West that would help both to tackle the great problems of the environment and of mankind together. This was the ultimate aim of the new thinking announced by Gorbachev. Often those who accompanied him to Summit Conferences were able to present his motives and aims more openly than Gorbachev himself, who was not meeting the American President as a political thinker, but to negotiate the details of the balance of missiles. It became apparent that, in the course of a few years, there had been a fundamental change in Soviet foreign policy, of a sort no one in the West had considered possible. Gorbachev had understood that *perestroika* in his own country could only succeed against an international background in which growing trust opened the way to arms limitation and disarmament.

Some of Gorbachev's initiatives, such as the zero option on mid-range missiles, had been goals of Western politics in the seventies. At that time Moscow had resisted steps towards disarmament, opposing them with propagandistic global demands. After 1980 the prevailing aim in the West was for parity, or even superiority, of a constantly increasing number of weapons. By the time Gorbachev tried to ease the rigid confrontation of world politics, foreign policy and security in both East and West had degenerated to an obsessive counting of military hardware.

With unfailing determination Gorbachev battled against the suspicion and mistrust of the Americans and Western Europeans. His proposals were always a few steps ahead of the Americans', and he was prepared to act unilaterally if the West was not yet ready to reciprocate. In 1985 he had called a halt to nuclear testing despite the resistance of the Soviet military. He withdrew Soviet troops from Afghanistan without negotiating more than formal reciprocity from the Americans.

When negotiations in Reykjavik on the reduction of mid-range missiles failed because the Americans refused to give up their Strategic Defense Initiative, Gorbachev did not break off negotiations. After a few months he amended his demands and created the conditions that, for the first time in history, enabled the USA and the Soviet Union to scrap an entire range of nuclear weapons.

Without insisting on reciprocity he withdrew Soviet troops from Eastern Europe. Soviet concessions made it possible to success-fully conclude the European conference on security and to get the Vienna negotiations on conventional forces in Europe moving again after years of stagnation. Step by step Gorbachev worked towards the realisation of his great goal: the treaty to limit and reduce the most dangerous weapons in human history, strategic nuclear missiles.

His aims seemed more credible to the West because the Soviet relationship to the Socialist states in Eastern Europe was begin-ning to change fundamentally. If countries like Poland and Hun-gary chose the road to reform, they were no longer threatened by Soviet military intervention. The Brezhnev Doctrine, which in 1968 had justified the invasion of Czechoslovakia, was aban-doned. For the first time it was possible to negotiate with the Soviet Union on the rights of people and nations.

Gorbachev had had to fight in his own country to win over the supporters of the old thinking in the Party and the army. He succeeded because he could call in scientists and experts whose arguments and statistics proved that urgently needed reforms could only be carried out in a climate of improved international collaboration.

The attitudes of the old men around Brezhnev had been formed by the Second World War. They were convinced that peace could best be secured by military strength, and supported the demands of the army chiefs that Soviet forces be as strong as any possible coalition of opponents. Now the army had to accept that the state would only finance a 'reasonable' defence capacity. The new policy could be justified by the country's colossal economic problems.

Gorbachev's new thinking also put military and economic fac-tors in a wider context. In his view the world was uniting because of its growing concern with the ecological dangers threatening mankind, and for this reason peaceful co-existence would need to become the permanent foundation of relations between states. This ultimately meant that people must be able to vote for and form their own political and social systems. If Gorbachev describes *perestroika* and the new thinking as a revolution, then no aspect of this new thinking is as revolutionary as the changes in foreign policy. During 1989 it became dramatically clear how profoundly Gorbachev's politics had transformed the world.

The changes broke like a storm over Eastern Europe. The factors that had long bound the Socialist states to Soviet rule had disappeared. The authoritarian structures of government handed down by Stalin had lost their justification with Gorbachev's policy of *glasnost* and *perestroika*. With the ending of the Cold War the conception of the world as consisting of rival military blocs also ended, and scope for individual reforms and independent policies increased. This was a direct result of the politics of Gorbachev and his Foreign Minister Eduard Shevardnadze, who had been advised by the experts at the Moscow Institute. The changes that took place in Eastern Europe were not merely set in motion by Gorbachev's reforms in the Soviet Union, they would have been unthinkable without them. They therefore did not occur against his will, even if their speed was beyond anything he had anticipated or wanted. He had personally committed the diplomats and foreign affairs experts to producing quick results, because for domestic reasons he needed demonstrable success for his peace policy. Such success was not attainable while Eastern Europe's development was considered solely from the viewpoint of Soviet security, as a military buffer zone whose highest principle was no more than the maintenance of Soviet control.

In the years of stagnation and change of leadership Moscow had watched with distrust as the governments of Eastern Europe gradually acquired greater freedom of action. But uncertainty about the aims of Soviet domestic and foreign policy forced even those Eastern European Communist leaders who kept the Party line to look for individual solutions to their countries' problems. The Soviet model of the late Brezhnev period no longer offered methods for overcoming economic problems. If the Socialist countries followed a Soviet policy that had rigidified into confrontation with America, then they too were committed to increased expenditure on arms or to the installation of new Soviet missiles that increased tensions in their countries and made an improvement in living standards more difficult. Each of the countries in Eastern Europe looked for its own formula. The political differences between them were significant, but each government gave the others propagandistic and tactical help in defending and increasing their limited independence from the Soviet Union.

Naturally it was also noticed in Moscow that Soviet policy was losing its conviction and becoming increasingly less suitable as a model for the Party leaders of the other Eastern Bloc states who were faced with forces demanding political and economic changes. When these forces revealed their full strength with the emergence of Poland's Solidarity movement, the leaders loyal to Moscow hoped for the intervention of the Soviet Union, while Communists wanting reform were condemned by Soviet pressure to a lack of any definite line, and thus to immobility. It was already apparent that a reduction of Soviet pressure might lead to the collapse of the entire Eastern European system.

Hungary had been the only country to adopt a consistent reform policy, and as a result the relations between the Party, the government and the people were freer of tension than in any other Communist state. But Hungary had to tread carefully if it wanted to press ahead with its economic reforms without alarming the Soviet Union and exposing itself to renewed paralysing pressure. When Andropov came to power, and for the first time there was talk of reform, the Hungarians risked saying openly what in other Socialist countries was only being whispered – that the common interests of the Socialist states could only be realised if account was taken of the national interests of each individual country.

In East Germany Erich Honecker was a confirmed opponent of Hungary's political and economic reforms. But he also felt abandoned by Moscow, and began building economic bridges with West Germany and speaking of the special community of the two German states. Moscow at first reacted sceptically, then warned of a so-called 'German-German Spring'. The comrades in East Berlin were themselves responsible for this policy, said a Central Committee expert, and care would be taken that these trees should not grow too high. Relations between the two German states could not develop successfully if they had to peer at each other through a fence of missiles.

As its only formula for Socialist success in the years before *perestroika*, Moscow demanded stronger bloc discipline. But in all of the countries of Eastern Europe, those eager for reform as well as those still in thrall to Moscow, the scale of the crisis had been recognised earlier and more clearly than in the Soviet leadership. The capacity for scientific and technical innovation was greater, and plans for reform more developed, in all of these states than in the USSR. The fear that Soviet stagnation would settle ever more paralysingly on their own states, making the resolution of social tensions impossible, had made the Communist leaders insecure. But most of them lacked the insight, political creativity and tactical skill to risk taking real steps forward on their own.

When under Gorbachev the floodgates of reform and free debate were opened, the dogmatic leaders of East Germany, Czechoslovakia, Bulgaria and Romania were unprepared, and were incapable of coping with the suddenly liberated social forces.

Gorbachev himself had hoped that the process of change in the Soviet Union and its allied states could be carried out without dramatic upheaval. He may have referred to *perestroika* as the 'second revolution', but he had a far-reaching, controlled process in mind. As late as 1986 he had written, in his book *Perestroika*: 'Since the end of the seventies contact between the leaders of the allied countries has increasingly degenerated to being merely representative, instead of dealing with serious political business. Trust in contact has faded. Today many things have changed. In the last two and a half years the Soviet Union together with its friends in the Socialist community has achieved a great deal. This we must and will continue. The entire spectrum of political, economic and humanitarian relations of the Socialist countries is at present being reorganised. The nature of this reorganisation is dictated by the objective requirements of both development in each individual country and the international situation. It will not be determined by subjective emotions.' Gorbachev is a politically rational man, and as a result he underestimated the scale of unrest that could be brought about by years of accumulated dissatisfaction combined with newly awoken nationalist feelings.

But when the great and general movement in Eastern Europe became apparent, Gorbachev knew that military intervention was not the answer. He expected the conservative Communist leaders who had balked at *perestroika* in their countries to nevertheless gradually adapt to a policy of reform, and to be able to defuse domestic tensions before they exploded. The changes in Poland, where the Communist Party was first ousted from power, were just acceptable to the Soviet Union because General Jaruzelski – even if under threat of Soviet intervention – had steered the way to a new political system. After Hungary, Poland became the most stable country in Eastern Europe by the end of 1989. The conservative Communist leaders who had refused change, on the other hand, were sitting on a powder keg.

This applied particularly to East Germany, whose leaders had hoped for too long that Gorbachev's reforms would be halted by the conservatives in Moscow. But *perestroika* continued, Gorbachev's position strengthened, and the situation in East Germany became visibly more unstable. Paradoxically, Gorbachev's policy itself seemed to make it possible for the East German leadership to keep to its rigid course, as one of the basic principles of the new thinking in the Kremlin was the renunciation of interference in the domestic affairs of allied countries. Now Gorbachev's team looked in vain for East German leaders who could command enough respect in their own country to be capable of getting through a new policy of reform. This would require an authority that did not rest solely on the secret service and armed might. On his visit to East Germany on the occasion of the fortieth anniversary of the founding of the state, Gorbachev had warned: 'Life punishes those who arrive too late.'

Gorbachev and Shevardnadze had known for a long time that the East German leadership was heading for serious problems, and that Honecker no longer understood the situation. But when Honecker was finally toppled by Party leaders who did see the extent of the crisis, his successor was not a man whose abilities were highly thought of in Moscow. Egon Krenz was an ageing Young Communist functionary, who on his lightning visit to Moscow gave the impression of not understanding his country's situation and of misreading the mood of the people. He also appeared groundlessly optimistic and sure of himself, and in his talk with Gorbachev seemed heedless of the General Secretary's warnings.

When Krenz finally gave in to the growing tide of refugees and granted East Germans the freedom to travel, the flood that had long been held back burst and swept him away. On 9 November 1989 the Berlin Wall came down. The Soviet Union, like the rest of the world, now faced a totally altered situation in Central Europe. No one could have predicted such a dramatic acceleration of events.

The toppling of the Berlin Wall was undoubtedly a consequence of Gorbachev's policies, even if it had not been their aim. Ten

213

years earlier, Soviet military intervention would have been virtually certain, but now it was not even considered. Gorbachev set about looking for peaceful and constructive solutions to the crisis. A return to the old power politics no longer seemed possible even to the conservative functionaries and army officers. It is not the least of Gorbachev's achievements to have convinced such people that the interests of the Soviet Union need to be secured not by tanks, but by negotiation and treaty.

Gorbachev knew that for a Soviet statesman German policy was a delicate area. For the old guard in the Party and the army, the victory over Germany in the Second World War had been the great event of their lives. Twenty million Russians died during the war, and the crimes and destruction of the German occupation are, even today, vivid memories for many Soviet citizens. East Germany, 'our Germany', was at the heart of Soviet security in Europe. The higher-ranking military found it difficult to stop thinking along these lines, and Gorbachev's opponents in the Party quickly began to revive the memory of the war. They claimed that the new policies had weakened the Soviet Union and lost its frontline bastion in Europe. Some said that Gorbachev had after all lost the war, forty-five years later.

Gorbachev knew his opponents, and had for a long time tried to keep the 'German question' off the political agenda. 'What has been formed by history is best left to history' was frequently his answer to questions about the future of Germany. But he had never fundamentally rejected German unification, and there was no need for him to see the toppling of the Wall as a failure of his policies. Like Shevardnadze, he saw the causes of the disintegration of Soviet power in Eastern and Central Europe as a consequence of decades of failed Soviet policy. Now a new order had to be achieved, by new means. But the collapse in East Germany was so rapid that there was no time for Moscow or the rest of the world to draw breath and steer the process by new political and military policies.

During this hectic period Gorbachev and Shevardnadze had to revise their assessment of the situation almost daily. What could have become a dangerous crisis in domestic and foreign policy was linked to a process of diplomatic negotiations. The new self-assurance and composure of Soviet policy was revealed by Shevardnadze's statement on the relations of the Soviet Union to the Eastern European states printed in *Izvestiya* on 27 February 1990. During the visit to Moscow of the new President of Czechoslovakia, Václav Havel, Shevardnadze said that he supported the democratic reform movement in Eastern Europe and that Moscow wanted to make this development irreversible. Relations with the reformed Eastern European governments needed to be founded on a basis of equality. Shevardnadze was repeating an assurance that Gorbachev had given in the course of his meeting with Havel. The Foreign Minister added: 'We consider everything that is now happening in Eastern Europe a democratic revolution that corresponds to our interests.' Gorbachev not only accepted the changes in Eastern Europe that were bringing non-Communist forces to power, but actually supported them.

This was only possible because relations between the Soviet Union and West Germany had developed more favourably than could have been anticipated at the beginning of the Gorbachev era. As late as 1985, on the fortieth anniversary of the German surrender, Soviet propaganda had attacked West Germany as a militaristic and revanchist state that supported the USA's hostile policy. The conservative West German government was at first hostile to Gorbachev's policies, which it considered merely a more skilfully presented continuation of the old Soviet quest for power.

The West German government's wish to involve German firms in the USA's Strategic Defense Initiative seemed deliberate provocation to Russian diplomats. Relations only improved when Foreign Minister Hans-Dietrich Genscher came to Moscow in July 1986. As well as extensive talks with Foreign Minister Shevardnadze, he also had a three-hour meeting with Gorbachev. This was, as the Soviet ambassador in Bonn, Yuli Kvizinski, explained, the beginning of an intensive political dialogue. Gorbachev himself said that his talk with Genscher went beyond the usual boundaries, and that a new page was now being opened in relations between the two states. In the Soviet press the attitude towards West Germany changed. Bilateral contacts that had been closed were reopened. The talks between Genscher and Shevardnadze continued in New York in August, and after the failure of the Summit Conference in Reykjavik the Deputy Foreign Minister, Vladimir Karpov, himself went to Bonn to inform the West

German Foreign Office in detail of the Soviet assessment of the summit.

In autumn 1986, however, relations deteriorated again. In a rash interview West German Chancellor Helmut Kohl described Gorbachev as a propagandist of the Goebbels type. In talks with the Soviet ambassador and in the Bundestag Kohl attempted to correct the impression that he had compared Gorbachev to Goebbels, but the Soviets now cancelled an arranged meeting of ministers, and there was only a brief discussion between Genscher and Shevardnadze at the periphery of the Vienna CSCE conference.

For several months relations remained strained. Talks at the highest level only began again in April 1987, when Deputy Prime Minister A.K. Antonov visited Bonn. The state visit to Moscow of West German President Richard von Weizsäcker brought about another significant improvement in the political climate between Bonn and Moscow. In his talks with Gorbachev it became clear that Weizsäcker shared Gorbachev's belief in a common European culture and the interdependency of all the countries of the continent. The West German people wanted *perestroika* to succeed, and Gorbachev stressed the importance of good relations between West Germany and the USSR. This, he said, was why the Soviet Union wanted West Germany to remain stable, as otherwise there was no hope for stability in Europe and the world.

Soviet distrust again awoke in summer 1987 when the West German government attempted to prevent the Soviet-American agreement on the reduction of mid-range missiles because it was unwilling to give up the Pershing missiles based on German soil. When at the end of August 1987 the West German government did after all give up the Pershings, the Soviet Union openly acknowledged this as a positive contribution to detente. The road to further political dialogue was again open. In the course of many talks Foreign Ministers Genscher and Shevardnadze came to regard each other as partners rather than opponents. Contacts between other ministers became more frequent, and German visitors to Moscow included Willy Brandt, who had always been highly regarded in the Soviet Union.

In October 1988 Chancellor Helmut Kohl came to Moscow. Early on in their ten hours of talks Gorbachev believed the ice had been broken. These were strictly political meetings, and there was little sign of any particular sympathy between the two men, but they were able to clarify their points of view and overcome each other's reservations. The visit was followed by the signing of a whole range of government agreements. For the first time a West German Defence Minister had detailed discussions with his Soviet equivalent, visited Soviet military units and gave a talk at the Military Academy of the Armed Forces.

Even at these meetings it was clear that the Soviet side believed that the two German states would remain separate for a long time, and that it was unrealistic to consider the 'German question' as central. Unofficial texts, however, make it clear that thought was already being given to the historical relations of the Germans and the Russians, and to their future prospects.

In July 1988 an article by Leonid Pozhivalov appeared in the respected *Literaturnaya Gazeta*, the title of which, 'The Germans and Us', brought a protest from the East German government. Pochivalov wrote that the division of Germany was not so old that one could talk of two nations. However, he felt that for the stability of the common European home there would have to be two German states, but urged collaboration with both of them, as they were equally important to the Soviet Union.

In a discussion on the future of Europe published in the IMEMO institute's journal, two political scientists debated the problem of a united Germany and put various opposing views. According to one, the German question had been finally settled. The other's view was that there could be no stability in Europe if a harmonious solution to the German question was not found. The political scientist Boris Orlov said that the problem of the national community continued to preoccupy the Germans, and that anyone who shut his eyes to this only encouraged those forces that might one day seek a violent solution to the problem. The common European home could only be built on a sure foundation if one did not evade debate on the German question. It was up to both German states to decide how the 'German community' should develop. A solution could however only be found in a new common European climate and in accordance with the interests of neighbouring states. The publication of this debate, if only in an information sheet for specialists, showed the climate of opinion in the foreign policy research institutes. The dogma of the unalterable existence of two German states was clearly being subjected to critical revision.

Mikhail Gorbachev's Bonn visit in June 1989 surprised even those Soviet observers who had witnessed the success of his previous performances abroad. Tens of thousands of Germans gave him an ecstatic reception. This would have been unimaginable a few years earlier. It was clear to Soviet television viewers that this was no organised jubilation, but genuine enthusiasm and friendliness. If for the German people Gorbachev embodied the hope for peace and a better future for Europe, then West Germany, for so long portrayed by Soviet propaganda as a threat, must also have changed, and could now become a partner in European collaboration. Gorbachev had become accustomed to success, and would have assessed his reception more soberly than the amazed Soviet viewers. But the experience must nevertheless have touched him, and he would have been well aware of the reaction these pictures would produce in the Soviet Union.

In the newly altered Europe the role of West Germany had significantly shifted in Moscow's view. The changes in Eastern Europe were irreversible, whether or not the interests of Moscow or Bonn coincided. Shevardnadze and Genscher had marked out a limited partnership in their talks, but everything had been made possible by Gorbachev's new policy, which created the prospect of a transformed Europe.

The results of this new policy alarmed the conservatives in the Party and many senior generals in the army. On the same day in summer 1990 that Gorbachev received Alexander Dubček in the Kremlin, Yegor Ligachev spoke on Soviet television about the dangers of the new policy to the security of the Soviet Union and the cohesion of the Socialist alliance. He said that the people of the Soviet Union were alarmed by the dismantling of Socialism and the return to capitalism and parliamentary democracy in Eastern Europe. It was not by chance that he spoke in front of the monument on the Field of Kulikovo, where once the Russian army had freed the country of Tartar and Mongol rule. Like other conservatives, he was of the opinion that Gorbachev's policy in Eastern Europe had lost what Stalin had won for the Soviet Union in the Second World War. The idea that the two German states might unite and become a member of the Western Alliance alarmed the Soviet Union's conservative politicians as well as its foreign affairs experts, who had been attempting for years to detach West Germany from NATO and to extend the Soviet sphere of power to the west. But a large majority of the Russian people were in favour of withdrawal from Eastern Europe and the reunification of Germany. Gorbachev had, once again, assessed the situation more accurately than his conservative critics.

Gorbachev and Shevardnadze succeeded in stepping up the Helsinki process in order to keep the course of change outwardly under control. As the process accelerated the dissolution of the eastern European empire, Gorbachev used it to secure political arrangements that would allow the Soviet Union to accept the new conditions without losing face. The prospect of new European security structures made it possible for him to justify NATO membership of a united Germany to his conservative critics. For that reason he had pressed for this at the special summit of the thirty-four nations, the summit that officially ended the era of confrontation in Europe, on 21 November 1990, two weeks before he was awarded the Nobel Peace Prize in Oslo.

The fact that a leader of the Soviet Union could now receive this prize showed the profound transformation of the international landscape. The extent to which the Soviet Union had changed was demonstrated by Gorbachev's first reaction to the award. He bowed to the memory of Andrei Sakharov, the only Soviet citizen to receive this prize before him. Sakharov, whom Gorbachev now honoured as one of the pioneers of peaceful change, had been in exile in Gorki under police supervision when he was awarded the prize and had not been able to accept it.

Gorbachev's achievement in foreign policy was of course more prized in the rest of the world than at home. Moscow citizens took a more detached view of the award. 'If only he could bring a little of his success in foreign affairs to his own country,' was the first reaction of the representative Igitian, and it corresponded to the opinion of many citizens who reproached Gorbachev with too many trips abroad and too little practical success in economic policy. While the controversy continued over Gorbachev's role in his own country, Gennady Gerasimov, Foreign Ministry spokesman, coolly concluded the debate: Gorbachev had, after all, won the Nobel Prize for peace and not for the economy.

It is due to Gorbachev that negotiated solutions can now be sought for the common future of Germans. If a peaceful and secure new order in Europe comes out of the unrest and confusion that accompany every period of transition, his place in history is safe. In any case, he remains the man who after decades of power politics opened the way for his people and the people of other nations to self-determination. It is said of Peter the Great that he opened a window onto the West for Russia, and it can be said of Gorbachev that he opened the door to a better future for Europe.

On 27 February 1990, the Supreme Soviet decided that in future the Soviet Union should have a President with new and increased powers. A few days earlier Alexander Yakovlev, Politburo member and Central Committee Secretary, had outlined why, at a time of radical change, the country needed a man at the top who was invested with great powers. The Soviet Union, he wrote in *Izvestiya* on 23 February, had no experience of democracy and therefore needed a symbolic figure of unity, a guarantor of democracy and security and a protector of the fundamental principles of the constitution of the state, who was accountable to the law and the people. A power vacuum had developed in the Soviet Union into which the forces of lawlessness and disarray were streaming. '*Perestroika* means democracy and people's power, but only the law can be relied on to guard democracy. The election of organs of power in the streets is not democracy but despotism,' he wrote.

The Soviet Union was in deep crisis. The controlled process of social change that Gorbachev had set in motion threatened to lead to disintegration and the dismantling of the Union. South of the Caucasus the republics of Armenia and Azerbaidjan were in a virtual state of war. Soviet soldiers, who were meant to separate the opposing factions and restore order in Azerbaidjan, had been fired on with machine guns and rockets. Azerbaidjanis had torn down the barbed wire on the border with Iran, burned the border posts, and were demanding independence or integration with Turkey.

In Georgia and the Moldavian republic, in the Ukraine and in Byelorussia, the strength of the nationalist movements grew daily. The parliaments of the three Baltic states were in favour of full independence and withdrawal from the Soviet Union. On 12 March 1990 Lithuania formally declared its independence. In the republics of Central Asia dissatisfaction and nationalist demands led to bloody clashes between various national groups. In large

Russian cities such as Volgograd and Sverdlovsk mass demonstrations had forced the removal of the entire local Party leadership. In the mining districts of Kemerovo strike committees of miners had practically taken over power in the administration after a long strike. Twice in February 1990 hundreds of thousands of people marched through Moscow, most of them demanding the rapid restructuring of society and the economy, but many also clamouring for the resignation of the General Secretary, the Politburo and the government.

The population of the Russian Federation was becoming restless. Forty-five years after the war, tens of thousands of refugees from the border republics of the Soviet Union were streaming back into the homeland of their ancestors – the newspaper *Argumenty i Fakty* estimated their number at half a million. Now a Russian national movement also formed, whose demagogic leaders made antisemitic speeches against Westernisation, reform and liberalisation.

The leadership in Moscow had underestimated the forces the reform process would unleash. When the conflict between Azerbaidjan and Armenia broke out, the Party and the government had held to the old Communist illusion that national conflicts were a dying remnant of bourgeois society which would vanish with an improvement in economic and social conditions. But promises of such improvement had not pacified nationalist emotions there or in other republics. It had not been possible, in so short a time, to realise the hopes placed since the beginning of *perestroika* in an improvement in the economic situation and in supplies.

After the nuclear accident at Chernobyl, faith in technology had been shattered. As a result of the fallout from Chernobyl vast areas of the country could not be cultivated for decades or even centuries, and many people had been affected, directly or indirectly, by radiation. From all parts of the Soviet Union came reports of ecological catastrophes that had destroyed huge stretches of land. One-crop agriculture and chemicals, the basis of centralised agricultural planning, had made the soil infertile and left thousands of farmers without work. Reports of malformations in children increased, and the life expectancy of people in the afflicted areas sank alarmingly.

But the reforms had not yet come into effect, as committees

of the Supreme Soviet were still working on their legal basis. Half a reform does not bring about a 50 per cent improvement in the living standard, but uncertainty and chaos. The selfishness of the enterprises and the special interests of regional authorities hindered the new economic policy. Republics and cities decreed that food supplies and other consumer goods could only be sold to registered local residents. Factories recruited qualified workers by promising them goods imported from the West. An intricate system of advantages and privileges now asserted itself against the common good.

Gorbachev had warned that things would be hard at first, but the great majority of the people no longer saw a convincingly directed course with attainable immediate objectives. What shaped their daily lives were rising prices, a rampant black market and an increase in crime. The Party's authority fell apart. The parliament, whose debates had at first fascinated Soviet citizens unused to democracy, now appeared as simply a forum for endless discussion, incapable of passing the laws that would improve supplies. It is easy for an outside observer to say that instability is to be expected during a process of profound change, but the people who experienced it found it confusing and painful after the initial enthusiasm for reform had worn off.

When Gorbachev became General Secretary he understood the problems that faced the Soviet Union better than anyone else in the Party leadership. But he also underestimated the difficulties of reorganisation, and assumed that the Soviet system was less fragile than it proved to be. He had come by his experience of the problems of nationalism with small groups of mountain peoples at the southern edge of the Stavropol region, groups whose nationalist feelings Stalin had broken by deportations and other enforced measures. Naturally he knew of the wider nationalist problems which had always existed in the Soviet Union, but he and his advisers concentrated on rational reform and projects for restructuring the Party, state and economy. He and his colleagues were well aware that this would lead to a new structure of the Union, and that central power and the rights of the republics would be reassessed, but the question of a federal constitution seemed less urgent than the general improvement of conditions in the Soviet Union. They only realised that nationalist tensions threatened to tear the Soviet Union apart when economic dissatisfaction in the republics combined with these strong nationalist feelings.

Gorbachev, his critics say today, should have taken stronger action much earlier, and sent in the Soviet Army. But this would have conflicted with his own political principles, and he hesitated during the unrest in Azerbaidjan until it was too late for the military to re-establish order. In July 1990, in a television interview that was never shown in the Soviet Union, Gorbachev said that he did not exclude sending in the army in a grave crisis. 'One must use force where it is required, and there are occasions when we have to protect our new revolution and the people themselves from danger. We have already been forced to resort to such methods. These were exceptional actions that were taken after great hesitation. Because measures of this sort are not simple. They leave their traces behind in the leading men and also in the regions affected. It is always necessary to seriously consider and assess the situation before resorting to force. This will all eventually pass. We will manage it. We are quickly learning how to conduct a dialogue and how to listen to each other. My chief aim is to allow this immense country, which has experienced such disruption, so many tragedies and such oppression, to start on a new path through life.'

Gorbachev knew that he would not gain majority support in the Party or the Supreme Soviet for a restructuring of relations between the Soviet Union and its republics until there was a clear awareness of the seriousness of the situation. Gorbachev has often held fire until developments reached the point of crisis. Then, against a background of apparently insoluble problems, he has driven his opponents into accepting his proposals for a solution. These tactics require patience and nerve, as well as swift resolution when the time is ready for action. Gorbachev hoped to win time, and was convinced that political and economic necessity would force a new relationship between the republics and the peoples of the Soviet Union, and that civil war and disintegration would not be the Union's inevitable future. The law ratifying the introduction of a presidential system was driven through the Supreme Soviet in two days. On 15 May 1990 Gorbachev was elected President by 57 per cent of the Deputies.

CHAPTER 12

President in Crisis

Even as he took the oath of office in the Kremlin, the new President was already under the pressure of time. Four days previously, Lithuania had unilaterally declared its independence from the Soviet Union. The disintegration of the empire had begun. Gorbachev responded with his first Presidential decree, requesting the Lithuanian parliament to withdraw its declaration of independence. Until that happened there could be neither dialogue nor negotiations. Gorbachev was taking a firm line, but what could he do to hold the country together? A year earlier the army had been sent into Tbilisi, resulting in an intensification of the crisis.

A partial economic blockade of Lithuania was ordered. In Vilnius, troops defended the offices of the Communist Party, and columns of tanks rolled through the streets. But now the limits of Presidential power became clear: to occupy Lithuania and use force to reconquer it from its newly elected parliament would go against everything Gorbachev had been trying to achieve as a politician.

The Soviet Union consists of fifteen republics. In the course of the next six months five of them declared themselves independent: Lithuania, Latvia, Estonia, Georgia and Armenia. Six others declared themselves in favour of sovereignty within a loosened Union: Azerbaidjan, Byelorussia, Moldavia, Turkmenistan, Uzbekistan, and the great Russian Federation, the heartland of the Soviet Union.

Once again Gorbachev seemed to hesitate. At first he sharply rejected the republics' demands for sovereignty. Then he began discussions with the Presidents of the Baltic states. Then he requested a new contract that would turn the Union into a voluntary confederation of sovereign states. The law that had been hurriedly passed in the spring, and that had been unacceptable to the nationalist movements, disappeared from discussions and seemed to go into storage. But the new negotiations over a contract for the republics proceeded hesitantly. Gorbachev demanded the right to determine foreign and defence policy, economic policy, finance and atomic power. But individual republics had already defied these conditions, and nothing indicated that they would turn back.

Gorbachev's alternating toughness and compliance was incomprehensible to the public, and seemed a sign of weakness. 'The maestro is improvising,' was the view of one of his closest collaborators. Alexander Yakovlev has said: 'I think the strength of Gorbachev is that he can change his point of view, even if there are people who reproach him for this. I like his readiness to take a fresh look at something, even when it's already set up. Not everyone is capable of saying: "What I wrote yesterday is nonsense." I myself can't do it.'

Gorbachev's critics reproached him with being one or two years too late in his decisions. Faced with a steadily deteriorating economic situation, they condemned his attempts to reform the economic system. As Prime Minister, Nikolai Ryzhkov appeared unimpressive and indecisive, and his programme for reform seemed to be a succession of compromises. Though he spoke of a regulated market economy, he offered no model for it, continuing to prescribe central steering and regulation, and as before restricting private entrepreneurs. Even worse, the disadvantages of a market economy were becoming visible to the people: recession, inflation, the closure of enterprises, and the announcement that 40 million workers could expect to be made unemployed. In the same breath that Ryzhkov promised a transition to a 'regulated' market, he also announced that the government would set new, considerably higher prices for bread, meat and other staples. The result was panic buying, and a collapse of supplies. Even salt became hard to get. But, according to the government's plan, a new economic system would not become a reality for six years.

Gorbachev had pressured his Prime Minister to accelerate the transition to a market economy. What Ryzhkov announced seemed to the people to be Gorbachev's programme, although Gorbachev had never publicly given it his blessing. He kept strangely distant from his Prime Minister, who was being attacked from all sides. Stanislav Shatalin, whom Gorbachev had brought into his Presidential Council as economic adviser, said quite openly in the summer: 'Neither in the Presidential Council nor on television has Gorbachev supported Prime Minister Ryzhkov's programme. Gorbachev spoke of the need for the transition to a market economy, and in principle supported the reform of the entire economic system. He was also definitely in favour of social support for the poorer sections of society. But if the government's economic programme is not completely changed, things could end badly.' Like many observers, Shatalin evidently foresaw a government crisis and Ryzhkov's removal. But Gorbachev held on to his Prime Minister, while at the same time asking Shatalin to develop a far more radical programme for the transition to a market economy.

Gorbachev fought on many fronts, which again made him appear indecisive. This further jeopardised his reputation among the people, encouraging the conservative functionaries in the Party to attempt open resistance. The Communist Party organisation in the Russian Federation, hitherto subordinate to the General Secretary and the Central Committee, decided to constitute itself a separate party, with a conservative programme hostile to reform and with a chairman who had proved himself an opponent of Gorbachev's policies. A move to the right throughout the entire Party was in the air, and in Moscow many people were even asking whether Gorbachev would survive the Twenty-eighth Party Congress. He himself gave the impression of being unsure of his future when he gave his first, lacklustre speech before the 5,000 delegates. The applause was weak. Yegor Ligachev was given a far better reception from the majority, which constantly interrupted him with outbursts of clapping. Close collaborators of Gorbachev's such as Yakovlev and Shevardnadze were attacked and booed. It seemed to be a triumphant victory for the opponents of reform.

But then, before the delegates voted for or against the General Secretary, Gorbachev made his closing speech. Now came a settling of accounts with the brakemen in the Party apparatus, indeed with the Party itself, sharper and more brilliant than had ever been heard from Gorbachev before. He appeared confident that, despite the sullen criticism of the delegates, his position was in no way threatened. Without compromising or holding back he presented his programme for reform. He left the Deputies in no doubt about the policies they were approving if they voted for him. There would, he said, be no return to the old command structures. The process of reform and democratisation could not be reversed, and anyone who disagreed with this policy should step down. He criticised the pitifully low intellectual and moral level of debate at the Party Congress, saying to the conservative delegates who reproached him with having lost Eastern Europe: 'Do you want to send in tanks again? Are we again to teach them how they must live?'

The delegates re-elected Gorbachev as General Secretary by a large majority. They may have cheered Yegor Ligachev, but now they rejected him both as Gorbachev's Deputy and as a Politburo member. A mere 600 delegates voted for Ligachev, too few for him to win a place in the new Central Committee. Without his position in the apparatus, the old functionary was lost. He returned to Siberia, and three months later he retired.

The Moscow Party chief Yuri Prokofiev, a representative of the centre right who had also been sharply attacked by the conservatives, believes that even the right recognised that if they had won it would have split the Party, bringing their own influence, their positions and the rule of the Party to an end. Perhaps the conservative functionaries who formed the majority at the Party Congress suspected that the rule of the Party was coming to an end in any case, and hoped that Gorbachev would at least be able to cushion their fall. In his closing speech, Gorbachev proposed a Deputy General Secretary and a new Politburo: his thoroughly mediocre list of nominees would clearly pose no threat to the Parliament or to himself as President.

If Gorbachev wanted to keep a firm grip on the apparatus, it made sense for him to fill the leading posts with weak people. This provoked the criticism that he preferred to surround himself with yes-men. His last major opponent, Boris Yeltsin, had marched dramatically through the immense Congress Palace to the speaker's desk, explained his reasons for leaving the Party, and then marched back to the accompaniment of booing and abuse, until the door shut behind him. 'This is the logical end of a process,' Gorbachev called after him. He appeared to consider Yeltsin's exit a victory.

Yeltsin had not attacked the delegates or the Party in his speech. On 30 May he had been elected President of the Russian Federation, and now he argued that as President of all the people he could no longer be committed to one Party. This high-minded explanation contained an implicit criticism of Gorbachev, who wanted to retain the offices of both President and General Secretary. But Yeltsin also knew that the Party, the majority of whose delegates had booed him, could be of no further use to him. He had learned from his disputes with the Central Committee in previous years, and had thought through and prepared his decision soberly and unemotionally.

It had been clear to everyone – except apparently Gorbachev – that Yeltsin had changed in the course of the year. He had survived a personal crisis, which had made the White House uneasy about his American trip and led to a scurrilous private scandal in Moscow. From the day that he was elected President in the Supreme Soviet of the Russian Federation he gained in confidence, political wisdom and stature, as if success had given him the strength to take on the leadership role for which he had striven so long. It was an astonishing change that surprised even his supporters. Yeltsin had needed to go through several ballots, and his final majority was even narrower than the one by which Gorbachev had been elected President in the Supreme Soviet: with 533 delegates, he had scraped in by only four votes.

Nevertheless, he won the support of a Russian parliament dominated by conservatives. Gorbachev had attempted to mobilise the moderate conservative delegates against Yeltsin – even at the risk of an extreme conservative such as the Russian Party chief Polozkov becoming the Federation's President. As so often in the battle between Gorbachev and Yeltsin, a rational explanation is hard to find. When Yeltsin speaks of his election, one notices his satisfaction at having inflicted a defeat on Gorbachev. 'A few hours before my election as Chairman of the Supreme Soviet of Russia Gorbachev brought together 250 Communists. He tried to convince them they had to use whatever means they could to prevent Yeltsin's election,' says Yeltsin, who sometimes speaks of himself in the third person. 'And leaving these instructions behind he flew off on a state visit to Canada and America. But the next day I was elected Chairman of the Supreme Soviet. My opponents behaved as usual: they did all they could to help me by their clumsy manoeuvres. After such wonderful publicity I could hardly lose. But behind their helplessness was fear, and out of fear came panic and chaotic behaviour. They fully understood what Yeltsin would do after his election: make Russia a sovereign state, allocate administrative functions in a new way, depoliticise the government apparatus and so on. Previously their problem was only Lithuania and the Baltic republics; now they had to add Russia to the list, and Russia cannot be threatened with a blockade. Russia can itself blockade everybody, although it will never do it.'

Gorbachev received the news of Yeltsin's election on the plane taking him to Canada. During the splendid state reception in Ottawa, he scarcely looked at the soldiers in their dress uniforms: he stared gloomily into space, clearly thinking about events in Moscow. Yeltsin's election as President of the giant republic of Russia was the hardest political challenge that Gorbachev had yet encountered. What made it even more difficult was that this crisis could not be resolved within the Party apparatus, over which Gorbachev had control. As well as winning the votes of the non-Communist, democratic representatives, Yeltsin had been supported by several hundred Communist Deputies. Representatives from the centre, and even conservatives, no longer cared about Party discipline, and perhaps they had used this opportunity to give Gorbachev a warning.

For his part, Yeltsin knew that he would be unable to control his parliament unless he had the moderate conservatives behind him. From now on he set his agenda with confidence. He gathered a circle of able advisers about him, marked out his tactical route, and made no more mistakes. In his first statement he found the theme with which he could draw the conservatives to him: Russian sovereignty. If 'sovereignty' was a favourite term of the democratic opposition, for the conservatives the word 'Russia' was full of patriotic resonance. Sovereignty within a restructured Union would mean that Russia could make its own decisions on the use of its rich natural resources, and on its own destiny. Yeltsin said in this first statement: 'The laws of Russia must stand above the laws of the Soviet Union. We will hire the central government to solve the problems that are important to Russia. We will pay what the work is worth to us. We have the right to independence and to leave the Soviet Union. If the central government falls out with us, with Russia, then it will have nothing left to lead. It should not argue with us, but look for compromises, and we will also make an effort to compromise.'

Not that there was much evidence of this to begin with. Both Yeltsin and Gorbachev seemed to actively seek confrontation. Yeltsin and the Presidium of the Russian republic declared Russia the sole owner of its natural resources, mines, power stations and factories. Russia's diamonds, for example, would now be sold directly through the Western diamond dealer de Beers, and the profit would no longer go to the Finance Ministry of the Soviet Union, but be credited to the government of the Russian republic. Gold, oil, and practically everything that Russia could export would also become Russian property. Gorbachev would be left empty-handed, and would have to plead with Yeltsin in order to finance his budget. He therefore repealed the Russian republic's decision by a Presidential decree. But even he saw that he was exposing himself to a conflict as difficult as it was unpopular: the demand that Russia's resources should be exploited for the benefit of Russia's inhabitants, and not for the Soviet Union and its republics, was a popular one with the Russian public, and the Russian Supreme Soviet was determined not to give in. Most of the other republics now made similar demands, leaving Gorbachev in danger of becoming a President without a realm.

The spectacle of recent summers now repeated itself with an altered cast. Previously it had been Ligachev who had pushed himself forward with speeches and television interviews during Gorbachev's holiday, and speculation about whether Gorbachev would now be dethroned by the conservatives was a proven means of exciting the world's press. In the summer of 1990 Yeltsin travelled throughout his republic, which stretched as far as the Pacific in the east. He flew as an ordinary passenger on normal scheduled flights. This was something new for a Soviet leader, and people approved of it. He went down the mines and came up black with coaldust. He was photographed in small cars and lorries. He knew exactly what effect to aim for. Meanwhile Gorbachev was in the state dacha at Foros on the Black Sea. Yeltsin scored points, but he also discovered that he faced problems similar to Gorbachev's. When he visited the Tartars, for example, they demanded from Russia what Yeltsin was demanding from the Soviet Union: a sovereign republic with the right of disposal

of its oil and other natural resources. The miners with whom
Yeltsin spoke may have directed their threats to strike at Prime
Minister Ryzhkov and the central government, but such a strike
would also cripple Yeltsin's Russia. As the new man he could
represent himself as everyone's understanding partner in a dialogue, but growing problems and the economic collapse suggested that a sharper confrontation with Gorbachev would be
inopportune. Gradually he drew closer to those compromises he
had described in his first speech.

It was difficult for Gorbachev to strike a balance with Yeltsin,
but developments left him no choice. The political forces he
himself had activated by his reforms were alien to him. He had
always been able to handle and manipulate the Party apparatus
with consummate skill, but new and incalculable political, economic and social forces were now in play, and his experience had
hardly prepared him for it. Indeed, the maestro had to improvise.

With scarcely a glance at his Prime Minister's economic programme, which he had never liked, after a five-hour talk Gorbachev came to an agreement with Yeltsin on a commission to
work out a new reform model. Stanislav Shatalin and Gorbachev's
experts contributed their ideas, which went far beyond Ryzhkov's
programme, and Yeltsin's experts prepared a plan for a 500-day
transition to a market economy. Both Presidents appeared on
television to affirm their common ground in the battle against the
economic chaos that threatened. It was an unusual scene: they
stood well apart and their body language betrayed the fact that
they had come no closer as human beings. Yeltsin, almost a head
and a half taller than Gorbachev, seemed visibly satisfied that he
was now Gorbachev's equal, and was full of tense energy beneath
his apparent composure. The television reporter as usual gave
Gorbachev more time to answer his questions, but one could see
that both Presidents were determined to have the last word.
Ultimately it went to Gorbachev, who stressed that there was no
personal or political tension between him and Yeltsin, but only
endeavour for a common goal.

Gorbachev was not used to dealing with an equal partner in
Soviet domestic policy. It was a different matter with foreign
statesmen, but as Party Secretary in Stavropol and General Secretary in Moscow he had grown used to taking decisions alone.
As President he had cast himself in the role of an arbitrator who

listened to varied opinions before making his own decisions. At times this made relations between the President and the government seem strangely distant and unregulated, and the functions of the Presidential Council, where strategic decisions were formulated, were also not clearly defined. Gorbachev had appointed sixteen men to this inner council. Some were there by reason of their office: Prime Minister Nikolai Ryzhkov, Defence Minister Dmitri Yazov, Interior Minister Vadim Bakatin, KGB chief Vladimir Kryuchkov. Alexander Yakovlev and Eduard Shevardnadze were there as trusted and experienced comrades-in-arms. Then there were the economists and social scientists, some of them from the reform camp, others of rather lower profile, and a few unusual people such as Stanislav Shatalin, who describes himself as a social democrat who only stays in the Party so as not to abandon it to the conservatives. The conservatives had protested in vain at his place in the Central Committee. Now he was the planner for reform for Gorbachev and Yeltsin at the same time. Another member is the right-wing metalworker Yarin, playing off workers' interests against market-economy reforms. The writer Chinghiz Aitmatov is a Khirghiz from the Asiatic regions of the Soviet Union whose ethical views are influenced by Christian values. And there is the writer Valentin Rasputin, a conservative Green, who for twenty years has protested in his novels against the destruction of nature and humanity by technology and materialism, and who in recent years, by emphasising traditional Russian values, has moved towards the extreme right of Pamyat.

Gorbachev himself says that these people, with all their differences, share his views. What is not clear is how they contribute to his policies. Stanislav Shatalin explains with his usual frankness: 'To be honest, no one, not even the President, is clear about the status of the Presidential Council. But now for the first time in the history of the Soviet Union there is a President, and it would be astonishing if the functions of the Presidential Council were already clearly defined. There is no formal voting in the Presidential Council: all give their opinion, but the President decides.'

Alexander Yakovlev believes that there is a wide spectrum of views in the Presidential Council, and that this guarantees successful discussion. Gorbachev himself admits that the Council has not yet found its role: 'We study the systems of other countries, we look at the roles played by mayors, prefects and governors. Even these questions have to be included in the general process of democratisation.'

Some of the members have a small staff of consultants at their disposal. Their function is chiefly advisory, but their political powers are vague. Shatalin, responsible for economic policy, is in contact with the leading men from the economic apparatus. He says: 'What exactly are our relations? Can I for example ask the Finance Minister to do something, or have I the right to order him to do something?' On the one hand Gorbachev has created the nucleus of a second government, on the other a discussion group that makes no decisions. Interior Minister Bakatin says: 'The President is what he is. He needs the Council for advice. It doesn't matter what gets recommended, the President himself decides and takes on the full burden of responsibility for his decisions. The President has to act within the framework of the Constitution, but the Constitution has been overtaken. He has to influence legislation, but at the same time can't change a comma in the existing laws, no matter what they are.'

Gorbachev himself says he wants to limit himself to political means and aims: 'The transition to market-economy relations and pushing ahead to draw up a Union contract are two sides of the same coin. The market will give people an incentive and strengthen natural relations; the new federal relations will make it possible for the republics to make use of their potential. We have to go this way if we want to revitalise society.' In Washington he stated this even more clearly before American politicians and intellectuals when he asked for understanding for the complicated process of restructuring the Soviet Union and spoke of the many and great tasks involved: political reform, renewal of the federal system, the sharing of power between the legislative and executive organs and the Communist Party.

'We have come to the simple conclusion that we cannot continue to live like this,' he said. 'Our society needs a new dynamism, it needs oxygen. This can be attained, but only with the foundation of freedom.' And yet, since taking up office Gorbachev has frequently intervened in the process of development with Presidential decrees and personal orders. He has attempted to block the way to sovereignty to the republics, forbidden demonstrations in Moscow's inner city, taken away rank, decorations and pension from a KGB general who criticised the KGB, threatened Armenia with sending in the army and then, faced with the danger of civil war, given the new President of Armenia two months in which to himself disarm the nationalist fighting units.

What is the power, what are the tasks of a President of the Soviet Union? Does he, as the Politburo formerly did, dictate decisions to the organs of government? Or does he only have authority to lay down guidelines in determining general policy? Or is he the arbitrator who stands above government, parliament, parties and new groupings? Gorbachev has not yet found his role as the first President of the Soviet Union. A year before he took up office, no one had thought the nation needed a President, not even, it seems, Gorbachev. He is now President of a country whose economic system is no longer viable and whose political structures and culture have been destroyed. New parties hardly exist in the new parliamentary system, and the old Party is reluctant to withdraw. In the small towns and districts its functionaries are still powerful, but at the centre of politics even the Politburo hardly has a part to play.

One thing is certain. Gorbachev's role is very much more President of the Soviet Union than General Secretary of the Communist Party. The Party Congress forced that office on him, although he wanted to abolish it and replace the head of the apparatus with a Party Chairman. Now he increasingly withdraws from the position of General Secretary, as if it were a merely transitional function. His power base is the Presidency. But he still needs to learn the extent and the limits of his authority.

In the search for his political position Gorbachev again began discussions with the intellectual reformers, some of whom in the meantime had taken over important political posts. The economist Gavril Popov was now Mayor of Moscow, elected by the non-Communist majority of the Moscow City Soviet, and had himself left the Communist Party shortly after Yeltsin. The jurist Anatoli Sobchak was in a similar position as Mayor of Leningrad. Gorbachev met with them and with Yeltsin for long talks, and Popov, who had been critical of Gorbachev in previous years, now saw a glimmer of hope. In his view Gorbachev had adopted a constructive approach to a reform programme, as the left liberals had long hoped he would. But Popov remained sceptical: with his political skill Gorbachev had always managed to triumph over the conservatives, but nothing had really been achieved by that. Gorbachev's policies had strengthened the centre right, but it was incapable of action and could not really guide the country. Nevertheless, one could hope for a change for the better with Gorbachev.

At the end of July 1990 the President unexpectedly invited thirty economists, social scientists and publicists to the Kremlin. All were supporters of radical reform. One of them relates how an unknown voice on the phone told him to come to Entrance 19 at twelve o'clock the next day for a talk with Gorbachev. Would that be Entrance 19 to the Central Committee? he asked. 'No,' said the voice. 'Entrance 19 in the Kremlin.' The next day the guests were seated at a long table. Punctually at twelve Gorbachev appeared with two members of the Presidential Council, Alexander Yakovlev and Yevgeni Primakov, who listened in silence to the discussion, which continued without a break until 6 p.m. One of the participants reports: 'Gorbachev seemed healthy, he was suntanned and very calm. Unusually, he spoke in a quiet voice, and some guests had to draw closer to understand him.'

Another participant, Anatoli Strelyani, thought that Gorbachev had evidently read a great deal on economic reform and the various alternatives, by Soviet and foreign writers, but seemed unsure how to evaluate so many varied points of view. Others thought the President seemed to consider himself superior to those present, as if he were saying: 'You're only theoreticians. I have to cope with reality.' Though Gorbachev listened to the experts' opinions, he did not react to their criticisms. At one point he brought the discussion round to developments in Poland, and seemed to consider applying the Polish economic reforms to the Soviet Union. But he decided they would not work. He then listened with interest as some of the economic experts described the difficulties and possibilities of the Polish stabilisation policy. Gorbachev took note of everything that was said, but did not adopt a position himself. To most of the radical reformers at the table it seemed as if he was still looking for a programme of compromise that would combine positive elements from all the proposals and programmes. They meanwhile argued that these proposals, the conclusions of numerous schools of economic thinking, could not be combined – least of all with the government's reform programme and its orientation to centralisation.

Among the President's guests were supporters of a Socialist-orientated programme, social democrats and liberals, but they only represented a part of the spectrum of political reform. The young economist Larissa Pyacheva, renowned for her sharply formulated criticism, left the discussion firmly convinced Gorbachev would sooner or later remove the government and radicalise the reforms. 'During the entire discussion,' she says, 'Gorbachev never used the word "Socialism". I believe, should he take the road of radical reform, that he'll probably remain silent on this question. And that's right. The only thing he can ban in a discussion on reform is the use of the words "capitalism" and "Socialism". That only leads down a dead end. We've experimented long enough with various ideological models. The time for a revival of Socialism, even Socialism with a human face, has passed.' But Gorbachev himself never gave voice to such thoughts. He merely stressed that there was no going back to the time before *perestroika*.

Gorbachev knew that the country had to continue on the road of *perestroika*, and faster than before. But in the jungle of countless problems he seemed uncertain which path to take, and did not commit himself. In previous years he had taken his time, allowing great, almost revolutionary decisions to ripen before choosing his moment to get them through. Now he jeopardised his authority and his reputation. The supply situation had dramatically worsened: food had become scarce, and some districts had introduced rationing. There were no more cigarettes in Moscow, and on the first Sunday of September no bread in the Moscow bakeries. The more the economy slid into chaos, the more the supply crisis turned into a crisis of confidence. In the glory of his foreign policy successes, which had made the Soviet Union an equal partner and participant in world politics, and encouraged by his success at the Party Congress, Gorbachev seemed to overlook the fact that disappointment with his policies and leadership was growing among numerous politically hostile groups throughout Soviet society.

On 1 May 1990, the forty-eighth day of his Presidency, Gorbachev suddenly discovered how the mood of the country had changed. The yearly demonstration of workers' solidarity on Red

Square was drawing past him: first the labour unionists in orderly rows, with banners bearing slogans of celebratory accord with Party and government, but also warnings against a market economy and unemployment. Gorbachev was well aware of the criticism of these groups, and had always been able to handle it. But then came the unorganised masses, those not officially representing anything – Gorbachev himself had decided to allow them to join the procession. Now the Moscow Voters' Organisation came marching, then the Lithuanian nationalists, the People's Front, the Christian Democrats, the Social Democrats, Monarchists, Greens, Anarchists and radical Marxist-Leninists. Everyone who wanted to protest had joined in. There had never been anything like this in Moscow. Every banner, every chorus of voices criticised Gorbachev's policies, reproaching him at the very least with a lack of decisiveness in the battle with the conservatives and the KGB. What the groups that stopped in front of the Mausoleum shouted at the President was drowned out by military music from giant loudspeakers, but Gorbachev had no need to hear the words to understand the mood that confronted him. He stood behind the stone balustrade of the Lenin Mausoleum, between Prime Minister Nikolai Ryzhkov and the liberal Mayor of Moscow, Gavril Popov. Below him lay the embalmed body of Lenin, behind him the tombstone of Stalin, before him the new forces of politics: not the people, but nevertheless the voice of the people. Gorbachev turned and left.

Soviet television had quickly switched off when the flags and banners of the unofficial groups came onto the screen. But all Moscow, and soon the entire country, was talking about the demonstrations and Gorbachev's departure. Many saw this as a defeat for the President; some because they regarded the Lenin Mausoleum as a captain's bridge no leader should leave, others because Gorbachev had not taken up the dialogue with the new forces.

Gorbachev understood *perestroika* as a process of democratisation, but as a regulated process, not a demonstration of power in the streets. When he turned and left the platform of the Lenin Mausoleum he seemed disappointed and bitter at what his policies had released. But is it a defeat or a triumph for Gorbachev if free speech, the will to freedom and democratic self-confidence – everything that *perestroika* was meant to awaken – begins to

unfold? Is it a defeat if the system develops independently beyond
its creator, if the child grows taller than its father? Yet the process
is painful for Gorbachev, as every advance, every success of his
policies at the same time limits his power.

The power of his office appeared to strengthen Gorbachev, as
he gave himself ever greater authority by means of presidential
decrees. In reality these were only improvised measures by which
he tried to prevent the emergence of a power vacuum. He had
his advisers draw up a new Union contract that was to establish
new relations between Moscow and the republics. In this 'union
of sovereign states' Gorbachev was envisaging a new form of
political community that embraced nearly one sixth of the globe,
with outlines that were only vaguely defined. It was a vision
which could hardly keep pace with the speed at which many
republics were becoming independent. In this community of
republics supposedly answerable to themselves, the president and
the central government would continue to determine policy on
foreign affairs, defence, transport, nuclear energy and tax. This
was not enough for many republics. Boris Yeltsin, as President
of the Russian Republic, was already demanding an independent
foreign policy and monetary policy and a Russian army. Such
decisions about a new division of power, between the centre and
the fifteen republics and their various interests, the form and
effects of which were not even fully clear to its advocates, could
not be made in haste. Even Yeltsin was prepared to give Gorbachev more time, but he named his price: the Russian Republic
should have the right to hold three key positions in the central
government – the offices of prime minister, minister of finance
and defence minister.

In the summer of 1990 Gorbachev and Yeltsin were to appear
in public alternately as allies and opponents. The dispute was
personified in Prime Minister Ryzhkov, retained by Gorbachev
without any clear signs of support, whose dismissal Yeltsin
demanded with increasing vehemence. When Gorbachev asked
his trusted economic expert Stanislav Shatalin to formulate the
radical reform programme of 500 days originally proposed by
Yeltsin it seemed as if Gorbachev had dropped the Prime Minister
and his cautious plan for economic reform. But then, shortly
before the Supreme Soviet decision, Gorbachev again interceded
for a programme of compromise, adopting certain guidelines

from Ryzhkov's programme and thus taking the dynamics out of the 500-day plan. Yeltsin's programme for reform had at least been defined by a framework of fixed deadlines, but Gorbachev presented the Supreme Soviet with a general declaration of the desire for reform, and one that set no clear dates for change and improvement in the lives of the Soviet people.

Gorbachev's relationship with Yeltsin broke down again when Ryzhkov unexpectedly decreed important price rises that were directly opposed to the economic ideas of the Russian Republic. But Gorbachev, in a tactical move completely in accordance with his general political inclination, had an economic programme ratified by the Party and the Supreme Soviet. Concepts such as 'private property' or 'market economy' without the restricting adjective 'socialist' were now set out quite openly, and the question of the rural possession of land was now no longer to be subjected to a referendum, but was to be 'regulated according to the will of the people'. Gorbachev had established the right to a new orientation in economic policy, on a scale that only a year earlier would not have gained a majority among the deputies. He hoped, with his far-reaching programme, to be able to determine the individual steps of the transition by presidential decree, while avoiding awkward and confused debate in the Supreme Soviet and with the governments of the republics.

But the country, living with the frightening reality of the steady disintegration of the power structure and the economy, was not satisfied with so general an aim and no longer seemed prepared to go along with the President. In the Supreme Soviet, in the newspapers and in the queues which had formed outside the poorly supplied shops, people spoke with increasing bitterness about the danger of a winter famine. In the opinion polls Boris Yeltsin had already far surpassed the President in popularity. And those groups on which the President's power depended also seemed to be withdrawing their support. The bureaucracy of the central ministries, holding the various parts of a gigantic country together with difficulty, felt they were fighting a lost cause. The supporters of reform in the Supreme Soviet, in the republics and in the parliaments of the big cities felt betrayed in their hope of a coalition with Gorbachev. The army saw its strength threatened by the new disarmament agreements and by the decrease in the defence budget; it also found itself forced into a hopeless role between fronts in the nationalist disputes and civil wars. Lieutenant Colonel Viktor Alksnis, speaking for the conservative wing of the army, demanded that Gorbachev either demonstrate his authority by proclaiming the power of the president or resign. In front of eleven hundred Soviet military men, who were also deputies in parliaments on various levels, Gorbachev could barely make himself heard over loud expressions of displeasure and was compelled to back down over the question of military reform and the transition to a professional army. Marshal Sergei Akhromeyev, whom Gorbachev had brought in to the presidential council, indicated that the army was ready to support a dictatorial seizure of power by the President, because it could not witness the state and social system being broken up by force. This seemed to be more a threat than a pledge of support.

Three days before he left for Paris to meet the heads of government at the special summit of the thirty-four-nation Conference of Security and Co-operation in Europe, the Supreme Soviet forced Gorbachev to account for himself in a debate. The deputies refused to deal with individual bills unless Gorbachev explained to them what measures he intended to take to meet the crisis. His opening report disappointed the deputies. It was a description of the problems with no outline of a solution. The Armenian deputy Igitian commented sharply that Gorbachev spoke as if he were an emigrant returning to his home country after a long absence and discovering with consternation what had become of it. But it was also clear the deputies themselves saw no way out, and they applauded with relief at the end of the session when Gorbachev announced that he would no longer wait for others, but take action himself.

So after two days of debate and disagreement Gorbachev had again secured the backing of the deputies and had again increased his power. He announced a profound reshaping of the power apparatus, 'a fundamental reorganisation, that subordinates the central executive to the president'. He shunted Ryzhkov to the side, without formally removing him. He dissolved his presidential council and announced the formation of a new government organ in which, under the name 'Council of the Federation', policy was to be determined jointly by him and by the leaders of the fifteen republics. The President put the influential industrial ministries directly under him because they seemed to be hindering economic change, and announced a reshuffle at the head of the army because men such as Defence Minister Yazov were not reforming the armed forces with sufficient speed. This time, however, Gorbachev's solution was less a personal victory than the postponement of a decision, as his opponents in their general powerlessness were unable to find any alternative. The sociologist Tatyana Saslavskaya described the mood of the country and its politicians as being one of a 'very high degree of tension and unrest, a kind of nervous exhaustion, together with widespread apathy – a strange and ominous mixture'.

The Supreme Soviet's approval of Gorbachev's latest plan for reform was an interim decision. It remains to be seen whether Gorbachev's authority is still sufficient to turn his programme into reality, or whether he has only driven the various opponents of his policies, themselves in disagreement, still deeper into opposition. The decisive factor will be whether he can achieve a viable collaboration on a basis of shared power with the forces for reform in the republics and cities and Boris Yeltsin, who effectively rules over almost half the Soviet population. His new 'Council of the Federation' would need to win the cooperation of the leaders of the republics, agitating more and more against the central government of the Union and against each other. He continues to need the generals, the majority of whom are not prepared to risk a military coup in spite of their dissatisfaction, but have now been made even more uneasy by Gorbachev's announcement of a re-shuffle at the top of the armed forces. And after downgrading Prime Minister Ryzhkov he needs to take control of the ministries, whose experienced bureaucrats until now have hindered reform, but have also prevented total chaos. In December 1990, when Mikhail Gorbachev received the Nobel Peace Prize in Oslo, he was experiencing at home a very serious crisis indeed.

It had been a long road to the top for Gorbachev, and also to the recognition that his country could only be saved by a comprehensive programme for reform, involving revolutionary and radical change. The road had not been straight, but looking back one can see a logical consistency to its stations. The gaping divide between real life and Soviet theory had been experienced at first hand by the boy from Privolnoye. He knew the true situation of the *kolkhoz* farmers, and how it compared to the propagandistic picture drawn in Moscow of Socialist country life. At Moscow University he met professors and students who often had to conceal their opinions behind a façade of conformity. He began his rise in the Young Communist League at a time when the revelations of Stalin's terror for the first time made it possible to doubt the legitimacy of the Party's claim to rule. He backed the renewal of the system that began, and failed, under Khrushchev.

In Stavropol he was a loyal and effective functionary, but his sense of justice and his democratic style distinguished him from other Party Secretaries. He had to follow changing directives from Moscow which destroyed new projects before they had a chance to succeed. He tried to resist ill-advised instructions, as far as a provincial Party Secretary could. He was independent in his thinking, but was still promoted by men who ruled the Party during a time of aimlessness and stagnation. It would be hard to say when exactly he recognised that the country needed greater changes than merely modernisation and a purging of the system. But everything indicates that, by 1980 at the latest, he had realised that only a profound and fundamental reform could solve the Soviet Union's problems. He also began to see that the great problems of ecology and the arms race could not be overcome by one country acting alone, and that a new world order and international co-operation would be necessary.

But the man with such far-reaching ideas was also a functionary of the apparatus who had grown up in the belief that change could only be effected from inside the Party. So, during his first year as General Secretary, he still hesitated to formulate his insights into a political programme. The Party apparatus would neither have understood nor accepted them. Gorbachev knew the weaknesses of this ponderous and rusty apparatus, but nevertheless believed he could not do without it, especially as he was usually able to manipulate it.

He had come far enough in his thinking to be able to set aside narrow Marxist formulae. But he still made use of classic quotations that Stalin, Khrushchev or Brezhnev might also have employed. 'For us Leninism remains the most important theoretical and moral force. Without Lenin's legacy our road leads no further,' he said in his speech on Lenin's birthday in 1990. But what seems to interest him most are the statements of Lenin's last years, which take a critical look at the outcome of the October Revolution. Gorbachev valued Lenin above all as a tough politician, who could be self-critical and revise his position, who in difficult situations could oppose the majority, threatening resignation if necessary.

Gorbachev is no dictator, and has no desire to be one. But he is too dynamic to merely preside over the decline of the Soviet Union. In keeping with his nature and his experience he has tried to implement his policies step by step, by way of compromise and with changing allies. Five years after taking office as General Secretary, he brought the CPSU to the point where it relinquished the rule of the apparatus over all areas of life and accepted a shift in power in favour of representatives elected by the people. For him the political development of the Soviet Union is an open-ended process: 'I don't consider a multi-party system a tragedy if it should correspond to the real interests of society,' he said on 15 January 1990. 'There's no need to fear the multi-party system like a devil fears holy water. But one mustn't artificially impose it. The multi-party system is no panacea. What is most important is democracy and *glasnost*, and the genuine participation of the people in all political and also social processes and institutions.'

Precisely because he was deeply convinced that Soviet society needed to be democratised if it was to be revitalised, Gorbachev was unable to impose change by a show of strength. He has said of himself: 'We will continue along the road of debate. I chose the road myself, and my fate is bound up with that decision.'

He had led the country from apparent and enforced stability into a period of change, where it is instability that is actually opening the way to new democratic structures. He is looking for new rules for a Socialist society. But the guidelines are no longer class interest and class struggle, but common human values.

And so he calls for new thinking for a world in which it is not only the Soviet Union that is undergoing crises and upheaval. Nikolai Portugalov, a Soviet German expert, once called Gorbachev 'our Luther'. Perhaps Gorbachev only wanted to be a reformer, but his new thinking has led from mere reform to revolutionary change. Out of deep conviction he has exposed his country to a process that will allow not only more freedom of opinion, but also genuine political freedom of choice. But he does not back change forced by 'the street'. 'Life has put before us the

necessity of fundamentally regrouping forces on the highest levels
of power. The mechanisms of executive power need to be strengthened so the laws function,' Gorbachev declared to the Supreme
Soviet when some delegates opposed the introduction of a Presidential office as being a step towards dictatorship.

Whoever is to lead the country out of crisis must have the
power to do so. But he must also be ready to allow this power
to be limited by the Constitution, the law and parliament. Gorbachev himself has repeatedly emphasised this. There is of course a
danger of a strong President, faced with growing crises,
impatiently using his executive power to override the inevitably
slower democratic process. The democratic opposition was afraid
of this when Gorbachev was elected. But the power of his office
was weakened by the declaration of sovereignty of the republics
and the decline of the central administration. Boris Yeltsin indicated – not without malice – that what would be left to Gorbachev
would be a role like that of the Queen of England. But there has
never been a parliamentary party system in the Soviet Union and
its republics. According to Gorbachev's convictions, if the Soviet
Union, with no democratic tradition, is not to exhaust itself in
the struggle of nationalities and break apart in the conflict of
group interests, it needs a period of guided transition during
which the new structures can develop – a fundamentally altered
economic structure, a parliamentary system of political parties
with equal rights, and new relations with the republics that today
want to leave the Soviet Union. Perhaps the Soviet Union must
first pass through a phase of disintegration before political and
economic necessity leads to new relations and ways of living – a
period in which a President, in unknown territory, must firmly
and patiently use all the reserves of his authority and political
experience. What this Soviet Union might look like in five or ten
years' time no one can tell. Gorbachev is well aware of the scale
of the crisis and the immense problems that face the country.

In just five years, Gorbachev's policies have changed the Soviet
Union and the world. This ensures him a place in history, even
if history follows its own logic and not the concepts of the President. The process is not yet over. The battle for the future will
continue. But Gorbachev has done more than anyone else to close
the door that leads back into the past, to the bondage of the old
system.

POSTSCRIPT

On the night of Sunday, 13 January, my mind kept going back to the last sentence I had written about Gorbachev's place in history. I stood among Lithuanians opposite the tanks and troops that had just occupied the television building in Vilnius. They had fired wildly from their Kalashnikovs, hit people with the butts of their rifles, brought up tanks to frighten the crowd. Finally they had brought in two busloads of party members to back up their claim of popular support. It looked like a replay of all the earlier communist coups in Eastern Europe.

People had been wounded near to where we stood. At the storming of the television tower, a few miles away, people had been killed. Near us four TV crews had lost their cameras to the soldiers, and one Spanish cameraman had lost his front teeth to a rifle butt. Now the Lithuanians were hiding us and our camera with their bodies so we could continue to document what occurred. They were calling Gorbachev a slaughterer, accusing the West of pampering him to the point of honouring him with the Nobel Prize for Peace. Now his troops were reconquering the Baltic republics with tanks and guns, perhaps ready to storm Lithuania's elected parliament.

I also thought of Peking, of Gorbachev's visit and the bloody day at Tiananmen Square that came a few days later. It had put a stop to reforms and democratisation in China. At that time many of my friends in Moscow feared that the orthodox communists in the Soviet Union would try for a 'Chinese solution' to end the process of liberalisation. But by then it seemed Gorbachev had eliminated the danger of a take-over from the right.

I kept thinking back to nights in Paris, thirty years ago, when the French riot police chased demonstrators who protested against the war in Algeria. There had also been fear of a coup from the right. There had been disappointment among my friends when General de Gaulle told the French settlers in Algeria that he understood their point of view. De Gaulle had finally ended the last colonial war and pulled France out of North Africa. But he had been a figure of towering authority among his people. There were no such unique qualities that Gorbachev could call upon to make the Russians in the Baltic Republics and the nationalists at home comply with devolution or the dismantling of the empire.

Even if he later disclaimed responsibility for the violent actions of the paratroopers it was he who had given the order to dispatch elite troops to the Baltic republics. If he would not or could not dissociate himself from the actions of the military his policy of *perestroika* was discredited and the course could lead only to more suppression. If the paratroopers and the special forces of the Union Ministry of the Interior had acted without authorisation, it meant that the troops were out of control, following either an unknown junta on the right or the leadership of local communist parties. Whatever the plan may have been, it failed when in Vilnius and Riga twenty people or more died. This price was too high for the occupation of some two dozen isolated buildings of no strategic or little political importance. The soldiers had neither broken the popular resistance nor effectively set up 'committees of national salvation' that could activate the fear of the Russian ethnic minorities in these republics. In the weeks before the tragic events, radical young officers, the 'black colonels', had called for a solution of this kind, asking Gorbachev to retire unless he would take a hard line to re-establish Moscow rule in the Baltics and other republics. But what looked like an attempt to put their thoughts into practice had failed. It had shocked the world and the majority of the Soviet people, who, despite attempts to muzzle press and television, had seen and heard enough of the shooting in Vilnius and Riga to understand that a military solution would not work.

Courageous Soviet journalists had used what was left of *glasnost* to report the events even though Gorbachev had installed a new chief of television and issued a decree putting the press under the control of the Supreme Soviet. He had used the new powers that the Congress of People's Deputies had bestowed on him at the end of the year. In theory he now held more power than any Soviet leader before him, including Stalin.

The Congress had granted these powers with the second largest majority Gorbachev ever received, second only to the approval of his foreign policy earlier in 1990. Gorbachev had even received grudging support from some members of the democratic opposition and almost all the votes of the rightwingers who had criticised him sharply in the weeks before. He had succeeded in pacifying those on the right. The Minister of the Interior, Vadim Bakatin, who tried to reform the police and prison system, was retired. In his place Boris Pugo, a former KGB chief from Latvia, was installed with General Boris Gromov, former commander of the Soviet troops in Afghanistan, as his deputy. Gorbachev had replaced Prime Minister Ryzhkov with an experienced financial technocrat, Valentin Pavlov. He had pushed through the election of Vice President Gennady Yanayev, who may not be the Stalinist he is called by the democratic opposition but is certainly a little-known functionary with ties only to the party apparatus. And Gorbachev had sacrificed his closest friend and adviser still in government, Eduard Shevardnadze.

In a moving speech before the Congress of Deputies Shevardnadze complained that nobody in the government or the parliament had defended him against attacks on his foreign policy and that there was talk among young colonels of liquidating him. He warned against preparations for a coup from the right and the establishment of a dictatorial system. Shevardnadze stressed that he still supported Gorbachev's policies of *perestroika* but his remarks on the danger of dictatorship were vague enough to leave the impression that Gorbachev himself might become part of it.

Gorbachev was clearly surprised by the resignation of his foreign minister but he made no serious effort, neither during the session nor in later conversations, to change Shevardnadze's mind. Shevardnadze, it seems, felt not only that he had become expendable since Gorbachev had begun to choose new allies but that he was being used as a figure to calm Western apprehensions.

He had not informed Gorbachev beforehand about his resignation. In fact there had been very little contact between them for weeks or even months, only telephone conversations about immediate top questions of foreign policy and no discussion of the worrying problems and developments of domestic affairs.

Gorbachev had never been an outgoing man but now he had completely withdrawn, at least from his friends. From Stanislav Shatalin, who for some time in 1990 had been the architect of Gorbachev's economic policies, we know that at the time of decisive changes in mid-December, when the outline of future presidential power for Gorbachev was defined, none of his advisers and collaborators for the early days of *perestroika* had been asked for opinions and advice: neither Alexander Yakovlev nor Yevgeni Primakov, neither Shatalin nor other members of the presidential council, not even prime minister Ryzhkov. Instead representatives of the right wing, from the leadership of the communist party of the Russian republic and from the Politbureau, participated in the decisive meeting – conservatives who had criticised or opposed Gorbachev's former policies.

From the party hospital in Barvikha near Moscow, very close to Gorbachev's dacha, Shatalin felt compelled to communicate with Gorbachev by an open letter published in the press. He reminded him that a reform by half-measures could only lead into a dead end and he claimed that Gorbachev himself had always understood the necessity of deep changes in the whole social and political system. He asked: 'I know that you can do it. Why don't you want to make the right political move? Why?'

Shatalin once more suggested that Gorbachev would be strongest if he relied on the democratic reform bloc rather than on an alliance with the right. Many serious thinkers of the democratic opposition had suggested this in the months before. Some of them had proposed to strengthen the powers of the president, arguing that only a more authoritarian system of government could push through the harsh and unpopular measures that were needed to move the country towards a market economy. But after the bloody events of Vilnius and Riga liberal reformers no longer believed in a benevolent authoritarian rule by Gorbachev. More than a hundred intellectuals, some of them cautious functionaries from the right, signed a document claiming that Gorbachev was leading the country back to 'labour camps, purges, fear, hunger and destruction'. Even close advisers of Gorbachev like the economists Stanislav Shatalin and Nikolai Petrakov signed a statement by the board of directors of the liberal *Moscow News* asking: 'After the bloody Sunday in Vilnius, what is left of our president's favourite topics of 'humane society', 'new thinking' and the 'European home'? Virtually nothing.'

There was no answer from Gorbachev. On 22 January he read a statement to the press deploring the violence in the Baltic republics but confirming the principles of the Soviet constitution superseding the legislative acts of the independent-minded parliaments. His words showed no way out of the deadly confrontation between the central power in Moscow and the republics. He did not even seem aware of it. Gorbachev entered the hall of the press conference with Alexander Yakovlev and Yevgeny Primakov, two old allies from the formative years of *perestroika*. But to sceptical observers in the hall and on the television sets at home this looked like mere window dressing directed at the West.

While he was reassuring the West on Soviet political support for the military sanctions against Iraq, editors and functionaries were informed of harsh measures to cut the money supply: banknotes of one hundred and of fifty roubles would be invalidated immediately. In theory this would hit the mafia and the black marketeers. In practice it hit millions of people who had saved a few dozen big banknotes for the day when they might be able to buy something in the shops.

Financially it may have been sound to take out of circulation some of the money the state had printed freely in the last years. Politically and psychologically the indiscriminate confiscation of banknotes was sure to erode confidence in Gorbachev and his policies even further.

Has Mikhail Gorbachev changed his political ideas? He insists that he is still working for *perestroika* and deep changes. He may have concluded that the move to a market economy, to democratic pluralism and to a process of devolution of the Union cannot be achieved all at the same time and by democratic means. He may be a prisoner of his new allies on the right he chose to pacify and rely on. Even his embittered former friends and advisers do not believe that he has been deceiving them for years, though some feel the taste of power has corrupted his thinking. Today there are none of his former friends around to interpret what the president thinks. He must be a very lonely man indeed.

Moscow, 24 January 1991

APPENDIX

Mikhail Gorbachev on Himself

In May 1989 Soviet citizens for the first time learned something about the life of their General Secretary. In January that year a publication reappeared that had existed between 1919 and 1929 and that reported on the work of the Central Committee. For sixty years the Central Committee had published no detailed information on its deliberations, and the refounding of *News From the Central Committee of the CPSU* was presented as another step towards greater openness. The fifth issue of the periodical carried, by Soviet standards, an unusually detailed interview with Mikhail Gorbachev.

The editors receive many letters from Communists and non-Party members that address direct questions to the Party leadership. The readers of *News From the Central Committee of the CPSU* are interested in the various activities of the people in the Party leadership, in their active participation in and personal commitment to the realisation of *perestroika*. A number of questions also refer to the private lives of members of the Party leadership – to their families, work and leisure.

Lately the editors have received many letters in connection with the publication of short biographies of members of the Party leadership and the Central Committee of the Party. While many readers welcome these publications, they also want more precise information about the careers of the members of the state and Party leadership than just dry enumerations of changes of workplace.

R. S. Bublik from Leningrad writes: 'Why are there no detailed biographies of our Party leaders published in *News From the*

Central Committee of the CPSU? Is this out of false modesty, or deliberate silence? This is how ill-intentioned people are given the opportunity to spread the most varied untruths. To fight these without having access to reliable information is difficult.'

N. F. Mukhin from Krasnoarmeisk, Moscow District, also shares this opinion: 'Bibliographical details on full members and candidates of the Politburo of the Central Committee of the CPSU are very sparse and incomplete. We know more about the President of the USA than about our own leadership. That is why many rumours and invented stories circulate among the population. Sometimes it is hard for me in my capacity as editor of the Society for National Education to answer such questions as how much members of the state and Party leadership earn per month.'

The letters of many of our readers contain similar questions.

Our correspondent L. Mikhailov has therefore asked the General Secretary of the Central Committee of the CPSU and Chairman of the Presidium of the Supreme Soviet of the USSR, M. S. Gorbachev, to answer readers' questions.

INTERVIEWER: Mikhail Sergeyevich, many of our readers would like you to tell them a little about yourself and your parents.
GORBACHEV: I have also had letters of this kind. First of all I should like to say that now, in the time of *glasnost*, a great deal is already being written about the activities of the higher organs of the state and the Party and its leaders – much more than was ever previously the case. The appearances of members of the leadership, their travels, meetings and talks with workers – all these have now established themselves in the nation's life. Soviet people – or at least those who are interested – can now inform themselves about the work of members of the leadership of the country, about their views on particular matters, and form a picture of their political, professional and human qualities.

Now to your actual question. What can I say that goes beyond what has already been published?

I was born in the Stavropol region. My parents and grandparents were farmers. My grandfather on my mother's side, Panteli Yefimovich, was an organiser for the co-operative for the joint cultivation of the land and then of the *kolkhozes*. He was the

chairman of one of these *kolkhozes* for many years. My father
Sergei Andreyevich and my mother Maria Pantelevna also
worked as farmers, at first on their own farm, then in the co-
operative and finally in the *kolkhoz* and at the machine and tractor
depot. My father worked for forty years as a mechanic. He took
part in the Great Patriotic War as a pioneer. He fought for Kursk,
freed Kharkov and Kiev and received a medal at the crossing of
the Dnieper. Shortly before the end of the war he was wounded
near the Czechoslovakian town of Košice and taken to hospital
in Cracow. During the war he joined the Party. His neighbours
valued him as a hard-working, modest and considerate man. I
am proud of my father.

Like all farmers' children, I had to lend a hand. At thirteen I
was already working regularly on the *kolkhoz*, and at fifteen I
helped on a threshing machine. Altogether I worked for five years
at the machine and tractor depot. At the same time I went to
school.

The atmosphere and the whole way of life in a farming family,
working with my parents from an early age, undoubtedly influenced my character and attitude to life. I finished school successfully, and in 1950 began my studies at the Law Faculty of Moscow
State University.

During my five years of study I was active in the *Komsomol*, and
in 1952 I joined the CPSU. I am grateful to Moscow University –
to the teachers, the Party and *Komsomol* organisations and to
student colleagues (I am in touch with many of them to this day)
– for the knowledge they handed on, for their friendship and
camaraderie. They were wonderful years, without which the
course my life took would not have been possible.

INTERVIEWER: Mikhail Sergeyevich, could you please say a little
more about your own family? What is its history, and what does
it mean to you?

GORBACHEV: I met Raisa Maximovna when I was at university.
She was born in the Siberian town of Rubtsovsk in the Altai
region. Her parents worked for the railway. She finished school
with distinction and then began studying at the Philosophy Faculty of Moscow State University. We met in 1951 and married
in 1953.

After getting our degrees we began working in Stavropol, my
home region. But I was not active for long in the legal profession

for which I had been trained. I was appointed to the *Komsomol*, and since then I have been active in the *Komsomol* and the Party. I worked for many years in the District Party Committee, nine of them as First Secretary. These were decisive years in my life.

As my work had a great deal to do with agriculture, I obtained a degree as an external student at the Economic Faculty of the Agricultural Institute, which proved a useful complement to my legal training.

Raisa Maximovna worked at various colleges. She wrote a dissertation on the life of *kolkhoz* farmers and became a lecturer. Altogether she taught philosophy for over twenty years. She worked with the Society for National Education. Our daughter Irina was born in Stavropol. She also grew up, studied and married there. She and her husband are doctors. Irina has a doctorate, and is an assistant at a medical institute. Her husband Anatoli is a lecturer, and for nine years he has been working as a surgeon in a Moscow hospital. His doctorate is in vascular surgery. In Moscow there have been additions to our family: we have two grandchildren, Xenia and Anastasia.

Raisa Maximovna now does social work and bears the responsibilities protocol requires of the wife of the Chairman of the Presidium of the Supreme Soviet of the USSR. I should say that my present responsibilities keep not only me, but my entire family fully occupied. And I appreciate the support and help of Raisa Maximovna and the rest of my family.

INTERVIEWER: Mikhail Sergeyevich, in the letters to our periodical there are many questions about your daily routine, about what your working day is like. Readers would also like to know something about your daily life and your income. Could you answer these questions?

GORBACHEV: If readers are interested in these questions, then they must be answered. About my work regime – that is a difficult question. My working day is determined by the times in which we live, by the problems society needs to solve, and naturally by the duties imposed on a Head of State and the Party. Apart from the few hours that I sleep, I never get away from work. It makes no difference whether I happen to be in the Central Committee, the Presidium of the Supreme Soviet or at home. And I don't suppose I need to point out that even on holiday I don't get away from work.

Now, about my income. Like all other Politburo members I get 1,200 roubles a month, regardless of the post I occupy. Candidates of the Politburo earn 1,100, Central Committee Secretaries 1,000 roubles. All fees that I receive for publications, lectures, addresses and speeches are paid into the Party funds.

I would particularly like to say something about the fees for the book *Perestroika and the New Thinking*, as this book was written at the request of an American publisher and appeared in a fairly large edition – more than 2 million copies – in over a hundred countries. The royalties from this were paid to the Party and to social organisations: to the fund for the earthquake victims in Armenia and Tadzhikistan, to the Soviet Culture Fund – for the erection of the Vassili Tyorkin monument – and for a children's playground in Moscow.

About my living arrangements: we have a city flat. State dachas are put at the disposal of members of the country's leadership, depending on the nature of their functions. Neither I nor any member of my family has ever had a dacha of our own anywhere. In the dacha of the General Secretary of the Central Committee of the CPSU and Chairman of the Presidium of the Supreme Soviet there are facilities necessary for him to carry out his duties, such as rooms where meetings of the Politburo and the Presidium of the Supreme Soviet can be held if necessary, or meetings with other heads of state. There is a study, a library and a communications centre with the most modern equipment. There are the technical facilities necessary for the Chairman of the Defence Council of the country to carry out his function. Some of the rooms are reserved for the personal use of the family.

Apart from this, the Central Committee and the government have at their disposal buildings that are used to receive important foreign guests and for other representative purposes.

It has been possible to hand over some of the state villas and dachas, for example in the Crimea and on the Black Sea coast, to health organisations as holiday homes for children and veterans as well as to cultural organisations and other institutions.

As for the transport at my disposal, this also depends on my duties. I will give you an example. After my appearance at the United Nations in New York I drove to Governor's Island for a meeting with President Reagan. We drove in his car. The mobile news centre was in one of our cars. While we were boarding the ferry to the island, a phone call came from Moscow. Nikolai Ivanovich Ryzhkov was on the phone and told me about the tragedy in Armenia. We immediately arranged to set up a Politburo committee and to take emergency measures. This technical facility makes it possible for me, at any time and from any place, to contact any part of the country, Soviet representatives abroad and heads of state in other countries.

INTERVIEWER: Mikhail Sergeyevich, what do you especially like to do when you have free time? Our readers often ask this in their letters.

GORBACHEV: I try to make full use of my few free hours. I have a variety of interests: literature, theatre, music, the cinema. What I like to do best in my free time is walk in the woods. But unfortunately I have less and less time for this.

INTERVIEWER: Mikhail Sergeyevich, I would like to thank you on behalf of our readers for what you have told us. I hope you will also be prepared in the future to answer questions from our readers.

GORBACHEV: I believe there should be more talks like this. I would like to take this opportunity to wish readers of *News From the Central Committee of the CPSU* well in their private lives and success at work in this difficult but interesting period of our history.

INDEX OF NAMES

☆

Principal entries on a particular person are given in italic type; material in brackets indicates their relationship to Mikhail Sergeyevich Gorbachev.

Index of Names

Index of Names